St. Tammany Parish

PUBLISHED UNDER THE AUSPICES
OF THE ST. TAMMANY PARISH BICENTENNIAL COMMISSION,
FRANK J. PATECEK, JR., CHAIRMAN

St. Tammany Parish

Parish

L'AUTRE CÔTÉ DU LAC

FREDERICK S. ELLIS

Foreword by Walker Percy

A FIREBIRD PRESS BOOK

PELICAN PUBLISHING COMPANY
Gretna 1998

Library of Congress Cataloging in Publication Data

Ellis, Frederick Stephen.
    St. Tammany Parish.

    Bibliography: p.
    Includes index.
    1. St. Tammany Parish, La.--History.   I. Title.
F377.S3E44   976.3'12   80-63
ISBN 1-56554-563-X   AACR1

Manufactured in the United States of America
Published by Pelican Publishing Company, Inc.
1000 Burmaster Street, Gretna, Louisiana 70053

FOR BETTY

Contents

Foreword

A good local history is an excellent and agreeable thing. It pleases on two counts. It satisfies the curiosity of the inhabitants of a region, whether newcomers or old settlers, especially if no adequate history had existed before. It dispels myths, corrects old wives' tales. And, if the history is first-rate, it goes beyond a factual account of persons and places, the particularities of a region, and shows the significance of these human happenings in a larger scheme of things, in this case the emergence of a new nation.

Ellis's history succeeds on both counts. It is a delightful and authoritative account of lore which not even St. Tammanyites may have heard of. Did you know, for example, that there was once a flourishing wine industry in St. Tammany Parish? That local vineyards produced excellent red and white wines, the red from Concord grapes, the white from Herbemont? Did you know that in 1891 a rice crop of 50,000 barrels was harvested, half the entire output of South Carolina? Did you know that the Choctaw Indians, whom most of us think of as the aborigines of the region, came into the parish after the white man? Did you know there was a silk factory in Lewisburg in 1883 and that silk cocoons, as fine as any in Europe, were being raised at Mulberry Grove on Lee Road?

One "myth" turns out to be the truth, more or less. One of the first things I remember hearing about Covington was that it was "the second healthiest place in the world" (I never found out what the first was) what with the wonderful curative properties of the "ozone" secreted by pine trees. Sure enough, it turns out that in 1890 the census commissioner in New Orleans reported only 25 deaths in a parish population of 10,000—of which only three or four occurred in Covington. Apparently this was a more or less average statistic in those years despite the fact that Covington, unlike other Southern towns, had always admitted refugees from yellow-fever epidemics in New Orleans. What with the pollution since of earth, air, and water, the death-rate may have changed.

Such are the sort of documented tidbits we locals like to read about—these and such items as Deed Smith's famous auto trip in 1910 in his new EMF 30 (he was the local Flanders and Brush dealer) from Detroit to Covington which took only eleven days and required 103 gallons of gas costing $16.75. Or the brief visit of the notorious Mme. Lalaurie, young beautiful housewife from New Orleans who was found to be torturing her slaves and escaped from an angry mob by schooner to the north shore where she hid out near the old courthouse at Claiborne before departing for Paris.

Of greater moment is Ellis's feel for the distinctive character of the region and its people. Though St. Tammany Parish is, by any reckoning, a backwater in the larger currents of history and though unflattering things have been said about it—Governor Claiborne mentioned "a great scarcity of talent" and "virtuous men," and Judge Ezekiel Ellis, one of the founders of the local Methodist church, is reputed to have called Covington "the wickedest place on earth"—what emerges in this history is a certain ornery independence of thought and action, an inexhaustible talent for dissent. In a word, St. Tammany folk usually found themselves on the losing side of most issues.

To begin with, many of the early Anglo-Saxon settlers dissented from the American proposition and as Tories fled the rebellious colonies for this pleasant English haven.

Yet in 1779 they insisted on taking an oath of allegiance to the United States even as they were becoming part of Spanish West Florida.

In 1810 they opposed the popular West Florida rebellion against the Spanish.

In 1812, when Louisiana became a state, they wanted no part of Louisiana and petitioned Congress to join the Mississippi Territory.

In 1860 they voted pro-Union in the presidential election and against secession at the state convention.

Yet in 1865, as a kind of ultimate contrariness, defying North and South alike, they were reported to have still owned slaves, as if the Civil War and Emancipation Proclamation had not occurred.

Such a talent for dissent, whether from a stalwart frontier spirit or plain unregenerate human cussedness, is remarkable. In either case, it is a distinctive people Ellis portrays here. Indeed St. Tammany Parish turns out to be a microcosm of the encounter of two cultures, the collision of the Creoles from the South with WASP invaders from the North—with mostly happy and always interesting results.

Ellis has rendered this pleasant and authoritative history in a graceful and lively style and with a genuine affection for the people he writes about.

Walker Percy

Preface

This is the story of a place. It is as accurate and authoritative as I could make it, but I cannot pretend that it is more than the bare bones of the whole story. There is much more work to be done in St. Tammany Parish, and if this volume can serve as a foundation for future research, I shall be well satisfied.

It has been, of necessity, a part-time project. If anything has emerged from this work, it is that, despite the substantial amount of new material turned up by the research, the surface has only been scratched. It soon became clear that if I waited until the research was complete to write the book, I would never begin to write. As new areas were explored, still other sources would appear, which in turn would lead to still more. Although the book is as comprehensive as one man could make it working within the time and space limitations imposed, there is still much original work to be done in all areas.

For instance, I have not used, or had access to or heard of any diaries or letter collections in private hands in St. Tammany Parish. My own research on the English period has not been as complete as I would have liked. I am certain that there are many undiscovered documents relating to St. Tammany Parish in the Archives of the Indies in Seville, Spain.

In writing the book, I have left all proper names as I found them in the original sources, so that the same name may be subject to spelling variations. I have used many quotations from contemporary works, because I believe they give a better feeling for the times than my own words might.

Researching and writing the book has been a voyage of discovery for me. I was surprised to learn that St. Tammany, although always rural, has never been a primarily agricultural community. Some other activity or commodity, such as tar, pitch, resin, turpentine, cattle, bricks, trade, and tourism, has always been the economic mainstay. Another surprise was the early date of settlement of the parish, only eight years after the founding of New Orleans. Earlier accounts had placed the first settlers about 50 years later, under the British regime.

A source of constant delight to me has been the people of the parish. Proud, independent, suspicious of government, and very suspicious of the law, they have marched through history to a different drummer. I am happy to be one of them, and like to think that their spirit still pervades and infects the newest of the newcomers.

The title of the book was chosen because all of the early French and Spanish sources refer to sites on the Tchefuncta River, Bayou Lacombe, and Bayou Liberty, which are many miles apart, as *l'autre cote du lac,* "the other side of the lake," as though they were on the other side of the moon. We are not so inaccessible today, but I think the name is symbolic of the history of the parish.
today, but I think the name is symbolic of the history of the parish.

There is no way this book could have been written without the help and encouragement of many people. First among these is Mrs. Bertha Perreand Neff, archivist, historian, and genealogist, who has opened many doors for me, and who has furnished much of the raw material on which this book is based. I am deeply indebted to the late Bob Fitzmorris, former Clerk of Court in St. Tammany Parish, and to Mrs. Lucy Reid Rausch, the present Clerk, for many courtesies extended. Elizabeth Millard, former librarian at the St. Tammany Parish Library, and her staff, went above and beyond the call of duty in obtaining material for me both at home and abroad.

Ghislaine Pleasonton at the Louisiana State Museum, who located and copied many of the early French documents and assisted in their translation, has my undying gratitude. The staff at the St. Ann Street Library of the Louisiana State Museum has been more than helpful during the many hours I spent there, both in locating materials of which I would have been otherwise unaware, and in suggesting other avenues of research.

Christine Westfeldt, who assumed responsibility for the illustration of the book, did much original research and contributed her own very special talent.

Valuable material has been furnished by J. C. Pittman, Ron Barthet, Philip Frederick Burns, Dr. and Mrs. Edwin F. Boagni, Dr. and Mrs. S. Harvey Colvin, Paula Patecek Johnson, and Mr. and Mrs. Roger T. Stone. Thanks are also due to the St. Tammany Historical Society for unlimited access to its archives.

Special thanks are due to Florence Chesnutt, who got me started as a historian, and to Walker Percy, who read the semi-final version of the history and gave valuable criticism of the work as a whole. Words cannot express my appreciation of Jeanine Guidry, who has typed this book in all of its versions except the first, and who has made my task a much easier one.

I must acknowledge the debt of love and gratitude I owe to two persons who will never see this book. My mother, Lelia Marguerite Rightor Ellis, assisted in the translation of some of the Spanish documents, and read the semi-final version of the book; but her greatest contribution was in the constant encouragement she gave, and in the educational background that was part of my heritage. Mother died in March 1979. My wife, Betty Dahlberg Ellis, was, throughout the research period, secretary, companion, critic, and organizer. She helped make sense out of nonsense and bring structure to chaos. Betty died in January 1978. I hope both of them realized that this work is as much theirs as mine.

Frederick Stephen Ellis
Covington, Louisiana

St. Tammany
Parish

Prologue

Pierre Le Moyne, Sieur d'Iberville, soldier, sailor, and explorer, scion of the great Canadian family; who captured the British posts on Hudson Bay in 1686; who defeated three British ships in a naval battle in 1694; who captured Fort Bourbon from the British, and enjoyed several more naval triumphs; who was received by the King of France with distinguished honors and was awarded the Cross of St. Louis; who established the first French Colony in the southern United States, and was the first governor of Louisiana; it was this Iberville, who by spending the night on Goose Point on the north shore of Lake Pontchartrain, became the official discoverer and first tourist to visit what we now know as St. Tammany Parish.

What he found, how it got that way, and what happened to it afterwards is the subject of this book.

CHAPTER I

Discovery

The combination of events and circumstances that brought Iberville to the shores of Lake Pontchartrain and the somewhat dubious hospitality of Goose Point, arose as the natural culmination of the rivalry among England, France, and Spain for domination of the interior of the North American continent.

The Gulf Coast was probably first seen by Amerigo Vespucci, the Italian navigator, explorer, and cartographer, who contributed his name, and little else, to the newly discovered lands of the New World. In 1497, he skirted the northern coast of the Gulf of Mexico, but if he put ashore, or noted the existence of the Mississippi River, he failed to report these facts. Over 20 years later, in 1519, Alonzo Alvarez de Pineda may have sighted the Mississippi River, although it is generally thought that the great river reported by him was actually Mobile Bay and the Mobile River.

In 1528, the ill-fated expedition of Pamphilo de Narvaez started out from Tampa Bay, and was almost entirely wiped out by Indians, disease, and starvation. On October 30, 1528, the few survivors, who included the famous Cabeza de Vaca, found the mouth of the Mississippi River.

In 1539, the Spanish dispatched the famous expeditions of Francisco Vasquez Coronado and Hernando de Soto into the interior of North America, Coronado in the west and De Soto in the east. In the spring of 1541, De Soto discovered the Mississippi River near the present boundary of Tennessee and Mississippi. In July 1543, the remnants of that unfortunate expedition, harried by the Indians, sailed down the lower 500 miles of the Mississippi River and made their way, via the Gulf, to the Spanish posts in Mexico.

As a result of these various expeditions, Spain claimed dominion over central and western North America, making the flag of Aragon and Castile the first to fly over St. Tammany Parish, the little corner of that vast territory which is the subject of this book. The Spanish, however, did nothing further to consolidate their claim, and, for over 150 years after De Soto, the lower Mississippi valley was undisturbed by European explorers. It was not until 1698, when they placed a small garrison in Pensacola Bay, that the Spanish once again took an interest in the area. By that time, however, the initiative had passed to the French.

In the latter part of the 17th century, French explorers pushed west from their early settlements in Canada. The explorations of Jean Nicolet, Fathers Raymbault and Jogues, Pierre Radisson, and others, had brought rumors of a great river in the west. By 1660, Colbert, the French Minister of Marine, and Jean Baptiste Talon, Intendant of New France, both feared that the vigorous British colonies on the east coast of North America would spread across the mountains and into the interior. To forestall this eventuality, explorations were pushed to the west, and, on June 17, 1673, Louis Joliet and Father Marquette, head of the Jesuit mission at Mackinaw, reached the Mississippi. They descended the river as far south as the mouth of the Arkansas River before turning back.

Finally, on April 2, 1682, an expedition headed by the famous Rene Robert Cavalier, Sieur de La Salle, reached the mouth of the Mississippi. La Salle formally claimed for France all of the territory drained by that great river. In his proclamation, he referred to the new territory as Louisiana, possibly for the first time, although this is not certain. The flag of Bourbon France became the second European flag to fly over what would become St. Tammany Parish.

In 1684, wishing to establish control over the Mississippi, the French sent La Salle to establish a colony near the mouth of the river. However, La Salle was unable to find the mouth of the Mississippi from the sea, and wound up in Galveston Bay instead. The expedition ended with the murder of La Salle and almost total disaster for the other members.

Interest in the lower Mississippi once again flagged in France, until it was revived in 1697 by the activities of two men, and by

French and Spanish flags ca. 1690

St. Tammany Parish
LEGEND

1. Ship Island
2. Cat Island
3. Chandeleur Islands
4. Entrance to Mississippi River
5. Future site of New Orleans
6. Bayou St. John
7. Lake Pontchartrain
8. Bay St. Louis
9. Bayogoula and Mougoulacha Indians
10. La Fourche
11. Quinipissa village
12. Mississippi River
13. Baton Rouge
14. Pointe Coupee
15. Houmas Indians
16. Iberville River
17. Lake Maurepas and Pass Manchac
18. Goose Point, Iberville's campsite, March 28, 1699
19. Grand Coquille
20. Desruisseaux's Island
21. Pearl River
22. Annochy village

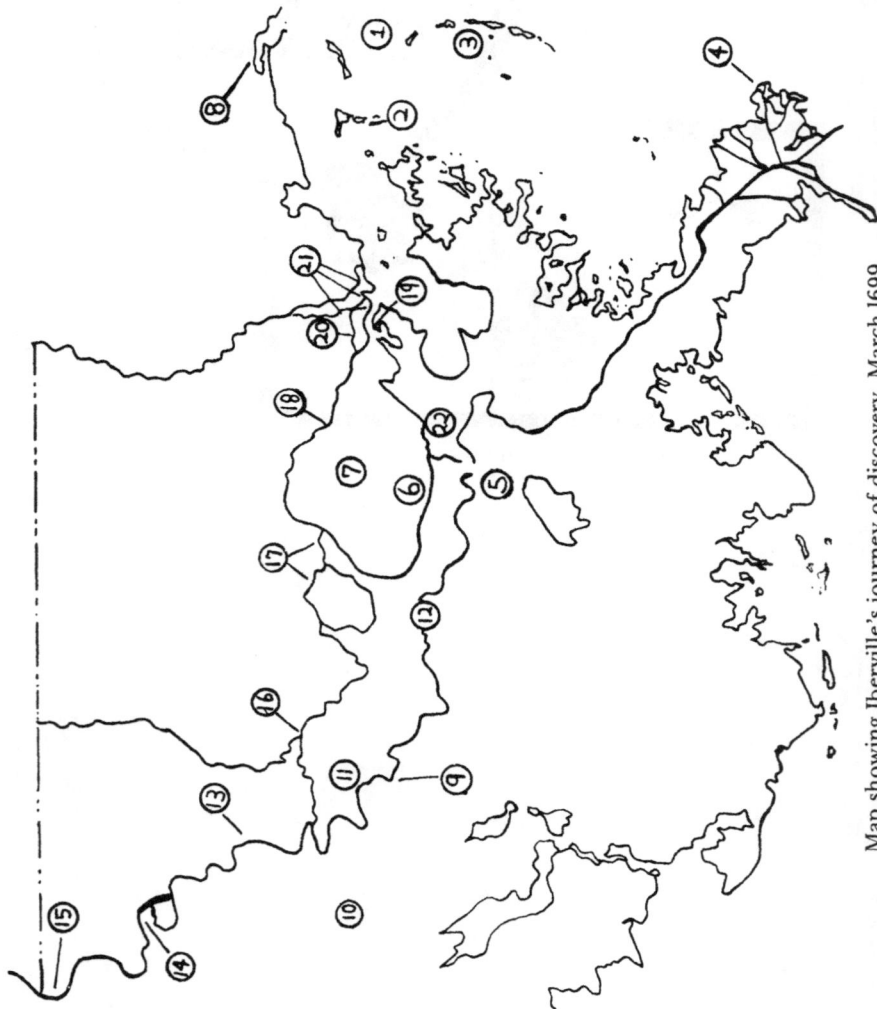

Map showing Iberville's journey of discovery, March 1699

rumors that the British intended to establish a colony on the river. The first of these two men was the Sieur de Remonville, an old friend of La Salle, who presented a memoir on the importance of the colonization of Louisiana to the French Minister of Marine, Louis Phelypeaux, Compte de Pontchartrain. The other proponent was Iberville, who had petitioned Jerome de Phelypeaux, Compte de Maurepas, son and successor of Pontchartrain, for government aid in establishing a colony on the lower Mississippi. As a result, a commission was issued to Iberville to carry out the plans at which La Salle had failed.

In 1698, Iberville's expedition departed from France in two ships, the *Marin* and the *Badine*. After a stop at the island of Santo Domingo, it reached the north coast of the Gulf of Mexico near Pensacola in January, 1699. There the Spanish had already established their post, and the expedition was refused admittance to Pensacola Bay. Iberville then sailed on to the west, exploring the islands bordering Mississippi Sound on the south. Eventually the ships anchored at Ship Island, from which point Iberville explored the Mississippi Gulf Coast between Bay St. Louis and the Pascagoula River. He then proceeded south along the Louisiana coast and, on March 2, 1699, during a violent storm, entered the mouth of the Mississippi River. The Sieur de Sauvole, Iberville's second in command, and Jean Baptiste Le Moyne, Sieur de Bienville, Iberville's 18 year old brother, were members of the party.

The little expedition went up the river, probably as far north as the mouth of the Red River. On the way upstream, they contacted a number of Indian tribes, including the Mougoulacha, the Bayougoula, and the Houmas. The chief of the Bayougoulas showed Iberville a stream, which the Indians called the Ascantia, and which he said would lead back to Ship Island. After contacting the Houmas tribe, Iberville began his return down the river. When he arrived at the Ascantia, on March 24, 1699, he decided to explore that passage back to the ships, taking with him four men and an Indian guide in two canoes.

Despite the illness of one of his men, Deschiers, and being abandoned by his Indian guide, Iberville continued his journey, traversing the waters which are today known as Bayou Manchac, the Amite River, Lake Maurepas, and Pass Manchac. He modestly named this route the Iberville River, after himself. On the evening of March 27, 1699, the party arrived at "a lake, the shore of which runs west-southwest, which we have named Pontchartrain." He also named Lake Maurepas, after Jerome de Phelypeaux.

On March 28, 1699, Iberville's diary says:

> We travelled along the shore of this lake about ten leagues to the east, a quarter southwest, the wind in the northwest. The water of the lake is too brackish to drink and camped on a treeless, grassy point, pretty bad, having no water to drink and many mosquitoes, which are terrible little animals to people who are in need of rest. For the last four leagues, there are prairies along the lake, which are about one league wide, back to the forest. I cannot see the other side of the lake . . .

On the next day, Iberville proceeded along the shore east southeast, and, about four leagues from his camp, came to the exit from the lake, which is now known as the Rigolets. (A league, as used in navigation at sea, equals about three miles. Iberville, a sailor and navigator, used this unit of measure.)

On today's maps, it can be seen that Goose Point lies about 30 miles from Pass Manchac and about 12 miles from the Rigolets, and is the only prominent point in the area. It is, therefore, likely that Iberville and his men passed the night there, and when they stepped ashore they became the first white men to set foot in St. Tammany Parish, an honor of which they were surely unaware.

After finding the Rigolets, Iberville made his way to the east, probably through Salt Bayou, since the southeast wind was too strong for the party to go through the Rigolets in canoes. He found the West Pearl River, and then passed to the east through Little Lake to the Pearl River, and thence out of the history of St. Tammany Parish. Sauvole tells us that Iberville said that the land along the lake was too low to be of value for settlement. So, what with the mosquitoes and the lake marshes, St. Tammany's first appearance in history is less than impressive.

Iberville was looking for a place to establish a fort which would give the French control of the mouth of the Mississippi and the lower Mississippi valley. It had to be reasonably accessible by ship, and had to have good communication with the river.

After returning to Ship Island, he rechecked the Gulf Coast

between Bay St. Louis and the Pascagoula River without finding a harbor which could be entered by boats of reasonable draft. He had decided to attempt to find a site for the fort on Lake Pontchartrain, despite his opinion of its unsuitability. However, on his way back from the Pascagoula River, he discovered an adequate channel into Biloxi Bay and selected a site on its east side, near the present railroad bridge, for the fort. He called it Fort Maurepas.

CHAPTER II

Geology and Geography

Although his choice of Biloxi Bay was a bad one, considering the requirements for its location, it is easy to see why he found the north shore of the lake unsuitable for the first settlement. In his journal he fails to mention any of the rivers and bayous that flow into the lake from the north. Since he carefully noted all of the tributaries of the Amite River, it is probable that he just did not see the mouths of the streams, which are extremely difficult to detect from the lake without navigational aids. All he was able to see was low marsh and swamp, with no harbors, and no access to the higher forested land which he could see beyond the marshes.

If Iberville had had the opportunity to look further, he would have found things somewhat better than his first estimate. The southern and eastern sections of the parish are flat, and rise slowly to the rolling hills of the north central and northwestern sections. The parish is drained by two major and four minor stream systems. Almost the entire western half is drained by the Tchefuncta-Bogue Falaya system, which also includes the Abita and the Little Bogue Falaya rivers, Pontchitolawa Creek, and other smaller tributary creeks and branches. The north central, northeast, and extreme eastern sections are drained by the Bogue Chitto-Pearl River system, which includes the famous Honey Island Swamp in its valley. The south central part of the parish drains into Lake Pontchartrain through Bayou Castein, Cane Bayou (or Big Branch), Bayou Lacombe, and Bayous Liberty and Bonfouca. In their lower reaches, all of the streams are quiet, winding and relatively deep, and furnish some of the loveliest scenery and most desirable homesites in Louisiana.

Except in the stream valleys, which are generally narrow and subject to periodic flooding, the surface of the parish is made up of silty to sandy clays of various colors, which are low in organic content, and therefore not very fertile. Deposits of sand and gravel are found adjacent to the stream beds in the northern and eastern sections of the parish. Many deposits of brick clay and pottery clay are found throughout St. Tammany, and the white sands of the rivers are excellent for glass manufacture and building purposes.

The various sediments which make up the surface of St. Tammany Parish, except in the river valleys and along the margin of Lake Pontchartrain, were all deposited during the latter part of the Pleistocene geologic epoch, which began about one and one-half million years ago, and ended about 25,000 years ago. The Pleistocene encompasses the entire history of modern man and the four great ice ages which sculptured and built the world as we know it today.

At the beginning of the Pleistocene, St. Tammany lay at the bottom of a shallow sea, which extended up into the State of Mississippi. As the first ice age, the Nebraskan, developed, great quantities of sea water were frozen into ice, causing a drop of several hundred feet in sea level, and exposing the surface of what would some day be St. Tammany Parish. Later, as the glaciers began to melt and recede, torrents of water, carrying enormous amounts of sediments, flowed down through the middle of the continent, depositing a layer of sedimentary material. The first Pleistocene stratum in Louisiana is known as the Williana Terrace. At the end of the first interglacial age, the waters of the sea rose to their former level, and St. Tammany lay once again on the floor of the sea.

This process repeated itself three more times, during the Kansan, the Illinoian, and the Wisconsin glacial periods, depositing successively the Bentley, Montgomery, and Prairie Terraces. The last terrace was deposited between 100,000 and 60,000 years ago, and exposed during the late Wisconsin glacial stage, which ended about 25,000 years ago.

As the Wisconsin glaciers melted, the sea level once again rose, reaching its present level about 5,000 years ago. At that time, the shore of the Gulf of Mexico was located approximately where the north shore of Lake Pontchartrain lies today, and St. Tammany Parish found itself permanently above sea level.

In addition to the rise in sea level, other changes were taking place. The great weight of the sediments deposited over south Louisiana during the interglacial stages caused a general subsidence of the strata located south of a line which coincides approximately with the north shore of Lake Pontchartrain. There was a corresponding slow uplift of the land lying to the north of that line. During the late Wisconsin glacial stage, the sea level fell to about 450 feet below its present level, which led to the cutting of fairly deep valleys by the streams of this area, and to substantial dissection and erosion in the higher sections. As the sea then rose to its present level, the deeply entrenched river valleys began to fill with their own sediments. This process can still be observed today. The Tchefuncta River is still quite deep in its lower reaches, and the same is true, to a lesser extent, of the other smaller streams.

The erosion in the higher sections led to the exposure of a substantial area of the Montgomery Terrace in the northwest and north central part of the parish, and a small outcrop of the Bentley Terrace is to be found in the extreme northwest corner of St. Tammany.

It is likely that by 5,000 years ago, the character of the interior of the parish, both in topography and vegetation, was substantially as it was when it was discovered by the white man. During the ensuing years, deltaic action of the Mississippi River has built up the land to the south of Lake Pontchartrain, cutting it off from the Gulf of Mexico almost completely, and leaving the area as we know it today.

Generally speaking, St. Tammany Parish offered to its discoverers a varied terrain, well-watered and well-drained, heavily-timbered with long-leaf pine, and having a healthy climate and beautiful environment. Extensive deposits of sand, gravel, and clay for bricks were available. The soil was relatively infertile, however, and the area was isolated from the surrounding country by lakes, rivers, and swamps.

CHAPTER III

Ancient Indian Cultures

History recognizes Iberville as the discoverer of this area, but he was not the first man to come here by a long shot. Although no definitive study has been made of the many prehistoric Indian sites in St. Tammany Parish, it is safe to say that the surface of the parish is virtually littered with the remains of those men who came here and lived here so long ago.

It is not known when man first appeared on the North American continent, but it is estimated that he made his appearance across the Bering Sea bridge 30,000 to 50,000 years ago, and by 10,000 years ago had spread to the tip of South America. Remains of the Paleo-Indian culture, the oldest of the American Indian cultures, have been found in Louisiana in the northwest part of the state, and at Avery Island in the south central area. These remains have been dated about 10,000 B. C.

Since the surface of St. Tammany Parish was uncovered before man came to North America, no remains could have been deposited at that time. When the Paleo-Indians arrived, the sea level was substantially below the present level and the shoreline many miles to the south, and it is probable that their habitat was in that vicinity rather than inland. However, some arrowheads found in St. Tammany have been identified as Paleo-Indian remains, so it is likely that the parish was occupied by man even at that early date.

There are three sites which have been identified with the Archaic Indians, who flourished about 5,000 years ago at about the time that the sea reached its present level. The Archaic Indians were hunter-gatherers who lived off the land, hunting animals and gathering other

15

Poverty Point cooking balls used by ancient Indians to heat water and cook ca. 1600 B.C.

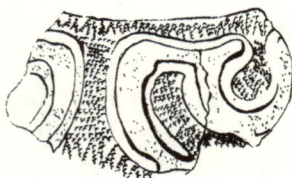

Indian pottery fragments

foods in their wild state. Other than their rather large spear points, there are few cultural remains of this primitive people, who did not make pottery.

The famous Poverty Point culture, which originated in about 1600 B. C., is also represented in St. Tammany Parish, although not with the spectacular earth-works which characterize the type site in northeast Louisiana. The Garcia site, in the southeastern part of the parish, is a local example. The Poverty Point culture is generally thought to be pre-pottery and pre-agriculture. It is characterized by cooking balls, balls of clay which were heated in a fire and then dropped into a skin-lined vessel to heat the water used for cooking.

The best known of the local prehistoric cultures is the Tchefuncta. It was first identified at shell mounds located in Fontainebleau State Park near Mandeville, which are the type sites for this extensive culture. It flourished between 600 B. C. and 400 A. D. and spread throughout the lower Mississippi valley and over as far as northeast Texas. It is generally thought to be the first pottery-making culture in this area. The type sites were fairly extensive shell mounds, or middens, located near the north shore of Lake Pontchartrain, and other sites have been located along the streams near the lakeshore. The Tchefuncta Indians were also the first in Louisiana to bury their dead in small earthen mounds.

The Marksville (200 A. D.-600 A. D.) and Troyville (400 A. D.-900 A. D.) cultures, which developed out of the Tchefuncta, are also represented in St. Tammany Parish. They are characterized by a fine pottery, used only in association with burials, and by burial mounds. It is known that they lived in round houses, and the presence of small stone points indicates that they may have used the bow and arrow.

The Coles Creek culture, which flourished from about 700 A. D. to 1300 A. D., was probably the first culture to engage in the cultivation of maize. The pottery techniques of these people were more advanced, and they built temple mounds, pyramidal in shape and flat on top. None of these mounds seem to be present in St. Tammany Parish, although there are some Coles Creek sites. The famous Pontchartrain Check Stamp pottery, which is typical of the period, is found at a number of sites in St. Tammany.

The Plaquemine-Historic culture grew out of the Coles Creek, beginning in about 1200 A. D., and still persisted in St. Tammany Parish when Ibervville made his appearance at the end of the 17th century. Apparently, during this period there was a decline in the Indian population in Louisiana, which continued into historic times. By then, the only tribe known to be in residence in St. Tammany Parish were the Acolapissas.

CHAPTER IV

St. Tammany Indian Tribes

Shortly after Iberville returned to Ship Island in March 1699 and selected Biloxi Bay as the site for Fort Maurepas, he departed for France, leaving Sauvole in command of the garrison, and young Bienville as second in command.

The French were interested in finding the Quinipissas, with whom La Salle and Tonti had been in contact in 1682, and Sauvole believed that the Colapissas and the Quinipissas were the same tribe. He persuaded Antobiscania, the chief of the Bayougoulas, who was visiting the new fort, to take Bienville to visit that tribe. In his journal, he says:

I enticed them to conduct M. de Bienville to the Quinipissas, to whom I also sent a present of a hood, of a calumet, of beads, and other things to win such people. The chief of the Bayo-goulas meditated a long time whether to go or not, telling me that he could not assure us that the others would not kill our people. I told him that we were not afraid of anyone and in case they took a false step, I would go and kill them all. Seeing that he could not keep him [Bienville] from going there, he de-cided to relent. He said all of this only in view of having every-thing for himself and not to give us knowledge of any other nation.

The 29th, M. de Bienville came back from the Coulapissas, this is how they called themselves. They have never heard talk of M. de Lassalle nor of M. de Tonty. He has been well received there. They are but four days' journey from us. They sent me two peace pipes; in spite of this, they have never approached

19

this place. The chief of the Bayogoulas must have intimidated them, making them believe that it was them that we were looking for, M. d'Iberville and me, when we questioned them so much about the fork of the river and about the Quinipissas. They are not more than a hundred and fifty men but very well built.

An early chronicle, generally credited to Bernard de la Harpe, describes the visit to the village:

May 20, 1699. M. de Bienville, with a Bayagoula chief and a detachment of twelve Canadians, embarked on a felucca and a bark canoe to go make an alliance with the Colapissa [Acolapissa] nation, who were located eight leagues inland to the right of Lake Pontchartrain.

May 22, 1699. The Bienville group debarked. The next day M. de Bienville took four Canadians and the Bayagoula chief to the Colapissa village. They found that this nation, numbering more than three hundred warriors, was armed and prepared to attack. Thus, while M. de Bienville and the other Frenchmen remained at a distance, the Bayagoula chief went to investigate the cause of the warriors' alarm. The chief learned that a short time before two white men, calling themselves English, had come with two hundred Chickasaws to attack the Colapissa village. The attackers had surprised the Colapissas and had taken prisoner many of their people. Thus, the Colapissas thought that the white men with the Bayagoula chief were the same as the recent attackers. When the Bayagoula succeeded in making them understand that the men with him were Frenchmen, enemies of the English, they put down their arms and received M. de Bienville and his men in a friendly manner. After distributing presents, M. de Bienville returned to Biloxi, arriving there on May 29, 1699.

In May 1700, Sauvole led a party overland from the head of Bay St. Louis to the village of the Colapissas, which had been moved considerably inland because of the attack led by the British the year before. According to the journal of Father Du Ru, a Jesuit priest who accompanied the party, the village was located about 40 miles up the Pearl River and about seven miles from the river, although we do not know in which direction. At that time the great village of the Acolapissas consisted of 15 or 20 bark cabins, surrounded by a palisade of pointed stakes. Du Ru says that the bark cabins were temporary and that permanent dwellings were to be erected.

There were about 500 people living there, including about 300 able-bodied men. Apparently there was no temple in the village, but a phallic symbol, which stood in its middle, was destroyed by the French and replaced with a cross.

Sometime later, probably in 1702, the Acolapissas moved once again, this time to Bayou Castein at the present day site of Mandeville.

In 1705, the Natchitoches Indians suffered a crop failure. They left their traditional home on the Red River and went for help to Juchereau de St. Denis, then in command of Fort de la Boulaye on the lower Mississippi. St. Denis sent Penicaut to take the tribe to live with the Acolapissas on Bayou Castein. Later that year, 80 of the warriors of the two tribes accompanied St. Denis and Penicaut on a raid on the Chetimachas, who were located on Bayou Lafourche.

In the spring of 1706, Bienville, who was by then Governor of Louisiana, sent most of his men to live with the Indians because of a shortage of supplies. Penicaut and eleven other Frenchmen spent the months from May until February 1707, living with the Acolapissas and the Natchitoches. In describing the visit, Penicaut gives us the only contemporary picture of the life-style of these Indians:

A week later we reached the Colapissas and the Nassitoches. That day we brought a great deal of game in our boats, having killed it the same day near the spot where we had spent the night. As we had had no more than two leagues to travel between our last stop and the Colapissas, we had hunted from morning till four in the afternoon, with the intention of carrying game to our hosts as an arriving present. And so in our boats there were six deer, eight turkeys, and as many bustards, killed that same day. When we got to their village with all this, they embraced us, the men as well as the women and girls, all being delighted to see us come to stay with them. Then they started cooking the meats that we had brought. And after supper the entire village began to dance, and danced far into the night.

We had in our group a companion named Picard, who had brought a violin with him. He could play it well enough to have these savages do some figure-dancing in step. They had us nearly dying of laughter, for the musical instrument had the whole village drawn up around Picard; it was the most comical sight in the world to see them open their eyes in amazement and every now and then cut the most comical capers ever seen. But it was quite another matter when they saw us dance a minuet—two boys dancing together. They would gladly have spent the whole night watching us and listening to the violin, had not the Chief of the Colapissas, fearing we were tired out, come to tell us that lodgings were assigned to us. All of them wanted to have us in their homes: the Chief of the Colapissas reserved the violin player to lodge with him; the most important men gave lodging to the others. For my part, I was lodged with the Chief of the Nassitoches. On my arrival, he had invited me to stay with him, and he led me away. I was the person that, acting for M. de St. Denis, had conducted this chief among the Colapissas the year before to live there with them. I knew him as one of the most honorable men among the savages of the region. Since that time, he had been indebted to me for saving his life, as I shall show later on.

I was not sorry that I was lodged with him, for in his house I received every possible favor. He had two daughters that were the most beautiful of all the savage girls in this district. The older one was twenty; she was called Oulchogonime, which in their language means the good daughter. The second was only eighteen, but was taller than her older sister. She was named Ouilchil, which means the pretty spinner.

I got up a bit late next morning because we had tired ourselves by dancing the greater part of the night. On getting up, I was surprised to see my host bring in a great platter of fish fricasseed in bear fat, and cooked very well. There was also some sagamite, which is a kind of bread that they make from cornmeal mixed with flour of little beans that are similar to our haricots in France. Just the two of us were to eat together, and I was surprised at not seeing his wife or his daughters; but half an hour later they came back together, bringing a big platter of strawberries, for as early as the first of May strawberries abound in the woods. That day they had put on their fine braguets of very white nettle-linen. I gave each of them a present of half an ell

of brocade of white background woven with little flowers
colored pink and green, out of which each could make a braguet;
but their father did not approve and begged me to keep this
material for the daughter of the Grand Chief of the Colapissas
because that chief outranked all others in their settlement. He
was absolutely determined that the younger daughter should
give her piece of brocade back to me; but when I showed him
another piece I was saving for that purpose, he thanked me at
great length and was beside himself with politeness, and the
mother was, too.

At this time two of my comrades came in to see me, one of
them being Picard, the violin player. As soon as my host's
elder daughter saw him, she kissed him. I was not so sorry about
this as I would have been if it had been the younger daughter
kissing him. Picard ate a bit of fish with us; and, when my
other comrades arrived unexpectedly, we all went together to
the house of the Grand Chief of the Colapissas. When we got
there, I embraced his daughter and also gave her a present of
half an ell of the same material that I had given the daughters
of the Chief of the Nassitoches, at whose house I was staying.
I think the father and mother would gladly have given me all
their possessions, they were so delighted with the present I
had given their daughter. We then went into all the huts of the
savages, one after the other, they vying with one another in
entertaining us.

Afterwards, during the after-dinner hour, we went to see
their methods of fishing. They pulled up their nets from the
lake filled with fish of all sizes. These nets, actually, are no
more than fishing lines about six fathoms long. All along these
lines, numerous other little lines are tied a foot apart. At the
end of each line is a fish hook on which they put a bit of sagamite dough or a small piece of meat. With this method they do
not fail to catch fish weighing more than fifteen or twenty
pounds. The end of the line is tied to their boats. They pull the
lines up two or three times a day, and they always catch many
fish when they do. Such fishing as this does not keep them from
working in their field, for it can be attended to in less than half
an hour. When they have pulled in all their fish, each person

takes some fish home, and after it is cooked and seasoned with bear fat, as I have already said, they begin to eat it, each in front of his door in the shade of peach trees.

When the sun had sunk low and all had eaten supper, we danced, as on the evening before, quite far into the night. Their dances, like the ones I spoke of in the article on the Natchez, are conducted to the sound of a little drum. Our musician endeavored to keep time with the drum and the singers' voices. Although he made a most painful attempt that drew upon all his skill and caused us all to laugh out loud, he never was able to approximate their rhythm; and, as a matter of fact, their singing is more savage than the savages themselves. Although it is an incessant repetition, Picard could not get their pitch; but he made amends by teaching many of the girls in the village to dance the minuet and la bourree.

Every day after dinner, which these savages usually have at eight o'clock in the morning, we would get together and then go hunting, and every day we would bring game back to the village, so that the savages were delighted to have us with them.

The Nassitoches are handsomer and have better figures than the Colapissas, because the Colapissas' bodies, men's and women's, are all tattooed. They prick almost their entire bodies with needles and rub the pricks with willow ash crushed quite fine, which causes no inflammation of the punctures. The arms and faces of the Colapissas women and girls are tattooed in this way, which disfigures them hideously; but the Nassitoches, men as well as women and girls, make no use of such punctures, which they loathe. That is why they are so much better looking; besides, they are naturally whiter.

As for their religion, they have a round temple before which they appear morning and evening rubbing their bodies with white mud and lifting their arms on high; they mutter some words very low for a quarter of an hour. At the portal of the temple there are some wooden likenesses of birds; within the temple are numerous little idols, of both wood and stone, representing dragons, snakes, and some toadlike creatures, which they keep locked up in three chests inside the temple, the key being held by the Grand Chief.

When a savage dies, a kind of grave is prepared, or, rather, a platform raised two feet above ground, on top of which the dead man is placed. He is covered completely with mud, and, further, bark is put on top of that, for fear of animals or birds of prey; and down below is put a little jug filled with water together with a platter full of meal. Every morning and every evening fire is lighted beside the platform, and here they come and weep. The richest people hire women to weep beside the platform. After six moons, the body is uncovered; if the flesh is consumed, the bones are put in a little basket and carried to their temple; if it is not yet consumed, the bones are taken from the flesh, and the flesh is burned.

They are rather cleanly with their food: they have an individual pot for each thing that they cook—that is, the meat pot is never used for fish. They cook all their food with bear fat, which is white in winter, when it is congealed, like lard, and is like olive oil in summer. It does not have a bad taste. They eat it with salad, use it in making pastry, in frying, and usually in everything they cook.

As for fruits, they happen to be few. They have, however, peaches in season that are even bigger than those in France, and sweeter; strawberries; plums; and a grape that is a bit sour and not so big as the grapes of France. There are also nuts which they pound into flour, using it with water to make pap for their children and mixing it with corn meal to make sagamite, or bread.

These savages have no hair on them whatever except the hair on their heads. The men as well as the women and girls remove the hair from their faces as well as from other parts of the body; they remove hair with shell ash and hot water as one would remove the hair from a suckling pig.

They have an unusual way to light a fire. They take a small piece of cedar wood, the size of one's finger, and another small piece of mulberry wood, which is very hard. They put them side by side between their hands and by spinning them together, like making chocolate froth, they make a little piece of fuzz come out of the cedar wood and catch fire. This can be done instantly.

When they go hunting, they go dressed in deer skins with the antlers attached. They make the same motions that a deer makes; and when the deer notices this, he charges them; and when he gets in good musket range, they shoot at him and kill him. With this method they kill a great many deer; and it should be acknowledged that in hunting buffalo as well as bear and deer they are more skilful than the French.

When winter came, we went out to the channel and into the woods to kill bustards, ducks, and wild geese that are much bigger than the geese in France. During that season unbelievable numbers of them are attracted to Lake Pontchartrain, and there they stay along the lake shore. Every day we brought back some of them, which we roasted inside the huts, where good fires were kept burning on account of the cold. The cold is not, however, so long or so severe as in the Upper Missicipy.

In this way we spent the greater part of the winter. As far as I was personally concerned, I was just as happy there in winter as in summer, for, to keep myself busy whenever I returned from hunting, I would sit close by the fire and teach my host's daughters to speak French. They made me die of laughing, with their savage pronunciation, which comes entirely from the throat, whereas French is spoken solely from the tongue, without being guttural.

Penicaut was once again sent to Bayou Castein by St. Denis in 1712, with instructions to return the Natchitoches to their former home on the Red River. The result was most unexpected:

The day after we got there he sent me in a boat, with two Biloxi savages, to the Colapissas village to get the Nassitoches and bring them with their families to Biloxi, so that he could then take them along with him to their old home on the Riviere Rouge. I was the person that had escorted them for M. de St. Denis to the Colapissas village five years before, so that they could live with the Colapissas. The night I got there, I was given a fine reception by the chiefs of the Colapissas and the Nassitoches; but the morning of the next day, when I set out with the Nassitoches and their families, the Colapissas were seized with jealousy or, rather, with rage. Seeing that the Nassitoches women, too, were leaving and were going away with their husbands, they fell upon the Nassitoches with blows of guns, ar-

rows, and hatchets and killed seventeen quite close to me without my being able to stop them. All I could do was save the
Chief by keeping him behind me. They seized more than fifty
women or girls—the others, men and women, having fled right
and left into the woods, wherever they could. When night fell,
they came like lost sheep and joined me on the shore of the lake.
All that I could get together I took away to M. de St. Denis,
who was greatly surprised at this grievous occurrence. He intended to take revenge for this at another opportunity and to
make the Colapissas give back the women and the girls they had
taken from the Nassitoches.

LePage du Pratz refers to an Acolapissa village on Bayou St.
John in 1718, which had been bought from the Indians by a Sieur
Lavigne.

According to Penicaut, the Acolapissas moved to the Mississippi
River in 1718, and they were visited at their river village in 1722 by
Father Charlevoix. By 1725, they were back at Bayou Castein. In a
memoir on the Indians of Louisiana, Bienville reported:

To the north of Lake Pontchartrain opposite the mouth of
Bayou St. John which is back of New Orleans are the Acolapissas. They now have only one hundred men from four hundred
that they used to have, very brave and great hunters. They furnish us almost all the fresh meat that is consumed at New
Orleans without however their neglecting the cultivation of
their lands which produce a great deal of corn, but as they do
not take the trouble to dress their skins we cannot obtain any
returns for France from them.

Shortly thereafter, the Acolapissas again left the shores of Lake
Pontchartrain and moved to a spot on the Mississippi River where
they eventually merged with the Houmas Indians and lost their
identity as a tribe.

Some authorities believe that some of the Acolapissas never left
St. Tammany, and that their descendants lived in the Bayou Lacombe area. One Spanish document in 1788 refers to "Chapa Atala,
captain of the village Callois." If "Callois" is a corruption of "Colas,"
a name by which the Acolapissas were known to the French, this
letter would lend some credence to that theory.

Other tribes which were located in the area included the Biloxi,

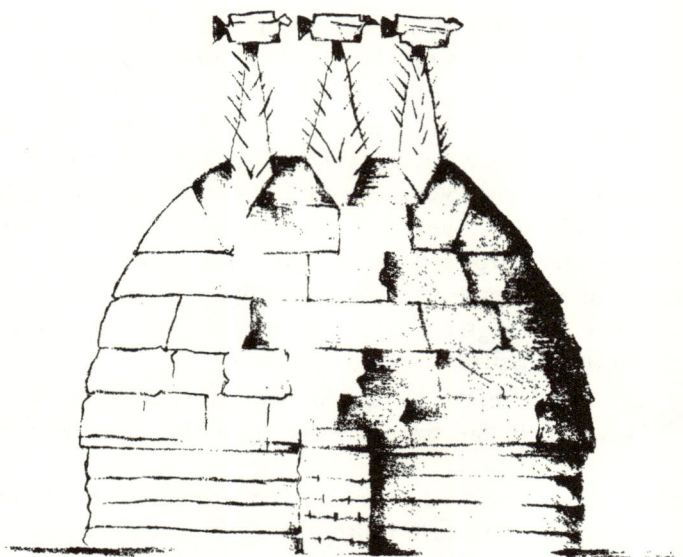

Acolapissa Indian temple ca. 1700 *(Original photograph courtesy The Historic New Orleans Collection)*

Choctaw Indian hut constructed of palmetto fronds and sticks ca. 1909

the Choctaw, and the Pensacola. The Biloxi, a Souian tribe, settled at the old Acolapissa village near the Pearl River in about 1722 and remained there for some years. A 1759 affidavit puts their village at Indian Village on the West Pearl River, where a Boy Scout camp now stands. In 1761, they are alleged to have sold all of their land between Bayou Bonfouca and the Pearl River to Marie Chenet, widow of Francois Rillieux.

In about 1725, the Pensacolas were, for a short time, settled in the same area as the Biloxi.

The Choctaw were one of the largest tribes in the southeastern United States. They do not seem to have made any permanent settlements in St. Tammany Parish until after white men had moved in, but they constituted a presence in the parish until the present century. French records indicate that in the mid-18th century, around 1748, there were a number of Choctaw villages in St. Tammany, but the locations are not given. Spanish records dated about 1790 suggest that there were still several Choctaw villages there. Later they are known through the work of Father Adrian Rouquette and of David I. Bushnell, Jr. However, in 1803, Daniel Clark was able to report to President Madison as follows: "There are no other Indians settled on this (the east) side of the River, either in Louisiana or West Florida tho' they are at times frequented by parties of wandering Choctaws."

There is also some evidence of hostile action on the part of the Choctaws during colonial and territorial times, but no particulars are known. In any event, the Indians do not seem to have been a factor in the development of the parish since early in the 19th century.

CHAPTER V

The French Colonial Period

In 1718, Bienville founded the City of New Orleans on the banks of the Mississippi at the portage from Bayou St. John, and, in 1723, moved the capital of Louisiana to the new city.

Prior to that time, no interest had been shown in the territory to the north of the lake, except for the visits to the Acolapissas. In August 1699, Sauvole had sent Bienville to explore Lake Pontchartrain, and Penicaut, who was a member of the party, described the latter part of the journey:

The next day we continued our route, always keeping to the channel of Pontchartrain, and one league from there found another river that the savages guiding us called Tandgepao, which in savage signifies white corn; the water in it is very good to drink. Three leagues farther, on the same channel, one finds a bayouque, or stagnant water, called Castein Bayouque, which means the place of fleas. The next day we left there and came five leagues away to a river that flows into the lake, which the savages call Taleatcha, which in French is Riviere-aux-Pierres; in it we found some of those shells, or cockles, about which I have already spoken, with which the savages scrape their boats after they have been burned. In these cockles, pearls are found. We gave two dozen of them to M. de Bienville, who was with us. This river is only three leagues distant from Pointe-aux-Coquilles. Here we left Lake Pontchartrain and took our way on this river, which conducted us, at a half league from there, to another of its branches that flows down to Isle-aux-Pois, only three leagues away. Here we spent the night because of the conveniences of the river, whose water is very good to drink and is of great help for all Frenchmen who come through these parts, for the water of Lake Pontchartrain is tainted with tidal salt water that comes into it.

Penicaut's account puts the Taleatcha River at the location of the mouth of Bayou Bonfouca, well inside Lake Pontchartrain, and he translates Taleatcha as "stone." Later, others picked up the name as Talcatcha, and translated the word as "pearl." As late as 1766, Lieutenant-Governor Browne of British West Florida was to locate the mouth of the "Pearl River" inside Lake Pontchartrain. It would appear that the Pearl River should have been called the Stone River, and should have been located at Bayou Bonfouca rather than serving as the border between Louisiana and Mississippi.

Either Penicaut's memory was faulty, or Bienville was not much of an explorer, because there is no mention either of the Tchefuncta River or Bayou Lacombe, two of the major streams on the north shore. We can forgive them if they missed Cane Bayou, which lies between bayous Castein and Lacombe.

In 1725, as first evidenced by Bienville's report on the fresh meat furnished to New Orleans by the Acolapissas, there was a definite commerce between New Orleans and the north shore of the lake. It was the beginning of an almost symbiotic relationship between St. Tammany Parish and the City of New Orleans, which was to last for over 150 years.

The first permanent white resident of the north shore of whom there is any record is Pierre Brou, who describes himself in a lawsuit filed on August 22, 1725, as a "resident at the Colapissas." He brought suit against one La Liberte, who had borrowed Brou's pirogue and then refused to return it, causing Brou to have to rent another pirogue in order to continue his business of carrying "Cajeu" from the woods to New Orleans. "Cajeu" is a word unknown in the French language. It must have been some local idiom, or the French version of an Indian word which unfortunately is untranslatable. We just do not know what Brou was carrying from the woods to New Orleans. Brou, whose signature is somewhat indistinct, shows up as "Barie" in the 1727 census. In 1745, he made his will in New Orleans, because he was afraid that death might overtake him at his northshore home, "a place so distant from all succor." At that time, his name is given as "Pierre Boyer, resident on the other side of Lake Pontchartrain."

Another early resident was Rene Chairman (or Chesneau) called du Chesne, who refers to himself, in a suit filed on January 3, 1726, as a resident at the Colas. He, too, had a problem concerning a pirogue with two men named Chapron and Rochon. As a result, he was forced to come from his house, with three men, in order to find and sell the pirogue, and wanted to collect four days' wages for the three men from Chapron and Rochon.

Du Chesne appears in the 1727 census as Le Sieur Duchesne, living on the north shore of the lake with one "Anion." Anion is certainly Francois Hamont, who was in business with du Chesne. They had two servants and 11 slaves in 1727, an extensive establishment for those days, but we can only speculate as to the nature of their business. Du Chesne died shortly after 1727, but his succession sheds no light on what he was doing on the north shore.

Others who are shown by the 1727 census as residing on the north shore of the lake are Lacombe, Lacroix, and Jean Vis and his son. Nothing is known of Lacroix. Jean Vis has been identified as Johann Weiss, a German, who later settled in Pointe Coupee Parish, and whose descendants still live there today. More is known about Lacombe, as we shall see.

During its early years, the colony of Louisiana was struggling hard to find some economic basis for success. Among the industries encouraged by the Crown was the production of pitch, tar, and resin from the pine trees which abounded along the Gulf Coast. At some time in the early 1730's, at least three, and probably four, of these tar works had been established along the north shore of the lake. The method by which tar was made was described by du Pratz:

> I have said, that they made a great deal of tar in this colony, from pines and firs; which is done in the following manner. It is a common mistake, that tar is nothing but the sap or gum of the pine, drawn from the tree by incision; the largest trees would not yield two pounds by this method; and if it were to be made in that manner, you must choose the most thriving and flourishing trees for the purpose; whereas it is only made from the trees that are old, and are beginning to decay, because the older they are, the greater quantities they contain of that fat

bituminous substance, which yields tar; it is even proper that the tree should be felled a long time, before they use them for this purpose. It is usually towards the mouth of the river, and along the sea-coasts, that they make tar; because it is in those places that the pines chiefly grow.

When they have a sufficient number of these trees, that are fit for the purpose, they saw them in cuts with a cross-cut saw, about two feet in length; and while the slaves are employed in sawing them, others split these cuts lengthwise into small pieces, the smaller the better. They sometimes spend three or four months in cutting and preparing the trees in this manner. In the mean time they make a square hollow in the ground, four or five feet broad, and five or six inches deep: from one side of which goes off a canal or gutter, which discharges itself into a large and pretty deep pit, at the distances of a few paces. From this pit proceeds another canal, which communicates with a second pit; and even from the first square you make three or four such trenches, which discharge themselves into as many pits, according to the quantity of wood you have, or the quantity of tar you imagine you may draw from it. Then you lay over the square hole four or five pretty strong bars of iron, and upon these bars you arrange crosswise the split pieces of pine, of which you should have a quantity ready; laying them so, that there may be a little air between them. In this manner you raise a large and high pyramid of the wood, and when it is finished, you set fire to it at the top. As the wood burns, the fire melts the resin in the pine, and this liquid tar distills into the square hole, and from thence runs into the pits made to receive it.

If you would make pitch of this tar, take two or three red-hot cannon bullets, and throw them into the pits, full of the tar, which you intend for this purpose: immediately upon which, the tar takes fire with a terrible noise and a horrible thick smoke, by which the moisture that may remain in the tar is consumed and dissipated, and the mass diminishes in proportion; and when they think it is sufficiently burnt, they extinguish the fire, not with water, but with a hurdle covered with turf and earth. As it grows cold, it becomes hard and shining, so that you cannot take it out of the pits, but by cutting it with an axe.

In early 1735, a Spanish *belandre*, a small, two-masted merchant ship, was wrecked on the Chandeleur Islands. From the affidavits taken during the subsequent investigation, we learn that La Liberte and Lacombe, together with Jacques Chauvin, a blacksmith, recovered a chest of silver coins from the wreck. All of them are said to be residents of "the other side of the lake," meaning the north shore. We also learn that Antoine Bunel and Company operated a *gaudronnerie*, or tar works, on the other side of the lake, and that Francois Gaspalliere, Joseph Gatoir, and one Perron were all employed there.

Originally Bunel and Michel Brosset were partners in the tar works. They had owned a boat, the *St. Anne*, in common with Antoine Aufrere, but bought Aufrere's interest on January 16, 1735. The *St. Anne* is the earliest boat known to ply the waters of the lake, except for Brou's pirogue. In August 1735, there was a suit filed against Bunel, who was alleged to have absconded, owing the plaintiff 8,419½ livres. We do not know what happened to this suit, but we do know that by March 1736, Bunel was dead. A new partner, Louis Cheval, was taken into the business during the next year, and in May 1737, they proceeded to sell the *St. Anne* to Michel Gerard, who did not pay, necessitating yet another sale of that well-travelled vessel.

On October 12, 1737, romance joined the partnership when Brosset and Mrs. Bunel were married. Their marriage contract shows both of them to be financially very sound, with personal assets well in excess of the value of the partnership. The last mention of Brosset was in June 1743, when he sued the estate of one Brunet, a blacksmith, for 155 livres worth of charcoal. This, of course, indicates that Brosset was still in the tar business at that time, since charcoal is a by-product of the tar manufacturing process.

On June 20, 1736, there is a contract among Claude Vignon, called Lacombe, Louis Joseph Bizoton, and Francois Hamont, by which Hamont, then a resident of Mobile, leased five slaves to Lacombe and Bizoton for use in their tar works on the shore of the lake.

The Bizoton-Lacombe partnership lasted until 1738, when it was dissolved and Lacombe went into a partnership with Jean Baptiste de Chavannes, "for the manufacture of resin and tar on the other side of the lake, in the place where the said Lacombe has already been working, until the present, in partnership with Mr. Bizoton. Under this contract, de Chavannes was to furnish 40 slaves, and Lacombe was to run the tar works and furnish three slaves and the various tools and work animals necessary for the operation.

In April 1739, Jacques Chenier was admitted to the partnership in return for furnishing some slaves. In March 1739, the partnership contracted for the construction of a boat, 44 feet long and 15 feet in beam, and the detailed specifications attached to the contract give a clear picture of the kind of boat used in the lake at that time. Unfortunately, the builders, although paid in advance, failed to live up to their contract, and the partners had to sue them.

It was in October 1739 that Lacombe purchased a very unusual boat, which is described as being 100 feet long, with a seven and one-half foot beam and a three and one-half foot draft. On January 4, 1739, Lacombe and de Chavannes contracted to sell all of the produce of their tar works to Gerard Pery of New Orleans. In fact, the partnership between the two became so close that on March 23, 1739, when de Chavannes made his will, he left everything to Lacombe. Alas, for true friendship, we find the partners in a legal dispute in August 1740, which was eventually resolved in favor of Lacombe. We do not know if de Chavannes changed his will.

In 1745, Lacombe was involved in a lawsuit with Nicolas Chauvin de la Freniere, because Lacombe was running cattle on de la Freniere's property on Grand Coquille Island, on Lake Pontchartrain. He not only refused to remove them, but told de la Freniere that he intended to bring in more cattle. Lacombe failed to show up for the trial, however, and lost the case.

On March 6, 1746, Lacombe leased a plantation and six slaves from Francois Hery, called Duplanty, to operate a tar works. Duplanty owned a plantation on the north shore, so it is likely that Lacombe was once again in residence in St. Tammany. On March 9, 1748, Lacombe settled in full with Duplanty a debt which he acknowledged to be 3,835 "piastres gourdes" of five livres each.

Lacombe had made his will on August 16, 1747, in which he left 50 livres to the Capuchins for his funeral and for prayers. He acknowledged the freedom of a Negress named Mariane and her children, Joseph and Pierre, and left them 100 piastres each, and acknowledged that he had already given them most of his cattle. The remainder of his estate was left to Michel Brosset, who was also named executor. Lacombe must have died shortly after satisfying his debt to Duplanty, since there is no further mention of him in the records. Other than the fact that he called himself a citizen of St. Alban des Roches in Dauphine, France, little is known of this man who was one of the earliest settlers on the north shore, and whose name lives on in Bayou Lacombe on which, in all probability, his tar works was situated.

Our old friend, La Liberte, who was sued by Brou in 1725, and was at the wreck of the *belandre* in 1735, was another pioneer of the tar industry. His name was Bertrand Jaffre, called La Liberte, and his tar works was located at Bonfouca on Bayou Liberty, which is named after him, its first known resident. Jaffre was living in New Orleans in 1721 with his wife and three slaves. Although he was involved in the Brou lawsuit in 1725, he may not have been a resident of the north shore at that time, since his name is not listed there in the 1727 census. In 1728, he and his wife were evicted from a property in New Orleans which they refused to surrender. Apparently, they were said to have killed some of the cattle on the property, and Mme. Jaffre was said by the plaintiff to have demanded 300 francs to refrain from cutting the throats of the cattle.

La Liberte had a shallop, a small sailing vessel, in partnership with his son, Ricard. In October 1739, the vessel, which was called *La Liberte,* was sold at judicial sale to Antoine Aufrere for 800 livres. This boat was undoubtedly used for commerce across the lake by both Jaffre and Aufrere.

On January 16, 1740, La Liberte contracted to sell to Mr. Pery his whole output of tar and pitch; tar for 10 livres a quarter, and pitch for 12 livres a quarter, delivered in New Orleans. La Liberte was successful at this and other enterprises, and, when he died suddenly in March 1740, he left an extensive estate. Gerard Pery was named his executor. The inventory of his estate on the north shore was made on March 28, 1740, and begins as follows: "Today, 28 March, 1740, we, the undersigned officials were transported from New Orleans, our residence, to the tar works of the said deceased La Liberte on the other side of the lake, at a place called Monsfoucart, a distance of ten leagues from this city. . . ." Monsfoucart is undoubtedly a corruption of Bonfouca, and this tells us that La Liberte's tar works was located on the west bank of Bayou Liberty, at the first high ground, the present location of Bonfouca. It is also the first place name of which there is a record in St. Tammany.

At the tar works, the officials taking the inventory found Michel Pacquet, who lived nearby on the bayou which bears his name today, and Jacques Chenier, who was to become a partner in the Lacombe tar works the next month. The inventory describes a property with one large house, in bad condition and poorly furnished, and three smaller cabins for the slaves, also in poor condition. There were 18 slaves, including three children, living on the place. A variety of tools used in cutting wood are described, as well as a number of oxen; a large boat, 40 feet long by 10 feet wide; a bateau three and one-half feet wide; a 30-foot pirogue; and two small pirogues used for hunting. The inventory also describes a tar kiln, 30 feet in diameter and 30 feet high, which was ready to be burned.

The Jaffre estate, after payment of all debts and charges, amounted to over 38,000 livres, half of which went to his widow and half to his heirs.

Mme. Jaffre did not spend much time in mourning the death of La Liberte. By May 1740, she had become engaged to Louis Cheval, of the Bunel tar works, and then broke this engagement to marry Jean Baptiste Gauvain, an innkeeper. Gauvain had to go to court to protect his interest in the lady when Cheval insisted on posting the banns for his supposed marriage to Mme. Jaffre. Gauvain apparently continued the operation of the tar works for a time.

Antoine Aufrere operated a tar works on the Tchefuncta River, alone and in partnership with various people. In April 1735, Aufrere leased 15 slaves from Jean Francois Pasquier for an enterprise in tar and pitch. He was originally in partnership with Sieur Charles de St. Pierre de St. Julien, who died on September 7, 1736, leaving most of his property at the tar works, where he made his home.

Aufrere's next partnership was with Jacques Larche, in June 1738, but their relationship did not last out the year. In December 1738, Aufrere entered into a partnership for making pitch and tar on the other side of the lake with Louis Tixerant, with Tixerant furnishing 25 slaves and Aufrere 15. Since both Tixerant and Aufrere had many other interests, it is likely that this partnership lasted no longer than the others.

In January 1739, Aufrere hired Fourcade, a cooper, to work in the workshop at the tar works for a period of three years, probably making barrels for the tar and pitch produced there.

Aufrere was a very successful businessman in New Orleans, but seemed to spend an inordinate amount of time in court. In one case, he was referred to as "Master Pettifogger," and another entry, in 1746, indicates that the Superior Council was seeking the aid of the governor in order to put M. Aufrere in jail because of his intransigence.

None of the proprietors of the north shore tar works seem to have obtained a government grant for the land on which they were situated, and, except for La Liberte's place, it is impossible to locate them precisely. There is no evidence to show where Bunel's *gaudronnerie* was located, and we can only assume that Lacombe's was on Bayou Lacombe because of the French custom of naming streams after the people who lived on them. The same is true of Michel Pacquet.

The interrogation of some Negro and Indian slaves in May 1748 reveals that Bayou Lacombe was already known by that name and that Brosset's place was located on it. The same interrogation tells us that Aufrere's works were located on the west bank of "Bayou Tchefuncte." The slaves were led by a Fox Indian slave named Cocomina. While on the north shore, they fell in with a band of Choctaws who tried to persuade them to attack the French settlers there. Apparently, they were taken to a Choctaw village or villages while on the north shore, because they were able to describe the merchandise there.

The north shore may have been a favorite place for fugitive slaves, since there is a record of an Indian slave who ran away in 1727 and joined a group of fugitives "beyond the lake."

Francois Hery, called Duplanty, owned a plantation on the north shore, which he at one time leased to Lacombe. He called it "Tauchipaho," and it was probably located somewhere in the Bayou Lacombe-Bayou Liberty area. After the British takeover of the Florida Parishes in the 1760's, Duplanty's claim was recognized by them.

Jean Baptiste Baudreau, who states that he was residing on "the other side" of Lake Pontchartrain in 1747, is distinguished only for his financial ineptitude and his libertine tendencies, as a result of which his wife obtained a separation and took back her dowry.

Jacques Milhet and his wife, Jeanne Poitier Milhet were residing on the north shore at the time of his death in 1763, after it had become British territory. The widow stated that the property consisted of a small cabin covered with canes and enclosed with posts, in which the following items of property were to be found:

One bottom of a cypress armoire, one cypress table, five stuffed chairs of white wood;

Item: four iron kettles, six earthen dishes, and four milk basins;

Item: two pairs of sheets, six napkins, three small tablecloths, all of linen and rather used;

Item: twelve men's shirts, all plain, some in good condition and some in bad condition; one waistcoat in bad condition; two coats, and two pairs of breeches in bad condition;

Item: a negro, named Jean, 52 years old;

Item: another negro, named Cupidon, of the Congo nation, 25 years of age;

Item: a negress, named Roze, 20 years old, with two children: one named Alexis, 5 years old, and the other named Jeanne, 18 months old; the said negress being subject to epileptic fits;

Item: twenty-six horned cattle, some small and some large, for part of which she declared she was indebted;

Item: eight hogs, some large and some small;

Item: one cypress bedstead, one featherbed, one moss mattress, one mosquito-net; . . .

If we are to judge by the possessions of La Liberte and M. Milhet, the early residents of St. Tammany did not live in very high style.

The Rillieux family must rank among the most important of the early settlers. As early as 1737 or 1740, Francois Rillieux, who had come to Louisiana in 1720, settled on Bayou Bonfouca, near the present city of Slidell. After Francois's death in 1760, his widow, Marie Marguerite Chenet, bought from the Biloxi Indians, who were then in residence at Indian Village, all of St. Tammany Parish lying between Bayou Bonfouca and the Pearl River, south of a line running from the headwaters of Bayou Bonfouca east to the Pearl. Since they neglected to have this grant recognized by the French, the family was still in court 90 years later, trying to have their claim recognized by the U. S. government.

Francois Rillieux's son, Vincent, for whom Bayou Vincent was probably named, made his home on the family plantation for many years. He was a soldier and sailor, a Revolutionary War hero, and apparently a man of wealth. His New Orleans home, which he built on Royal Street in 1795, is now Brennan's Restaurant. Among his descendants were the Musson and Freret families in New Orleans, and he was the great-grandfather of Edgar Degas, the great French impressionist painter.

The family sold a large tract on Bayou Bonfouca to Bartholomew Martin in 1825 and, on his death, the tract was inherited by John Gusman. Gusman eventually had his claim recognized by the U. S. government, and the Gusman grant, containing 4,400 acres, is one of the three largest in St. Tammany Parish.

Another large tract which was included in the Rillieux purchase from the Biloxi Indians is the island bounded by the Rigolets, Lake Pontchartrain, and Salt Bayou. Through the years it has been referred to as Rousseau's Island, Petite Coquille, Las Conchas, Weems' Island, Prevost's Island, and Geoghegan's Island. The first settler was one J. Desruisseaux who established himself there in the 1750's. He had a substantial place, with a two-story house, a number of fruit trees, cattle, and other improvements on the property. Desruisseaux claimed to have bought the island from the Biloxi Indians, who were apparently not above selling the same property twice, thereby setting a precedent which would be followed by later real estate promoters in St. Tammany. After a lawsuit over ownership of the property, during the Spanish regime, Vincent Rillieux settled the case by paying Desruisseaux $1,000 and taking full title to the island.

Besides running a number of cattle on their properties, the Rillieux family was also engaged in manufacturing pitch and tar, and were still doing so as late as 1824, when Vincent's succession was belatedly opened in St. Tammany Parish.

Generally speaking, under the French regime, St. Tammany Parish was exploited for its natural resources, and little substantial development took place. There is virtually no mention made of the north shore in the French records after 1750. By that time, however, events in Europe and in the northeast United States were bringing about the first of a series of changes in dominion which were to bring St. Tammany under five national flags in less than fifty years.

CHAPTER VI

The English Colonial Period

In 1755, the Seven Years War, which involved France, Spain, and England, broke out in Europe. The American branch of that war, which we call the French and Indian War, was in full swing at the same time. The ultimate British victory, which was confirmed by the Treaty of Paris of 1763, resulted in the loss to France of all of her North American dominions. Under the terms of the treaty, the British were ceded all of the French territory east of the Mississippi River except for the Isle of Orleans, which is all of southeast Louisiana lying east of the Mississippi River and south of a line running from the river down the centers of Bayou Manchac, the Amite River, Lake Maurepas, Pass Manchac, Lake Pontchartrain, and the Rigolets to Mississippi Sound. As a result of the treaty, St. Tammany Parish fell into the newly constituted British territories and the British flag became the third national flag to fly over it. At the same time, France secretly ceded the rest of Louisiana, including the Isle of Orleans, to Spain.

Both Spain and England were somewhat slow in taking actual possession of their newly acquired territories, although the British did organize politically almost immediately. By a proclamation of October 7, 1763, King George III created the ". . . government of West Florida, bounded to the Southward by the Gulph of Mexico, including all islands within six leagues of the coast from the River Apalachicola to Lake Pontchartrain; to the Westward by the said lake, the Lake Maurepas, and the river Mississippi; to the Northward by a line drawn due East from the part of the river Mississippi which lies in 31 degrees North latitude, to the river Apalachicola, or Catahouchee; and to the Eastward by the said river."

The capital of the new province was established at Pensacola, the Spanish having been forced to surrender their territory in Florida to England under the terms of the Treaty of Paris. In 1764, the northern boundary of West Florida was shifted north to 32 degrees 30 minutes north latitude, which was approximately the mouth of the Yazoo River.

In 1766, Montfort Browne, Lieutenant Governor of West Florida, reported on a tour of inspection through the new province, demonstrating a somewhat shaky knowledge of the geography of the area:

> From Mobile on my way to Pascagoula, we visited the Islands, Ship, Horn, Deer, Cat and Round Islands, they scarse deserve mentioning being mostly all sand, there are some cattle on them but very few inhabitants. From Pascagoula, an old French settlement of some consequence, I sail'd thro' the Regulies, to Pearl River, on the Bank of which we found choice land well stored with Oak of several kinds, red and white Cedar and Cypress trees, thence by way of St. Louis and thro' the Lake Pontchartrain to Tanchipaho, another old French settlement, the land of which is only fit for the breeding of cattle. Here my Lord, I administered the oaths of allegiance to a good many French families of property, who from being much disgusted against the Spanish Government have brought their families, negroes and cattle and have established themselves on our side on the Creeks of La Combe, and on Grand Coquille, so called from the mountains of shell that are upon it. There are many French families inclined to come over if allowed the liberty of Religion, which I promised them.

Captain Harry Gordon, who visited New Orleans in 1766, made the following notes in his journal:

> Our Boat and Baggage being carried to the Bayou de St. Jean, for which we Paid 20 Dollars for the Boat alone & is only 2 miles distance, we left New Orleans the 15th in the Evening & lay that night at the Bayou. To this place the Trade from Mobile comes, & all manner of Smuggling: There are three Schooners, constantly ply between the East side of Lake Pontchartrain and here employed in bringing Tar.

In his "Observations on West Florida" written in 1766, Jacob Blackwell said:

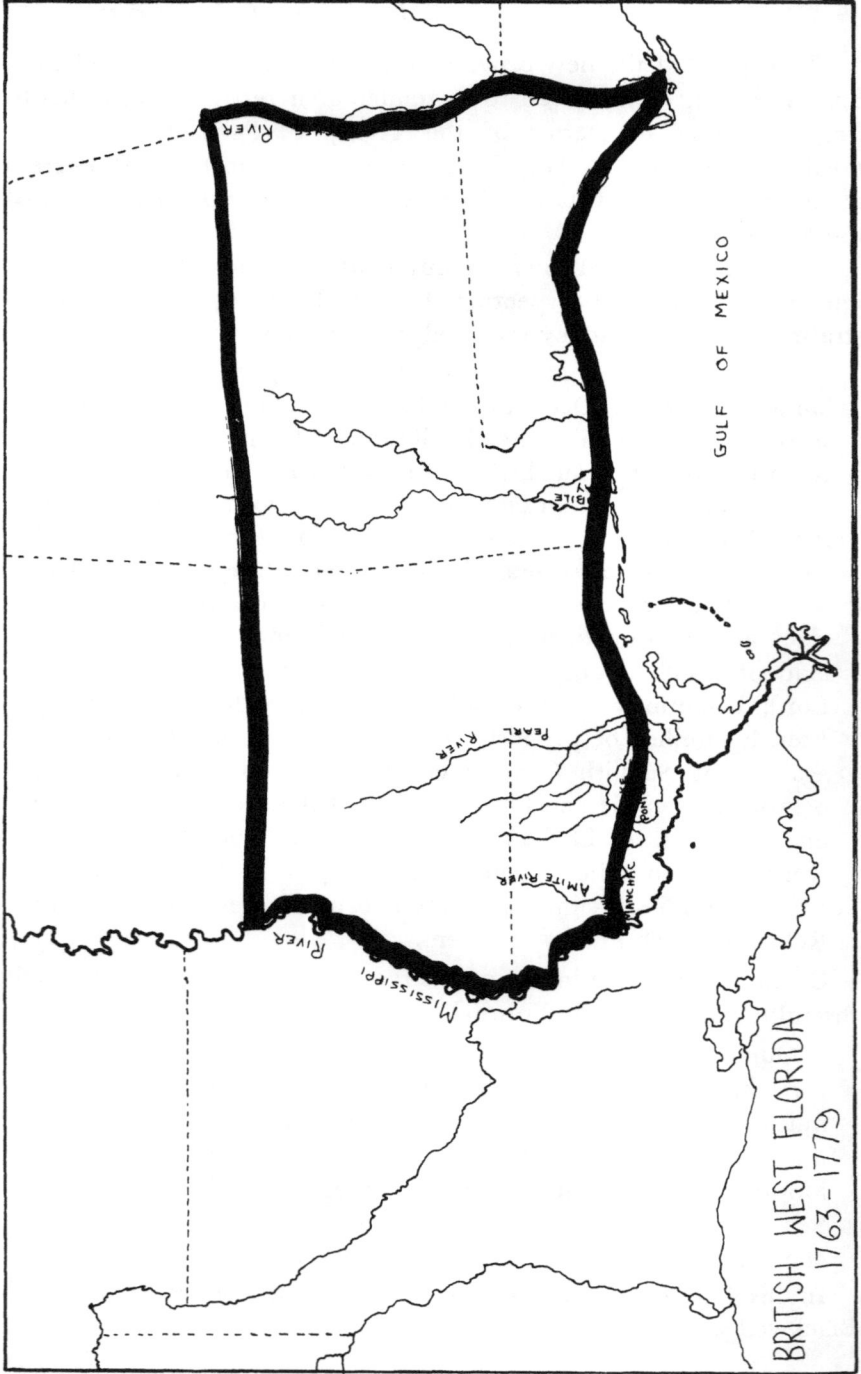

GULF OF MEXICO

MISSISSIPPI RIVER

PEARL RIVER

AMITE RIVER

MANCHAC

BRITISH WEST FLORIDA
1763 - 1779

The Trade of N. Orleans if in the Hands of the Spaniards will become very valuable, as they will take our Linnens &c. which they will Run into Vera Cruz in their own Vessells, which Vessells will come there with Goods from thence, & also with Cash to pay the Troops—Where—as the Trade of New Orleans during the time the French have it, is a loosing Trade to us for the following Reasons—

First—it Chiefly consisted in running Wine, Brandy, Rum, Sugar, Coffee & french Frams into Mobile & notwithstanding the Great diligence of the Custom house Officers, who made many Seizures, it did not prevent Great Quantity's being Run into the Province for which they had most part hard Dollars in payment.

Second—The Deer Skins which should be Brought to Mobile & shipp'd for Gt Britain were carried by our Indian Traders on Pack horses to a Town on Lake Pontchartrain call'd Tangipahou, which Town stands on our Land but is inhabited by frenchmen & Choctaws, who with the assistance of two British smugling Merchts. send over these Skins in large Cannoes & small Schooners belonging to N. Orleans to that place where they sell for as much as they do in London; in paymt of which Skins the English Indian Trader takes Liquors &c. & Runs them into our province. The Chactaw Indian receives in Return from the french, Rum, Powder, Ball & Blankets & Strouds—& what is worse, the French give them bad talks and poison their Minds against the English—further This Town call'd Tangipahou doth supply N. Orleans with Pitch, Tar & Lumber, contrary to Act of Parliamt, also with Charcoal & Lime some Cattle; all which I Endeavoured to prevent by sending an Armed Vessell in the Custom house service to lay off said Town; upon her Arrival there Two hundred Chactows & all the French came down to the Water side & threatened to Burn the Vessel. The vessell then Hauled off from the Shore and whilst she lay there kept her great Guns Loaded & during her stay that trade was totally stop'd.

These Estates at Tangipahou belonging to Great Britain should be Granted to British Subjects in case these frenchmen do not take the oaths of Allegiance & live under the Laws of Great Britn. To prevent the Continuance of their shameful

Trade it is necessary to have a small Schooner with 6 Swivils & 6 Sailors with a Corporal & 6 Soldiers to Cruize on the Lake & also to have a small Stockaded fort Built at Tangipahou with an Officer and 50 Men therein which will give us actual possession of that fine Country which we only have now in imagination & even supposing the Spaniards are in possession of N. Orleans it will be Necessary to have such a post at Tangipahou but no occasion for a Custom house Schooner as she may be of Prejudice to the Spanish Trade which cannot be too much Encouraged.

The settlement of Tangipahou would appear to have been located in the area of Bayous Lacombe, Liberty, and Bonfouca, judging from what Montfort Browne said and from our knowledge that most of the early French settlers were in that vicinity.

Both the British and the Spanish wanted their colonies to be able to trade only with the mother country, and so forbade intercolonial trade. As can be seen, the French and the Indians resented these restrictions on the traditional trade across Lake Pontchartrain, and smuggling was carried on between New Orleans and the north shore during the entire British period. Because of this and because the British recognized that the water route from Pensacola through Mississippi Sound and the lakes to the Mississippi River was vital to the life of the colony, they maintained an armed sloop in those areas.

The earliest British land grant in St. Tammany was to "Francis DuPlanly," of a plantation called Tanchipaho on Lake Pontchartrain. The grantee is almost certainly Francois Hery, called Duplanty, and the property the same tract that was leased to Lacombe in 1746. Although it appears that the British were willing to recognize the rights of the settlers to land already occupied by the French, very few such grants were actually made. Evidence indicates, however, that for the most part, the French settlers were left undisturbed.

A few British settlers began to trickle into the area as the government became established. On July 28, 1766, John Jones was granted 500 acres on Lake Pontchartrain, "on a creek named Chefuncte." Another early settler was Richard Dixey, who was granted 500 acres on Lake Pontchartrain at "Bayou Chief Mentieno." It may be that this was the Chef Menteur, which was not even in British territory.

Two grants were made on September 29, 1767. Jerome Matulich

received 1,000 acres "at the head of Lake Pontchartrain." John Gradinego, who had a wife and family of 10, was granted 1,000 acres adjoining land on Lake Pontchartrain granted to Jerome Matulich. The grant was made conditioned on the land being vacant and "not occupied by St. Martin."

On December 18, 1767, Cornelius Bradford, William Marshall, John Moore, Edmund Milne, and George Hawkins were granted 5,000 acres adjoining the lands of John Gradinego on the west side and extending towards the Rigolets, including an island called "Rousseau," and an additional 5,000 acres to be by them located wherever they should appoint, provided same was vacant and did not interfere with land already granted to French settlers, and that 1,000 acres thereof, including the Isle Rousseau, be part of William Marshall's land.

The Isle Rousseau must be Desruisseaux's island, which, of course, was already occupied by him. This fact, and the mention of the Rigolets, enables us to locate the grants of Gradinego, Matulich, and Bradford *et al.*, at the east end of the lake. Another piece of evidence is a later grant, in 1768, to Babe de St. Martin, of 500 acres on "Bayou de la Combe."

The last of the early grants was 250 acres on Lake Pontchartrain granted to Peter Miller in 1767, but there is no evidence of its exact location.

After these early settlers came in under the British regime, there was a long period during which no grants were made in St. Tammany, probably because the settlers preferred the lands closer to Pensacola or the more fertile tracts along the Mississippi River. In 1775 the Revolutionary War began, and, probably as a direct result, settlers soon began to appear in greater numbers. In 1776, Matthew Arnold, James Connett, Lewis Davis, William Webb, James Kirk, Paul Labyteaux, John Loofbarrow, and Thomas Loofbarrow settled around Bayou Castein. Arnold and Connett are said to be artificers from New York. Davis came from Georgia seeking asylum with his wife and child and 13 slaves. Webb, who settled next to Davis, was also from Georgia, and brought with him his wife, a grown son, a daughter, and five slaves. Kirk, Labyteaux, and the Loofbarrows were all from New York. Kirk brought his wife, Labyteaux and John Loofbarrow had a wife and five children each, and Thomas Loofbarrow had no family. The latter three men were artificers.

Also in 1776, Francis Fisher, Edward Foreman, William O'Brien, James Oliphant, and John Simpson settled on or near the Tchefuncta River. Fisher, who had first arrived in the province in 1772, had a wife and eight children. James Oliphant had a wife and three children. Nothing further is known of the other three men.

Another group which came in 1776 and settled along the Pearl River included Jacob Bell, who came from Connecticut with two apprentices; James Donald, who came from Virginia seeking asylum; Robert Donald, also from Virginia, who brought one Negro and settled next to James Donald; John Payne, a reduced master in the British navy; and Edward Tyng, a reduced subaltern, who settled next to James Donald.

Two 1776 settlers received grants on or near Lake Pontchartrain in unspecified locations. They were Jesse Kirkland, from Georgia, and Thomas Farrell.

In 1777, settlers continued to arrive in St. Tammany, and once again, the bulk of them settled around Bayou Castein. Jacob Ambrose and Rebecca Ambrose settled near the mouth of the bayou. Mathias Ardis came from South Carolina with his wife and three children. Nathan Gamble, John Perry, and John Spell also settled near the bayou. John Perry had actually settled there in 1774, with his wife and three children, and his grant was confirmed in July 1777. He then requested permission to move to the Pascagoula or Chickasawhay rivers, but was refused. John Spell was a British army major, who was granted 100 acres on Lake Pontchartrain and 350 acres on Bayou Castein. Many of his descendants still live in St. Tammany Parish today.

Grants of unspecified location on Lake Pontchartrain were made to William Bryan, Stephen Eubank, and Samuel Ferguson. Others who received grants in 1777 were John Gaston on the Tchefuncta River; John Favre on the Pearl River, about five leagues above its mouth; and James Falconer, who left Virginia because of the rebellion, on the Pearl River.

Hugh McCree, who came from Baltimore in 1776, was granted 200 acres on an island in Pearl River in 1778. James Sutherland, a reduced navy lieutenant, received 1500 acres on the west side of West Pearl River in the same year. Another settler for a short time in 1778 was John Sakeld, who first settled in 1764 at Petit Gulph on the Mississippi River, but moved because of Choctaw Indian trouble.

He then settled on Lake Pontchartrain at Lacombe Creek and became an English pilot on the Mississippi River. He later moved to Pensacola because he was mistreated by the Spanish.

The last of the British grants was 200 acres on the north side of Lake Pontchartrain made to Morris Smith on September 10, 1779.

Bernard Richardson, an artificer from New York, settled for a time on Jackson's Creek, about two miles west of the Tchefuncta River, but later moved on to a grant on the Amite River. Jackson's Creek is probably the stream now known as Black Creek.

Unfortunately, we can only speculate as to how the St. Tammany Parish settlers made their living. Surely, all of them could not have been manufacturing tar and pitch or engaging in trade with the Indians. It is probably reasonable to assume that most of the new settlers were farmers or cattle raisers, and that the economy of the north shore was based more on agriculture than on exploitation of the natural resources or trade.

Although many, if not most, of the English settlers had come here to escape the Revolutionary War, their respite was to be short lived because by 1777 the war was beginning to come to them.

CHAPTER VII

The Revolutionary War

As early as the spring of 1776, before the Declaration of Independence was signed, there had been trouble between American and British ships on the Mississippi River at New Orleans. The British had made prizes of several American vessels there, without objection by the Spanish authorities. After that time, however, the Spanish attitude took on a strong pro-American cast.

In 1776, Oliver Pollock, a wealthy American merchant who lived in New Orleans, wrote to the Continental Congress offering his services to the new nation, and in 1778 he was appointed Commercial Agent of the Congress in New Orleans. Pollock, an unsung hero of the Revolutionary War, gave financial support which made possible the successful campaign of George Rogers Clark in the Northwest Territory. He was to impoverish himself by using his own credit to obtain supplies for the United States. Pollock immediately busied himself trying to ship needed goods from New Orleans by sea to the east coast of North America and up the Mississippi River. His efforts were seconded by his close friend, Bernardo de Galvez, the young and able Spanish Governor of Louisiana, who was very sympathetic toward the American cause.

Since January 1776, the British had maintained an armed sloop, the *West Florida*, on patrol in the lakes and in Mississippi Sound. The *West Florida*, which was the only armed naval vessel in the area, gave the British control of the lakes and Mississippi Sound, and protected the lines of communication between Pensacola and the settlements on the Mississippi River. In April 1777, the *West Florida* captured three boats in Lake Pontchartrain which the British contended were American boats engaged in smuggling tar to New Orleans from the north shore. Galvez, contending that the captured boats were Spanish and not American, immediately retaliated.

For some time, trade had been carried on openly between the British and Spanish at Fort Bute, a British post situated at the point where Bayou Manchac meets the Mississippi River. Galvez seized all British shipping in the river south of Bayou Manchac, claiming that they, too, were engaged in smuggling. This charge was technically all too true, although the activity had been known of by the Spanish and winked at by them for some years. Among the vessels taken was the *Norton*, of British registry, which was owned and commanded by William Pickles, a Philadelphian.

Lengthy diplomatic negotiations relative to the incidents were carried on between Galvez and Peter Chester, the British Governor of West Florida. Just as the trouble seemed to be dying down, an American military expedition again strained British-Spanish relations to the breaking point.

In the spring of 1778, a force of Americans under James Willing came down the Mississippi River. After capturing the settlement at Natchez and obtaining neutrality oaths from the settlers there, Willing continued on down the river. Apparently, he did enough looting and burning of the British plantations in the Baton Rouge area to make his name hated by the residents and his presence in the area an insult to the British. The expedition captured Fort Bute and a British ship, the *Rebecca*, which was anchored there. Willing then went on to New Orleans, where he was welcomed and given asylum by the Spanish.

When the goods captured by the expedition were auctioned off, Pollock bought the *Rebecca* for the account of the United States, renamed her the *Morris*, and proceeded to outfit her as a man-of-war. Then, using a blank commission sent him by the Congress, Pollock appointed Pickles a captain in the United States Navy and placed him in command of the *Morris*. Pierre George Rousseau, a French national who was a lieutenant in the U. S. Navy, was named as second in command.

The presence of the Willing expedition in New Orleans caused further deterioration of British-Spanish relations, and further fuel was added to the fire when the *West Florida* was suddenly refused permission to enter Bayou St. John, a privilege which she had enjoyed for some time. In retaliation for that insult, the *West Florida* captured two more boats in the lake, one belonging to Vincent Rillieux and the other to a Mr. Cousin. Both of these vessels had come from the north shore, but at the time of their capture they were anchored in Spanish waters off the south shore of the lake.

In June 1779, Spain declared war on England. Word of the declaration was sent out to the colonies prior to its being made known to the British, so that Galvez knew of the war in August 1779, before the word had reached West Florida. He resolved to launch an immediate attack on the British at Fort Bute and at a new fort just constructed at what is now Baton Rouge. On August 18, 1779, however, a terrible hurricane in New Orleans sank all of the boats and ships in the river, including the *Morris* (ex *Rebecca*), which was by then fully outfitted and ready for sea.

Somehow in the next few days, Galvez was able to mount his expedition against the British. In order to prevent reinforcements from coming from Pensacola, it was necessary to gain control of the lakes by getting rid of the *West Florida*. A small vessel, called the *Morris's Tender*, which was manned by Captain Pickles, Lieutenant Rousseau, and members of the crew of the *Morris*, including some American marines, was sent out to engage the *West Florida*. Where this vessel came from is not known. Galvez says that he gave it to the Americans, but with all shipping in the river sunk, it is difficult to say where Galvez got it. Of course, it may have really been the *Morris*'s tender, the boat which serviced the *Morris* when it was anchored out in the river.

Be that as it may, the little ship embarked on its quest, the results of which were reported by Captain Pickles to Pedro Piernas, the acting commandant in New Orleans.

Sir:

I touched at Ship Island to see if the enemy frigate was there but she had gone. I came to the Lake where I found the ship, which I have fought, which I have captured, which I have with me. We had a very violent battle which lasted about 20 minutes, with many injuries on both sides. I will be obliged to you if you would have the goodness to keep an eye on our wounded, which is a favor I beg of you.

I am having one of my corsairs leave immediately to guard the Rigolets, and if I can be of any service to the village of Galveztown, just send word by my surgeon. In any event, I will leave immediately for wherever you think is best. If you could send me some sailors, I have great need of them. All of mine are dead and wounded and I have only soldiers left.

I have the honor of being, Sir
Your humble obedient servant
William Pickles

Aboard the Schooner
Morris, September 12, 1779.

Lieutenant Rousseau wrote a more detailed account of the fight:

Having arrived in the lake the 10th of this month at one o'clock in the afternoon, we discovered the boat the West Florida and gave chase to him, and he gave chase to us at the same time. Our Captain Pickles cleared ship and ordered everyone to turn out to hear his orders, and ordered Lieutenant Rousseau to be ready to board and the swivel guns to fire after the volley of musket fire; came about on the other tack, and ran alongside the boat. After having spoken to him and demanding who he was, he told us he was the West Florida of Pensacola, and demanded of us in his turn from where we came. Having answered him that we came from the same place, he told us that he was satisfied; upon which Captain Pickles told him he would soon change his mind, and instantly, having struck the English flag, we hoisted the American flag. Immediately the fight began, very violently on both sides, and, after the first volley, having touched him on the starboard side aft, the Captain ordered the crew to board. Lieutenant Rousseau, one sergeant, and three others, tried to climb up, but were repulsed by blows of lances back to their ship; Mr. Rousseau turned again, being only slightly wounded in the hand, seeing his Captain who repeated the order to board and who followed himself immediately, the said officer having climbed up by the quarterdeck, the Captain with him, and everybody having followed them, the Master surrendered to them. They found the Captain of the boat wounded to the death at their feet with three other men, and the remainder on the bridge who asked for mercy, and all surrendered. Captain Pickles and Mr. Rousseau made every effort to pacify the fury of their men on those who asked mercy which was given to them immediately. Captain Pickles, finding himself master of the boat, made Lieutenant Rousseau Captain.

The said boat was armed with two cannons of six and two of four pounds, barricades the height of a man, with a siege barricade nine and a half inches thick, and with ten swivel guns mounted on the bridge at the same height, which made them tower over us, giving them a considerable advantage; further they had lances, battle axes and many other implements of war. The number of men they had on board was twenty-eight or thirty, among whom were found several Americans who had been forced to serve.

The schooner of Capt. Pickles was armed with only four little cannons with two and a half pound balls, and another of one and a half, with ten little swivel guns on board, without any barricades, so that, because of the construction of the boat, the whole crew was exposed from head to foot. His people numbered 51 men and six cabin boys, of whom three of the crew were killed.

Fort St. John, 12 Sept., 1779.

Pierre Rousseau
American First Lieutenant

Captain Pickles shortly after came to the defense of the north shore inhabitants, revealing at the same time certain educational shortcomings, in this letter, written to Pedro Piernas:

I am informed that theare is a small Vesel afitting out in ye Corrutor of acrusor. I am told she is a privit proporty if so she is only fitting out to go ovor ye lakes to plundor ye inhabitanes, if so I could Abeen adoing of that, but its my opinion its not right I am sarten we have anumbor of frends theare, & they hav been obliged to stay thear own acct. of theare Familes & what littel proporty they had, & now we to go & take it away from them it undoubtedly will Mak them ower Inemes, in my Opinien its Ower business to make all ye frends we can, in the rume of making of Inimes, if I had amind to plundored them i cout adun that sum time ago but my mining is to secure ye lakes, & take Care if Enemy dont slip out of ower hands, if ower friends was to be destressed I can soon do that.

I may cum across this vessel in ye night & may do hir som

mischeaf dont blame me for it For I trust to none, for what trifel can be got From them is no obgect at this time, & I am shure in my own opinien that so smal a vesel, as I undorstand she is cant be own any other desire only plundering of ye inhabitanes.

Shortly before the Battle of Lake Pontchartrain, Vincent Rillieux had his revenge on the British for their earlier capture of his schooner. As reported by Caughey in his fine work on Galvez:

The most spectacular victory was that of Vizente Rillieux, the commander of a Spanish ship in this locality. Having sighted an English transport on its way to Manchac, Rillieux landed his crew and artillery at the pass between the lakes, felling a few trees for their concealment. When the English ship was directly under his guns, he blazed away at it, and raised such a bedlam of bloodcurdling yells that the English, persuaded that they were beset by four or five hundred men, with one accord sought refuge below deck. Rillieux and his men straightway jumped on board and made them prisoners. What was their surprise to find themselves, numbering fifty-six soldiers of the Waldeck regiment and ten or twelve sailors, apprehended by fourteen creoles, the entire command of Rillieux!

Captain Pickles continued to patrol in his vessel in the lake and in Mississippi Sound, where he captured a small British vessel which was carrying a number of slaves. On September 21, 1779, he landed on the north shore and accepted the surrender of the British citizens there. They signed the following surrender document:

We whose Names or Marks are hereunto set and Subscribed being Settlers and Inhabitants on Lake Pontchartrain between the Bayou LaCombe and the River Tanchipaho, do hereby acknowledge ourselves to be Natives as well as true and faithful Subjects to the United Independent States of North America. And whereas on the Tenth Day of last month William Pickles, Esquire, Captain in the Navy of the said States did arrive in this Lake and make Prize of the English armed Sloop West Florida who had kept possession of the Lake for near two years before, and the said William Pickles, Esquire, did on the Twenty first of the same month land some of his People and take Possession of this Settlement and gave us all the Protection against Indians and others that his Force would admit of, and suffered us to remain on our possessions till further Orders; We therefore consider ourselves belonging to the said States, and are willing to remain here and enjoy our Property and Privileges under the said States.

October 16th, 1779

Paul Pigg	Jacob Ambrose
James Farro	Alex^n McCullogh
Daniel Tuttle	Fred^k Spell
Abel Goffigon	James Mosely
Matthew McCullogh	Benjn Curtis
Edward Torriman	Mary Smith
Francis Fisher	Willm Fisher
William Dickinson	Samuel [his X mark] Smith
John Spell	Jerard Brandon
William Stiel.	

Of all of the signers of the surrender, only Edward Foreman, Francis Fisher, Jacob Ambrose, John Spell, and William Stiel had been recipients of land grants from the British, and a number of the grantees of whom we know do not appear on the document. The others who signed must have been settlers who had not yet received grants.

However, by signing the surrender, these early residents of St. Tammany became the first Louisianians to swear allegiance to the United States.

It is doubtful that it can be claimed that Betsy Ross's flag officially flew over the north shore, because on the same day that Captain Pickles landed on the north shore, the British fort at Baton Rouge surrendered to Galvez, who also received the surrender of the post at Natchez. During the next two years the Spanish under Galvez took the British forts at Mobile and Pensacola, and the entire province of West Florida fell for the second time into Spanish hands.

Under the Treaty of Paris of 1783, which concluded the Revolutionary War, and the concurrent wars between England and the French and Spanish, West Florida was ceded to Spain by the English. Due to ambiguities in the treaties, there resulted a dispute between the Spanish and the Americans as to the location of the northern boundary of the province, but the dispute did not affect St. Tammany Parish, which had become Spanish territory.

CHAPTER VIII

The Spanish Colonial Period, 1779-1803

It was during the Spanish colonial period that the first marked growth of the population of St. Tammany took place. Settlers first began to move into the area from New Orleans, and subsequently they came from the American territories to the north. The former group settled along the rivers and bayous in the southern part of the parish, near the lake, and the latter along the rivers further into the interior. The American State Papers show that only seven grants of land, all English, which were ultimately recognized by the American government, antedate the Spanish period. However, 77 grants were made based either on Spanish patents or on occupancy which commenced during the Spanish regime from 1779 until 1810.

Shortly after the Spanish took over, the province of West Florida was split for the first time into smaller political subdivisions. St. Tammany Parish fell into the District of Chifoncte, the boundaries of which coincide almost exactly with the boundaries of present day Washington and St. Tammany Parishes. It was also during this period that we learn the names of the first local public officials.

The first commandant of the District of Chifoncte was Charles Parent, who settled on a large land grant just to the north of present day Madisonville in about 1785. Parent came from an old Louisiana family, his parents having come in 1719 to Mobile, where he was born in 1738. After serving in the French army at St. Louis (Missouri), he returned to Mobile and married Jean Rochon in 1773. They were the parents of six children.

Parent's major business in St. Tammany was probably cattle raising, since the inventory by his succession showed him to own between 1,200 and 1,500 head.

58

Painting of Choctaw Indians in St. Tammany Parish by Francois Bernard created in 1869 (*Courtesy The Historic New Orleans Collection*)

Parent's duties as commandant were quite varied. In 1788, he was called on to investigate the purchase by some local residents, including himself, of horses and sheep allegedly stolen by the Indians in other localities. It appeared that Joseph Janty, a Mr. Dunquerque, Hilaire Boutte, a Mr. Badon, and Parent himself had bought animals from the Indians. Janty had bought a horse and a sheep from Chapa Atala, who is said to be the "captain" of a village called Callois. In 1790, Parent was asked to find two Negro slaves who were being held by the Choctaw Indians. He was asked to learn in what village they were, the name of the chief, and, if possible, the names of the Indians who were keeping them. This indicates that there were several Choctaw villages in St. Tammany at that time.

Parent was also called on to settle disputes over money between Morgan Edwards and his neighbor, Daniel Coyle; to collect back wages owed by Paul Labertu to George Callwell, and by John Spell to George Sharp. John Spell was also sued by Ann Spell and William Hewit for money, and Hewit was, in turn, sued by John Joyce for the same reason. James Spell was sued on his note for 100 barrels of resin and 25 barrels of tar. This, of course, indicates that tar works were still functioning on the north shore in 1794 when the suit was filed. Another suit for money filed in 1792 was against James Goodwood and a Mr. Brassols by Thomas Spell. Others who suffered the same fate were Joseph Cultida, Jacob Miller, and Madame Widow Krebs.

Parent was also called on to settle a land dispute between Morgan Edwards and Henry Richardson, and a dispute over a horse between Morgan Edwards and a Mr. Richard. He also was ordered to make inventories following the deaths of Jaque Constan and Mr. Cuilleris in 1793, and of Morgan Edwards in 1798. He also had to serve summonses on our old friend Vincent Rillieux, who was involved in two lawsuits in New Orleans.

On two occasions Parent had to entertain and furnish transportation to Franchimastabe or Talanchymastabe, the great chief of the Choctaws, who, with the King of the Chicasaws and other chiefs, visited the Spanish Governor in New Orleans in 1789 and 1792.

Other names mentioned in Parent's correspondence were Mr. Allard, who was his neighbor to the north; David Ross, who received a large grant to the north of Allard; Sieur Millon; Honore, a free

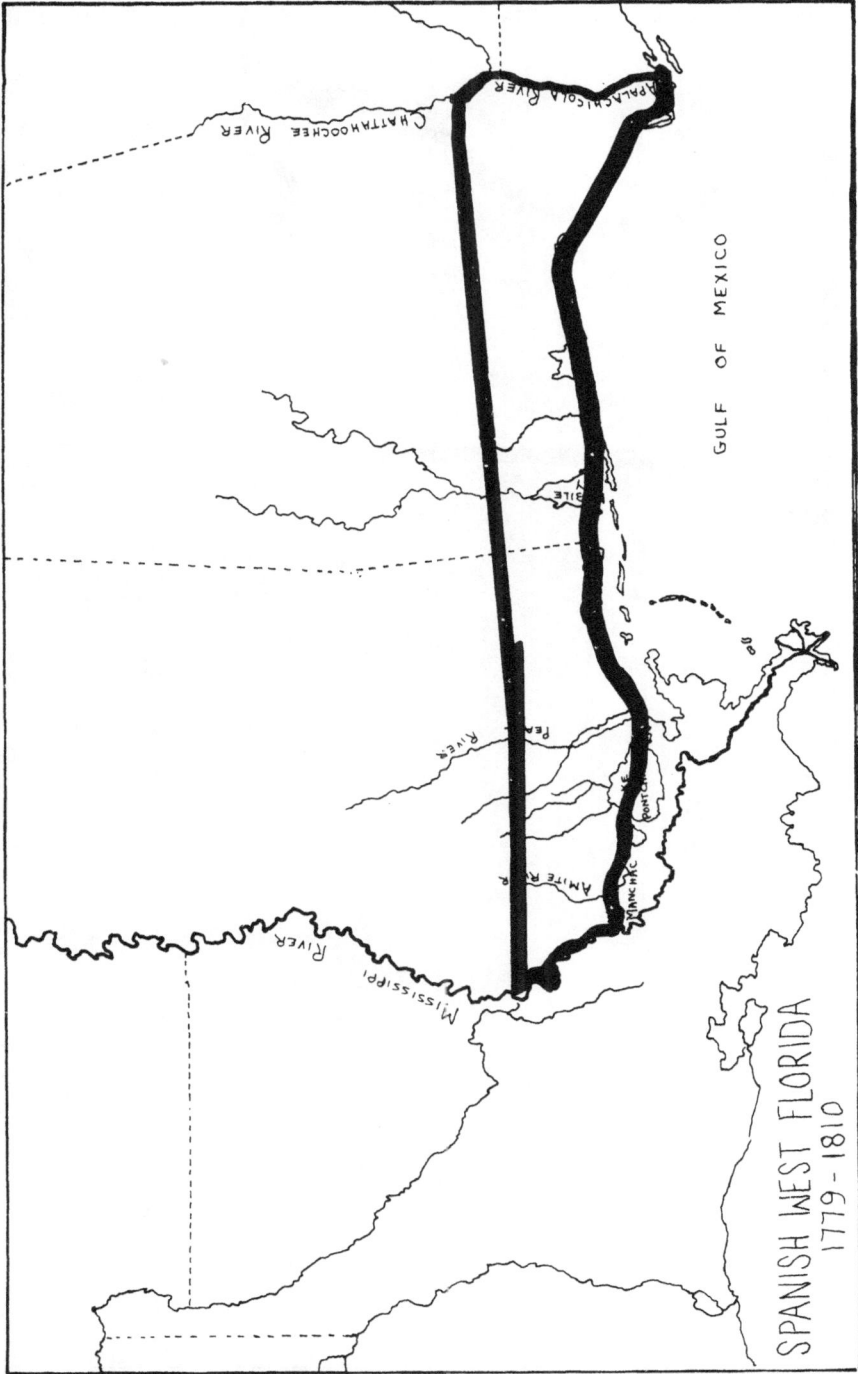

GULF OF MEXICO

APALACHICOLA RIVER

CHATTAHOOCHEE RIVER

MISSISSIPPI RIVER

PEARL RIVER

AMITE RIVER

PONTCHARTRAIN

MANCHAC

MAUREPAS

MOBILE BAY

SPANISH WEST FLORIDA
1779 - 1810

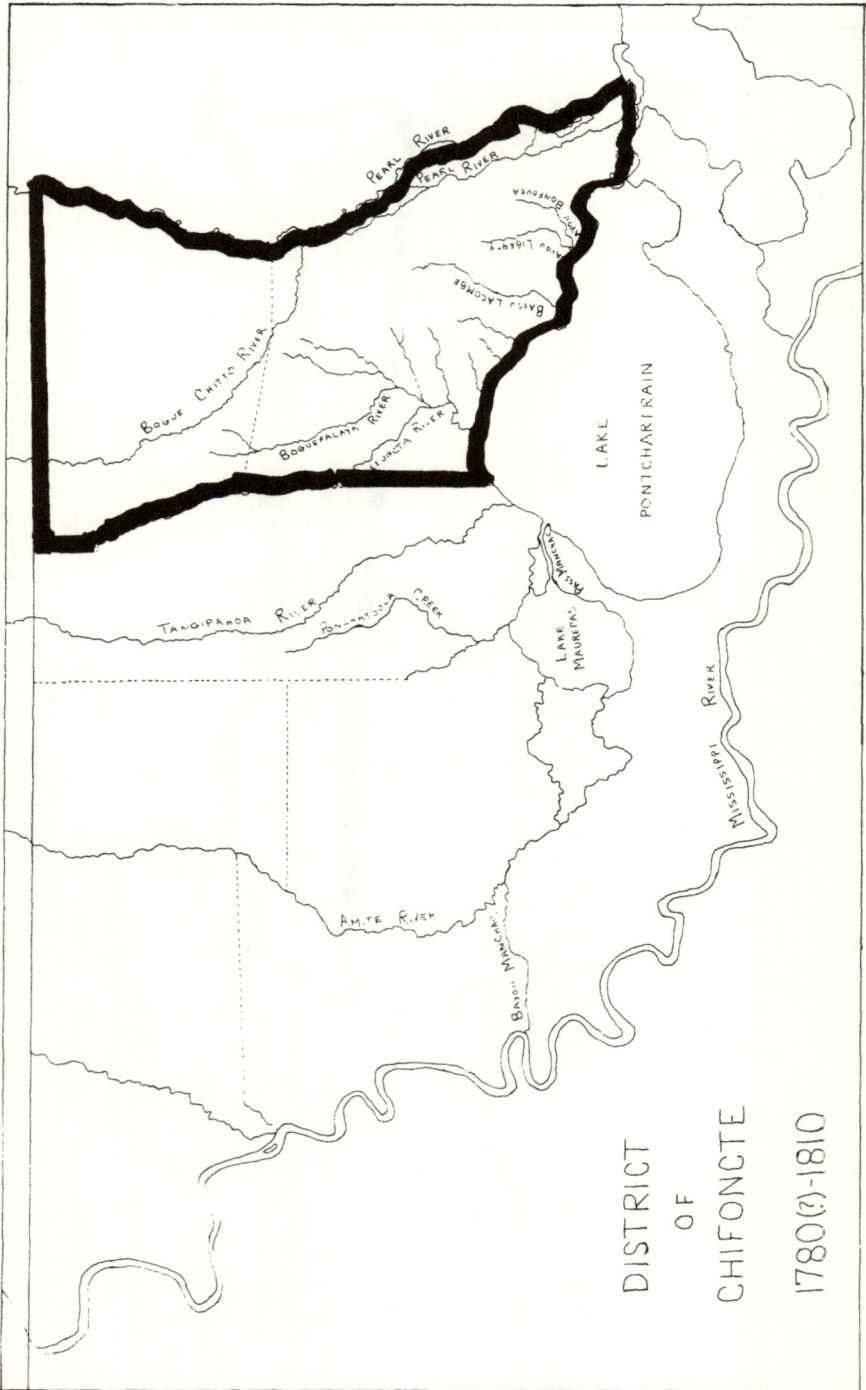

DISTRICT
OF
CHIFONCTE

1780(?)-1810

mulatto; and Thomas Rees, who died, leaving his property to Daniel Coyle.

The Spanish maintained a detachment of troops on the north shore under the command of the Baron de Sterntal, but they were recalled to New Orleans in November 1799, because there were scarcely enough troops to protect New Orleans in the event of war.

Parent died in 1804, and his succession is the first full judicial proceeding affecting the north shore of which there is any record during Spanish times. Parent's son, Charles Parent, Jr., continued to live on the family property where he raised cattle and operated a brickyard, until his death in 1868. One of Parent's daughters, Francoise Aimee, married Andre Bienvenu Roman, who was to serve twice as Governor of Louisiana after it became part of the United States.

Some of the settlers who came into the area during the Spanish regime were Morgan Edwards in 1781; James Melon and Francois Bernard in 1784; Dominick Jung, Widow Badon and Philip Le Dols in 1786; Antoine Foucher in 1787; F. Dubuisson in 1788; Antoine Bonnabel, Stephen Rene, and Mrs. Floriar in 1789; Jose Reboaca and James Goodby in 1790; V. Judiff in 1791; Zed Melon, Brazil Kreps, and Richard Barrell in 1794; and David B. Morgan in 1795.

After a lapse of three years, Samuel Lloyde, John Baam, William Rose, P. de la Ronde, and David Ross came in 1798. In 1799, Dr. White came, but he was driven off by the Indians after one year. Also in 1799, J. White, B. Howard, Joseph Bonner, John Campbell, William Joiner, and James Lee moved into the area.

Jacques Dreux, on whose property the City of Covington now stands, first took possession of his property in 1800. Others who came in 1800 were David Clark, Joshua Kennedy, Joseph Baham, John Barkley, and Madam Dupont.

Also arriving before the time of the Louisiana Purchase were T. Richardson in 1801, Robert Rancival, Samual and David Caradine, and C. de Reggio in 1802, and John Jones and T. Canon in 1803.

All of the above names are given as they appear in the source materials, although in many cases the spelling is incorrect. V. Judiff, for instance, is almost certainly Urban Judice, Baam and Bahan are undoubtedly other spellings for Baham, a well known family in the area.

As a result of the Louisiana Purchase in 1803, New Orleans and all of the vast Louisiana Territory became American property. The United States claimed that West Florida was included in the Purchase, but Spain contended that West Florida, which had been acquired by conquest from the British, formed no part of the property it had received from France in 1763, and had transferred back to France in 1803. Whatever the merits of the respective claims, Spain remained in control of West Florida and maintained a major base at Baton Rouge, which is where the records pertaining to the District of Tchefuncta were kept after 1803.

CHAPTER IX

The Spanish Colonial Period, 1803-1810

The Louisiana Purchase brought about substantial changes in a number of ways. First, there was less government by the Spanish, since West Florida was a relatively minor province. Second, the old southern boundary, through the lakes, was once again an international boundary. Third, the character of the economic base, although still largely based on cattle and naval stores, began to change slightly, as Chifoncte, as the Madisonville area was then called, and the Barrio of Buck Falia, as the Covington area was known, began to develop as trade and transportation centers.

Even before the coming of the white man, there were three major Indian trails through St. Tammany, each having its terminus near Covington or Madisonville. The first of these seems to follow the approximate course of the present Covington-Bogalusa highway, and intersects the second trail near Covington. The second trail starts at Lake Pontchartrain, probably near Lewisburg, and goes north past Covington, approximately along the route of the present Highway 25, toward Natchez. The third appears to begin at the intersection of the other two roads, and to go west across the Tchefuncta near Madisonville and then northwest to meet the Natchez-Baton Rouge trail just above the present Mississippi line.

There must have been some use made of these trails since Jacob Blackwell talks of the use of pack-mules to bring goods to Tanchipaho for trade with New Orleans in 1766.

In 1804, a survey made by Carlos Trudeau of two parcels of land being granted to Joseph Bahan, located west of Madisonville on Black Creek, shows a road running east and west across the properties. A contemporaneous survey of the grant to Juan Bahan, which encompasses the present site of Madisonville, shows a road coming in from the west, and running to the Tchefuncta River at about the present location of the bridge. A fork of the road crosses Bayou Desert and runs to the river on the Charles Parent property. This is probably the road which later maps show running west and then northwest towards Natchez.

Another 1804 survey, depicting a 25,830 arpent grant made to Don Enoul Felipe Dugues, shows two roads intersecting just south of the Bogue Chitto River. One of these, which runs northwest, is called the road from Pearl River to Natchez. The other, which runs about north and south, crossing the Bogue Chitto, is called the road to Buck Falia. From the physical features shown on the survey, it is apparent that the Buck Falia Road is almost exactly where the Old Military Road was formerly located in that area. From other surveys of the period, we find that the Barrio of Buck Falia encompassed the Covington area.

On October 18, 1804, the Syndics of the District of Baton Rouge voted to build a road from the fort at Baton Rouge to connect with "the road which extends from the District of Tchefuncta and crosses that from St. Helena." The road was to cross the Amite River and continue to the Tickfaw River. This road probably connected Baton Rouge with the road running west from Madisonville, where it crossed the Tickfaw River.

Contemporary writings also point to a recognition of the growing importance of "Chifoncta" and "Buck Falia" as trade and transportation centers. In October 1803, John Sibley, writing to Governor William C. C. Claiborne of the Orleans Territory, reported that the best roads from Natchitoches to New Orleans would always be through Natchez and then south across Lake Pontchartrain. In November 1803, Daniel Clark, writing to the Secretary of State of the United States, reported that General Wilkinson "took his route across Lake Pontchartrain, that he might arrive with more expedition at Fort Adams," which was located on the Mississippi River just north of the present Louisiana-Mississippi state line.

A final piece of evidence is the report of the activity in the Port of Bayou St. John, which shows that in 1803, 314 boats left the Bayou bound "across the lake" for St. Tammany Parish. The most active of the sailors was Terence Carriere, who had a land grant on Bayou Lacombe, where he later operated a large brickyard, and who crossed the lake no less than 28 times that year. Pedro Bahy (probably Baham) made 20 trips. Bartholomew Martin, who at first managed the Rillieux plantation on Bayou Bonfouca and later became its owner, made 15 trips. Other active sailors were Luis Brasier, with 14 trips, and Joseph Laurent, who made 13. Uriah Smith, a resident of the west end of the parish, crossed 12 times. Other familiar names on the list are Robert Badon, Joseph Janty, Charles Parent, Sebastian Milon, Zenon Milon, and Pierre Robert, who owned the land just to the north of the Rillieux property on which the Town of Slidell would eventually be built. Nicholas Ducre, the alcalde, made four trips. Eugene Dubuisson, who owned property on Bayou Liberty; Jacob Miller; Francois Cousin, who was to be the recipient of the largest land grant made in St. Tammany; and Gabriel du Bertrand were others who made the crossing. In all, 70 different individuals, many of whom were not residents of the parish, made trips to the north shore in 1803. This, of course, indicates that trade across the lake was sufficient to attract outsiders, even at that early date.

Boat building, another important industry, began to develop during the latter part of the Spanish regime. The list of ship registers or enrollment of New Orleans, from 1804, shows that a number of vessels were built on the north shore during that time. In 1797, the *Esperance*, a schooner, was built in the Tchefuncta River. *Catiche*, a schooner, was built in Lacombe in 1802. In 1803, *Friend*, a schooner, was built on the border of Lake Pontchartrain. The schooners *Mary* and *Precious Ridicule* were built in the Tchefuncta River in 1804 and 1806, respectively. *Gourmand*, a schooner, was built in Bayou Bonfouca in 1805, and *La Redoubtable*, belonging to the Rillieux family, was built there in 1806.

The United States did little to discourage this trade with its neighbors on the other side of the lake from New Orleans. The policy of the United States toward the disputed territory was outlined by Albert Gallatin, Secretary of the Treasury in his letter of February 27, 1804, to N. B. Trist, the Collector in New Orleans:

> The United States claim as part of Louisiana under the treaty of cession, all that tract of country which formerly made part of the British province of West Florida and which lies south of

the 31st degree of latitude, between the Mississippi on the West & the river Perdido on the East.

It is however understood that owing to instructions received from Spain, the Officers of that government have not delivered possession of that Territory. This subject being considered as proper matter of negotiation between the two countries, it is not the intention of the President of the United States to occupy the same by force; and you are therefore to exercise no act of Territorial Jurisdiction within the Said limits, though part of your district, nor to commit any act which may endanger the peace of the U. States.

But in the meanwhile the inhabitants on both sides should enjoy the advantages of a friendly intercourse; and some regulations are necessary for the protection of the revenue and to prevent the sufferance of possession in Spain from being abused for purposes injurious to the United States.

With that view the following rules must be observed.—

1st   All articles of the growth, produce or manufacture of the said disputed Territory may be freely imported into the ports of New Orleans & of Bayou St. John as American produce and without paying any duty.—

2d   Boats and vessels of less than (blank) tons burthen which are employed solely in the River or Lake trade, and owned by persons residing within the said Territory, may when coming direct from the place where owned and laden solely with articles not liable to pay duty, be admitted without paying Tonnage duty in the ports of New Orleans & Bayou St. John.—

And Boats & vessels not decked or if decked not masted, thus employed, owned & laden may in the River Mississippi & Lake Pontchartrain respectively be considered as American Boats and vessels of the same description.—

The settlers continued to come in, but more from the American territories to the north than from New Orleans. An interesting survey of a grant of land lying between Bayous Liberty and Bonfouca, shows the locations of a number of the residents at that time. At the site of Bonfouca, on the west side of Bayou Liberty, was the property of D. Morana. Immediately to his north was the concession of Mr. Blau, which had been sold to Mr. Cousin. Continuing upstream, we find the properties of M. Dubuisson, Sanlarge Milan, and Urban Rose. Between the bayous lies the large grant of Dona Maria Caue, widow of Don Gabriel Payroux. Bordering her on the west side of Bayou Bonfouca, to the north, is property of the Widow Rillieux, Vincent having died in 1800. To the north of Widow Payroux, on the east side of Bayou Liberty is the concession of Mr. LaChaise, which was sold to Mr. Ducre.

Since the United States officially claimed West Florida under the Louisiana Purchase, it refused to recognize any grants made by the Spanish after 1803. However, it did recognize the claims of actual settlers between 1803 and 1810, regardless of their Spanish titles or lack thereof. Moving into the area in 1804 was Joel Ott; in 1806, John J. Ricks, Isaac Broomfield, and Charles Baldwin; in 1807, R. Tenchez, Joseph Durbin, Jemima Smith, and Charles Smith. The pace picked up in 1808, when James McDaniel, David Robertson, Isaac Irwin, Francis Clarider, Thomas May, F. Claron, John Adams, John D. Singleton, and William Vardeman settled in the area.

In 1809, new settlers were Joseph Clayton, Henry Badon, John Irwin, John Dicks, E. Coneilly, and J. Williams. In 1810, a large group moved in and became the last of the colonial settlers. They were John Chapman, Sr., John Chapman, Jr., James Burrell, Jesse Parker, William P. Bon, Robert Hickber, Jacob Tabley, William Brown, Sherard Adams, T. Mitchell, George Ellis, John Tanner, Ebenezer Ford, N. Trippler, Leopold Crownvalley, James Foster, William Bickam, Samuel Neily, Reuben Jones, Nancy (a free woman of color), James Bryan, Michael Jones, James Gwinn, F. Cousin, W. Franklin, Thomas C. Hunt, Thomas C. Holmes, John Clark, Samuel Hide, Newhampton Tapley, Isaac Graves, and Elizabeth Bevins.

Many of the above people did not settle in St. Tammany Parish as we know it today, but since the parish originally took in everything in the Florida Parishes east of the Tangipahoa River, they are officially among our pioneers.

The most active local public official of whom we have knowledge during this period was Nicolas Ducre, who is officially referred to as "Alcalde of the Tchefuncta" and "Syndic of Bayou Lacombe and its dependencies." His first acts were to make the inventory and perform other official chores in the Succession of Charles Parent.

Another action was a suit by Thomas Brooks against Hugh

Sheridan in 1808 for 450 pesos which Sheridan owed Brooks for a Negro named Blaize. Ducre went to the Sheridan house and collected the money from Mrs. Sheridan in the absence of her husband, which apparently settled the matter.

The Succession of Christina Weeks Goffigon in 1808 was a long and complicated proceeding which involved very little property, but which gives the names of a number of residents of the area. These include William Owens, who was the husband of Mrs. Goffigon's daughter, Leah; John Edwards and Samuel Sims, who acted as witnesses; William McDermott and John Wood, who testified as to the death of Mrs. Goffigon; Jacob Miller, who claimed to be a creditor of the succession; Uriah Smith and Zachariah Cloat who testified in the case; William Hewit, who had predeceased Mrs. Goffigon, and who referred to her as his cousin in his will; and, of course, Nicolas Ducre himself. The entire estate consisted of three slaves and some miscellaneous clothing and furniture.

Another 1808 proceeding involving Marselle Soulange Millon, of Bayou Lacombe, Maria Clara, a slave belonging to his brother, and the brother Zenon Millon. Soulange accused his brother of threatening to shoot him and of great cruelty to the slave. Eventually, it was determined that Soulange was of "weak character" and mentally deranged. Zenon took no action against him or Maria Clara, who was returned to Zenon's custody without punishment.

The Spanish records also contain a sale of a piece of property between Bayou Liberty and Bayou Pacquet, made by Castagnio Fremont and Margarita Blount, his wife, to Nicolas Girod, who was later to be mayor of New Orleans. The deed states that the property had been formerly purchased in 1804 by Manuel Toledano, Mrs. Fremont's first husband, from Gabriel Dubertrand. The latter sale had included 11 slaves, a number of cattle, horses, and sheep, all of the implements of the 1,240-arpent plantation, a 25-ton schooner, a pirogue, and a scow.

CHAPTER X

The West Florida Rebellion

As time passed in the years between 1803 and 1810 and as more and more Americans moved into the Florida Parishes, Spanish administrative control grew weaker and weaker. The inhabitants, feeling that they were being abused, began to demand a voice in their government. Pressure on the Spanish administration increased, but the more that concessions were made to the citizens of West Florida, the greater were their demands.

Finally, on July 25, 1810, a convention of men from the various districts of West Florida was held. The "District of Tanchipaho and Chifuncte" was represented by William Cooper, a North Carolina Tory who had been serving as one of the alcaldes for the Spanish. Cooper was at the time, and remained, a staunch Spanish loyalist.

The convention, which did not then anticipate revolution, listed a number of grievances which they felt needed redress:

On Motion of Mr. John W. Leonard seconded by Mr. Thomas Lilley, it is unanimously Resolved, That it is the immediate object of this assembly, to promote the safety, honor, & happiness of his Majesty's province of West Florida (we mean Ferdinand the 7th.) to guard against his enemies both foreign and domestic; to punish wrongs and to correct abuses dangerous to the existence and prosperity of the State.—

On Motion of Mr. John W. Leonard seconded by Mr. Thomas Lilley it is resolved unanimously that this convention consider themselves legally authorized by the Decree of his Excellency hereto prefixed, to exercise the powers and perform the duties expressed in the proceedings of Yesterday.

71

On Motion it is agreed that the convention do now take into consideration the existing greviances of the country which require immediate redress, whereupon the following being proposed were unanimously agreed to Viz:

On Motion of Mr. Lilley seconded by Mr. Haws that we consider it a greviance that while the country is a place of refuge for the deserters and fugitives from Justice of the neighbouring States & Territories, Men of character and fortune are prohibited from settling among us, by which means a population is daily increasing dangerous to the peace and safety of the country, while we have no increases of such as are interested in maintaining order and obedience to the Laws.--

On Motion of Mr. Thomas seconded by Mr. Hicky resolved that we consider as a grievance the want or almost entire neglect of Laws respecting Roads, Slaves, and live-Stock of every description in the country.—

On Motion of Mr. Lilley seconded by Mr. Spiller it is ordered that a committee of five members be appointed to draft a plan for the redress of the existing grievances and for the defense and safety of the Country; and that the said Committee report to the convention by Bill or otherwise.—and it is further ordered that the members of the said Committee be elected by ballot—when Messrs. John H. Johnson, Thomas Lilley, John W. Leonard, Philip Hicky and John Mills were duly elected.—

Other grievances were related to methods of taxation, neglect of petitions filed by the citizens, no system of weights and measures, permitting the French who were exiled from Cuba to settle in West Florida, inability of settlers to obtain land titles from the government, and a failure to prescribe punishments for assault and battery and slander. These and other demands resulted in concessions which effectively stripped de Lassus of his authority and placed it in the hands of the convention.

On August 24, 1810, the convention adopted this resolution:

On Motion of Mr. John W. Leonard seconded by Mr. Spiller, Resolved that Chefuncte, Bogchitto and Pearl River Settlements lying between the east Side of Ponchitoola and the West side of Pearl River, and extending from the lakes to the line of Demarkation become a District, and entitled to an equal representation with the other Districts of this Jurisdiction according to the number of their Inhabitants.

On August 29th, elections were ordered:

On motion Resolved that Abner Beckham Esqr be directed to cause an election to be made in the Settlements of Tanchepaho, Bogcheto and Pearl river, by the free voice of the inhabitants to represent them in the next Convention to be held at St. John's Plains on the first monday of November next— And that three members may be elected by the said inhabitants including Mr Cooper who still continues a member of the Convention.

On October 24th, the convention received this certificate:

By order received from the Convention of West Florida, through Col. William Spiller for an election to be held in the District of St Ferdinand for two members to be elected to represent said District, We therefore do certify that said election was sufficiently notified and that Abner Bickham Senr, and Champness Terry were unanimously elected. Given under our hands, Sept 29th, 1810. (signed) Wm. Lawrence, Isaac Erwin Superintendents of the Election.

Cooper refused to go along with the more extravagant demands of the convention, and wrote to Folch, the Spanish governor in Pensacola, warning him that the Spanish government might be overthrown. Cooper, for his efforts, had his property destroyed by loyalists who disapproved of the actions of the convention, and thereafter, was branded a traitor by the leaders of the republic which was to be established.

It was not until the first week in October that Folch, who was preparing to take action, learned that on the morning of September 23, 1810, the conventionalists had attacked and captured the Spanish fort at Baton Rouge. Colonel Philemon Thomas, in command of the convention force, reported on the attack:

My orders were not to fire till we received a shot from the Garrison, and to cry out in french and English Ground your arms and you shall not be hurt. This order was strictly attended to by the volunteers, till we received a discharge of musketry from the guard-house where the Governor was stationed, which was briskly returned by the volunteers. We received no damage on our part, of the Governor's troops Lieutenant Louis Grand Pre was mortally wounded. Lieutenant J. B. Metzenger commandant of Artillery was also wounded one private was killed, and four badly wounded. We took twenty one prisoners among whom is Col. Delassus, the rest of the Garrison escaped by flight.

The officers of the force occupying the fort immediately acknowledged the convention as the "legitimate organ of the Sovereign people." The convention then proceeded to make a Declaration of Independence from Spain, adopt a Constitution, and call elections for a Senate and a House of Representatives. The flag of the new Republic of West Florida, a white star on a field of navy blue, became the fifth national flag to fly over St. Tammany, which now lay in the newly named District of St. Ferdinand.

On September 30th, fearing local opposition to the revolution in the Districts of St. Helena and Chefoncte, the convention ordered Philemon Thomas, now a Brigadier General, to take a detachment of troops to those areas. His orders further read:

You will resort to force chiefly for the purpose of securing the designing and unprincipled men who have attempted to seduce and mislead those inhabitants.—Having too much reason to suspect that one of the members of our body, and one of the Judges of the Supreme Court, William Cooper and Shepard Brown may be of the number, you will take all prudent and proper measures to take them into your custody, and bring them to answer to us the charges, which may lie exhibited against them.—You will carry with you a copy of our declaration of the Independence of this Commonwealth, and receive the signatures of such as may choose to engage to support it.

General Thomas was given the following proclamation to use in convincing the people to join the revolution:

Inhabitants of St. Helena & St. Ferdinand! the Convention call on you for the last time to unbosom yourselves to Genl. will abandon you at the hour of danger, by a man who accepted, meaning to betray, an appointment from the Convention of the highest trust & importance to the People, you will no longer suffer yourselves to be misled by the Cameleon, Brown; & much less by the Traitor from our own Bosom, whose Murderous cruelties, even at an age when the youth of his Beard might have taught the most criminal in lieu of the most innocent Captives, to expect mercy, will not allow him to remain quiet.— Cooper! After approving, & sanctioning with his signature all our Ordinances, endeavored with Brown to stir your bloods to anarchy & discord.

The Convention secure in the purity & patriotism of their cause, as they are in their strength, & support from abroad, still address you as Friends & Brethren, whom nature one common interest, & the ties of blood, call all to rally under the glorious star which now presides over their liberty & regeneration.

Inhabitants of St. Helena & St. Ferdinand! the convention call on you for the last time to unbosom yourselves to Genl. Thomas, the plain and virtuous Chief, who leads a Band of Heroes, & to learn from him the words of Peace, Union, & Independence.—The Convention in the name of their Constituents, & of all the Inhabitants of Florida, ask of you, if complaints you have to depute & send to them from among yourselves, men of principle & moderation. With such men the Convention will concede all to satisfy you, except Liberty and Independence & good Government, but they will make no Compromise with one of their own Members, and an officer of their own appointment who betrays them, & seeks to plunge the Country into anarchy & civil War.

Signed John Rhea President

General Thomas, at the head of 400 men, departed from Baton Rouge on October 1st. He first met with Michael Jones, an influential loyalist, who was persuaded to sign the Declaration of Independence. On October 3rd, he dispatched an advance guard under Majors Johnson and McCausland to attempt to catch Brown and Cooper at their fort in Springfield. They found it had been abandoned ten hours before. On October 5th, Thomas sent a "considerable force" to Tanchipaho and Chefuncte under Colonel Kimball.

Under the new constitution, the District of St. Ferdinand was authorized to elect one senator and three representatives. Champness Terry was chosen as senator and Daniel Edwards, John Verner, and Abner Bickham became the representatives.

On November 19, 1810, the newly elected legislature of the tiny

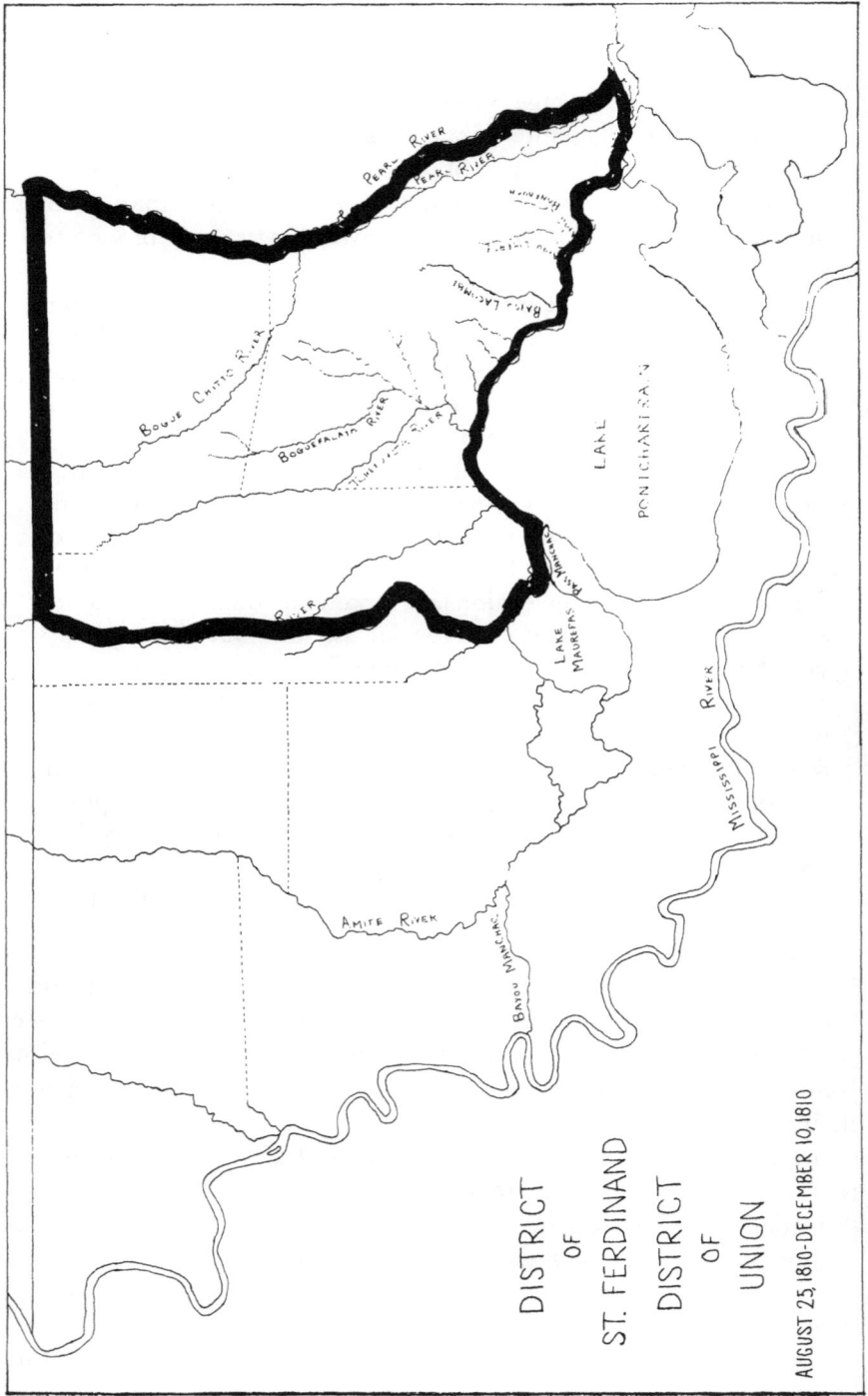

Pearl River
Pearl River
Bayou Bonfouca
Bayou Lacombi
Bayou Lacombi
Bogue Chitto River
Bogue Falaya River
Tchefuncta River
Tangipahoa River
Tchefuncte River
Pass Manchac
Lake Maurepas
Lake Maurepas
Lake Pontchartrain
Amite River
Mississippi River
Bayou Manchac

DISTRICT
OF
ST. FERDINAND

DISTRICT
OF
UNION

AUGUST 25, 1810-DECEMBER 10, 1810

new republic met for the first time. Champness Terry of St. Ferdinand and Philemon Thomas of Baton Rouge were there, but it was not until November 21st, when John Rhea of New Feliciana took his seat, that a quorum was present and the Senate could do business.

The House of Representatives had the same problem. Daniel Edwards of St. Ferdinand was there, but again there was no quorum. On November 20th, John Verner, "Abner Bickum," and other late comers took their seats, and the House was also able to transact business.

On November 22nd, Fulwar Skipwith was elected Governor of the new republic by the legislature. The legislature also started up a judicial system, organized an army and a navy, and began preparations for the further conquest of Spanish West Florida, beyond the Pearl River. The expedition was to be launched from the principal naval base, which was located at Chifoncta. Among less momentous actions, they passed an act changing the name of the District of St. Ferdinand to the District of Union. However, all of these ambitious plans were to come to naught.

On October 27, 1810, President James Madison of the United States, issued a proclamation declaring that West Florida formed part of the Louisiana Purchase, and directed Governor William C. C. Claiborne of the Orleans Territory to take possession of the new nation. On December 7, 1810, Governor Claiborne raised the flag of the United States in St. Francisville without opposition. Three days later, on December 10, 1810, supported by a force led by Colonel Leonard Covington, Claiborne lowered the flag of the Republic of West Florida in Baton Rouge, and the short life of that nation came to an end. The 15-starred flag of the United States was raised and became the sixth flag to fly over the Florida Parishes and St. Tammany.

CHAPTER XI

The American Colonial Period

Governor Claiborne lost little time in setting up the government of the newly acquired lands, which now formed part of the Territory of Orleans. On December 22, 1810, he issued a proclamation creating four parishes between the Mississippi River and the Pearl River.

Be it known that "for the execution of process civil and criminal," I do, by virtue of the powers in me vested, under the ordinance of congress, for the government of the territory of Orleans, ordain and decree, that there be established within the county of Feliciana four parishes whose limits shall be as follows: All that tract of country lying below the boundary of the Mississippi territory, and between the most eastern branch of Thompson's creek and the river Mississippi, shall form the first parish, and shall be called the parish of Feliciana: all that tract of country lying between the most eastern branch of Thompson's creek and the river Iberville, and extending from the river Mississippi to the Amite, shall form the second parish, to be called the parish of East Baton Rouge: all that tract of country lying below the boundary of the Mississippi territory, and between the Amite and the river Ponchitoola, which empties into the lake Maurepas, shall form the third parish, to be called the Parish of St. Helena: and all that tract of country east of the Ponchitoola, including the settlements of Chiffonta, Boquechitto and Pearl rivers, shall form the fourth parish, to be called the parish of St. Tammany: within the residue of the county of Feliciana, there shall be formed such other parishes as may thereafter be deemed expedient.

Claiborne never explained why he named the new parish St. Tammany. The name is generally thought to come from Tamanend, a Delaware Indian chief, who was reputed to be a great friend to the white man in the early days of the colonization of the east coast. His name lived on in a political society called the Sons of Tammany, which eventually gave its name to Tammany Hall in New York City. The title of "Saint" was purely honorary, although Tamanend was renowned for his goodness.

On April 24, 1811, the territorial legislature adopted an act re-subdividing the territory between the Mississippi and the Pearl:

8. I.   The county of Feliciana shall be divided into six par-ishes, the first shall be called the parish of Feliciana, lying be-tween the lower line of the Mississippi Territory to the mouth of Thompson's creek, and a line running thence due east to the river Amite, and its western boundaries shall be the Mississippi.

9. II.   The second shall be called the parish of East Baton Rouge lying between the parish of Feliciana and the Iberville and between the Mississippi and the Amite.

10. III. The third shall be called the parish of St. Helena which comprehends that tract of country lying below the line of the Mississippi territory, and between the Amite and the river Tanchipao.

11. IV. The fourth shall be called the parish of St. Tammany lying east of the Tanchipao, to Pearl river and south of the Mississippi Territory.

Despite the obvious weakness and indecision of the Spanish, who were still ensconced at Pensacola, there was apprehension that they might retaliate against the United States, and attempt to recapture their lost territory. Governor Claiborne was particularly concerned about St. Tammany. Writing to Colonel Covington on December 25, 1810, he said:

From information received as to the very exposed situation of our newly acquired settlements on the Lake Ponchartrain, and of the description of Inhabitants, I am impressed with the expediency of establishing a military post somewhere on that Lake or its waters. I must therefore Sir request of you to detail

William C. C. Claiborne ca. 1815 *(Courtesy The Historic New Orleans Collection)*

for duty under the command of a proper officer about one hundred men with orders to the commanding officer, to proceed from hence by the way of New Orleans to the Fort on the Bayou St. John, and there to await my instructions as to the Position he is to occupy.

Shortly thereafter, a cantonment was constructed on the banks of the Little Bogue Falaya River, a few miles north of Covington, although when and to what extent it was occupied by troops is not certain. It is likely that the cantonment was occupied by the 3rd Regiment of Infantry of the United States Army during 1812. It had as many as eight companies totalling 435 men. The 3rd Regiment was transferred to Pass Christian, Mississippi in the latter part of 1812. In 1813, the cantonment was described as "an elegant range of barracks and officers' houses, sufficient for a regiment of men, which have been built, and occupied by the United States troops: they are now vacant."

In addition, a navy yard was constructed near Madisonville, probably two miles upstream of the present site of the town. On June 26, 1814, the headquarters of the Seventh Military District were established there by Brigadier General Thomas Flournoy. The Seventh Infantry Regiment had been transferred to the Navy Yard earlier in that month, and Major John Nicks was placed in command. Apparently, the Navy Yard was not looked on with affection by the men stationed there. Captain William McClellan, temporarily commanding the regiment, wrote to General Andrew Jackson on July 10, 1814:

I can't say what General Flournoy's motives were in ordering us to this place. We have been here twelve days and lost three men. The river is on our front. We are surrounded by a marsh in our rear. The spring water we have to make use of, a Tennessee horse would nearly blush to drink it. This climate proved fatal to the Tennessee troop. I have lost fine soldiers of my company since I left Tennessee. If I stay here during the sickly season, I may calculate on nearly half of them dying. The 7th Regiment would like to be stationed with the General. I am fully persuaded that if you were to see our regiment you would be pleased with it. Our music is very good. The officers of the regiment have spent upwards of $400 in purchasing instruments for the musicians. Major Nicks has just come in and took command of the regiment. Perhaps he will write you on the subject. From here to New Orleans is upwards of forty miles. From the Pass Christian is sixty miles. The latter is very healthy, and this has no claim to health.

Claiborne also directed his attention to appointing officials for the new parish, although not without some difficulty. Writing to Robert Smith, who was then Secretary of State of the United States, on December 24, 1810, he said: "Judges for the parishes of St. Helena and St. Tammany have not yet been named;—there is in that quarter a great scarcity of talent, and the number of virtuous men too, (I fear) is not as great as I could wish."

Despite that problem, he appointed Joseph Spell to the office of justice of the peace on February 1, 1811, the first man named to hold office in the new American regime. On March 2, 1811, he named Baptiste Baham as a justice of the peace. Finally, on July 18, 1811, he issued a commission to Thomas Cargill Warner as Parish Judge, an office which, at that time, combined both the executive and judicial functions. The judge not only performed the usual judicial duties, but also acted as president of the police jury. On August 1, 1811, a proclamation calling for the election of one representative from the Parishes of St. Helena and St. Tammany was issued, the election to be held on the first Monday in October 1811, and on the two following days. Until statehood, the political organization of St. Tammany Parish was complete.

Outside of the appointing of the officials and pardoning James Graham of St. Tammany Parish, who had been convicted of selling liquor without a license, Claiborne took no further action relative to St. Tammany during 1811.

After an extended debate in Congress, Louisiana was admitted to statehood on April 8, 1812, as the eighteenth state. It was the first state outside of the original boundaries of the United States, as established by the Treaty of Paris of 1783, to be admitted to the Union. Under the bill originally adopted, the Florida Parishes had not been included in the State of Louisiana, and there was a sharp difference of opinion among the citizens of the Florida Parishes as to whether they wished to be included. In the more heavily populated areas around Baton Rouge and the Felicianas, the people generally wanted

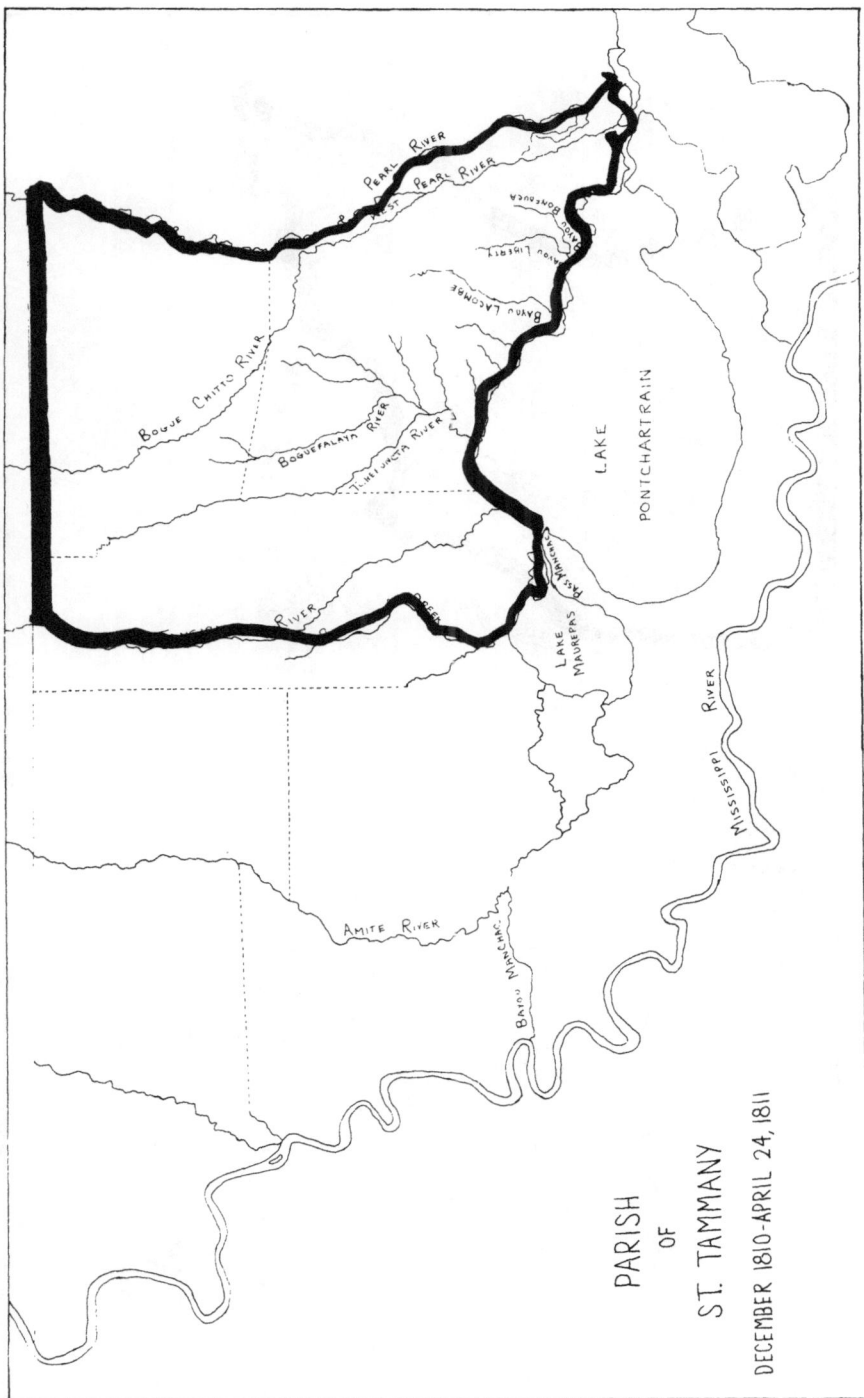

PARISH
OF
ST. TAMMANY
DECEMBER 1810-APRIL 24, 1811

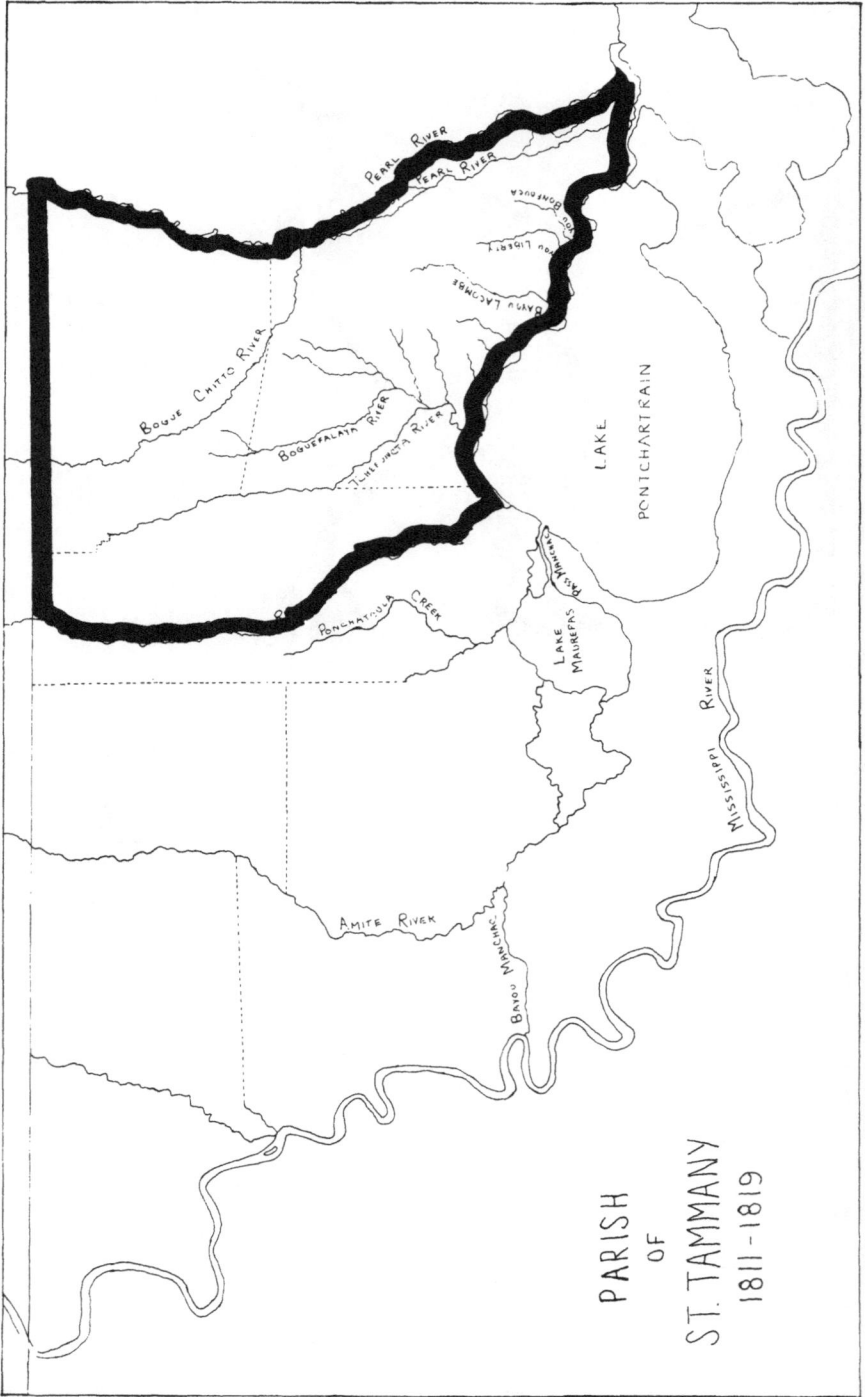

PARISH
OF
ST. TAMMANY
1811-1819

Pearl River
Pearl River
Bayou Bonfouca
Bayou Liberty
Bayou Lacombe
Bogue Chitto River
Boguefalaya River
Tchefuncta River
Ponchatoula Creek
Lake Pontchartrain
Lake Maurepas
Pass Manchac
Mississippi River
Amite River
Bayou Manchac

to be part of Louisiana. On the other hand, the people in St. Tammany Parish petitioned Congress to be made part of the Mississippi Territory. On April 14, 1812, despite the resistance, a bill was signed by President Madison which included the Florida Parishes in Louisiana, conditioned on their being accepted by the State Legislature. Finally, on August 4, 1812, the State Legislature accepted the Florida Parishes, and St. Tammany Parish became part of the State of Louisiana.

This was the third time that the people of St. Tammany had been opposed to their political destiny, but were unable to prevent it. The first time was in 1779, when the local people took the oath of allegiance to the United States, just before becoming Spanish citizens. The second was when they were opposed to the West Florida rebellion, but found themselves part of the Republic of West Florida. The third time was not to be the last.

In his message to the legislature on August 8, 1812, Governor Claiborne reported that in 1811 there were "in St. Tammany from 17 to 18 hundred free people and three hundred slaves. I have understood that in the course of the present year, 1812, there has been a considerable emigration to the four Parishes above mentioned, particularly to St. Tammany."

Claiborne continued to hold his low opinion of St. Tammany, however. On August 14, 1812, he reported:

> On turning my attention to the interior of the State, I perceive with regret, that within the parishes of Feliciana, Baton Rouge, St. Helena and St. Tammany (which have recently been annexed to Louisiana) the Civil Authority has become so weakened and relaxed, that the laws have lost much of their influence, and in the parish of St. Tammany particularly are scarcely felt.

The governor's estimate of both population and immigration appear to be quite realistic. The 1811-1812 tax roll compiled by James Gaines, the first sheriff of St. Tammany, shows 162 taxpayers, who paid a total of $981.11. The biggest taxpayer was Francois Cousin, who paid $93.25, almost ten per cent of the total. Other big taxpayers were John Lorance, Madame Vinsant, Thomas Spell, R. Baddon, and R. Baham.

The 1812 tax roll, which was made by Benjamin A. Hickborn, an attorney, after Mr. Gaines had absconded, shows a total of 355 taxpayers on the roll. There was a total of 322 men, 239 women, and 835 children, as well as 301 slaves in the parish, for a total population of 1,697. Some of the more affluent citizens were Francois Cousin, who owned 42 slaves, 2 schooners, and 1,300 cattle; Madam Vinzant, who owned 22 slaves, a schooner, and 500 head of cattle; and John Lorance, who owned 16 slaves, a schooner, and 1,000 head of cattle.

There were also eight persons who were licensed to sell liquor in quantities above one quart, which indicates either a healthy consumption by the local citizenry, or a considerable transient trade. In the light of the future history of the parish, it is likely that both of these conditions existed in 1812. The names of the eight gentlemen were Renez Baham, Robert Badon, John Gustavus, Henry Hill, William Lawrence, John Thawarth, Rice Wells, and Luke Lea.

The tax list also shows that there were 305 "improvements" in the parish, probably meaning houses, 18 schooners, 11 stud horses, 13 wagons, 511 work horses, and 9,922 stock cattle. This would indicate about the same economic base as in 1803. The sale of one piece of property which includes a cotton gin among the things transferred, tells us that some cotton was being raised at that early date.

As to immigration, the American State Papers show 61 land grants based on occupancy beginning in 1812, which is by far the largest year for settlers coming to St. Tammany up until that time, and for many years thereafter.

CHAPTER XII

Statehood, 1812-1820

The early years of statehood were eventful in St. Tammany. Indian trouble broke out in the latter part of 1812 and apparently persisted for some time. In September 1812, Governor Claiborne wrote: "About the same time (9th ult.) I received sundry letters from respectable Citizens of the parishes of St. Helena and St. Tammany within this State, informing me of the frequent menaces of the Chactaws and requesting that measures might be taken for the safety of the settlements."

In the spring of 1813, the Governor reported to the Secretary of War: "In the course of the last year, their safety was seriously threatened, so much so that several farms were abandoned, and the frontier settlers fled to the interior for surety."

Governor Claiborne later visited the parish to take some measures for the safety of the inhabitants. It is not known what he did, but whatever it was, it worked. There is no further mention of Indian troubles in St. Tammany. Of course, the presence of the troops at the cantonment and at the navy yard may have had something to do with this fact.

The first two towns were founded in 1813 and 1814, although there had been settlements of sorts at Chifoncte and at the Barrio of Buck Falia for some years. Jacques Dreux, who settled in St. Tammany in 1800, received a Spanish grant on the west bank of the Bogue Falaya River, at the head of navigation. Possibly as early as 1805, he had laid out a small town called St. James or St. Jacques, but there are no records of its exact location. In 1813, the Dreux tract was acquired by John Wharton Collins, who, on July 4, 1813, dedicated the Town of Wharton. By legislative act adopted March 11, 1816, the town was formally incorporated, and its name changed to Covington.

There are two versions of how the town got its new name. One of these is a legend, handed down in the family of Jesse R. Jones, and of general circulation in the town:

> One day, according to the story, when Jesse Jones, then a rising young lawyer, who had fought with Andrew Jackson behind the breastworks of Chalmette, was enjoying a convivial glass with some of the town officials in a tavern, he suddenly quirked his lips in a smile as he gazed at the amber liquid in his tumbler. It was Kentucky whiskey of excellent quality they were drinking, despite its honest price of forty cents a gallon.

> "Gentlemen," said the future judge, gesturing toward the label on the jug before them, "I have a suggestion to make. If we're going to confer honor on anything when we rename this town, let us choose something worthy of the honor. I don't know of anything that's given us all such mellow and consistent pleasure as this Blue Grass whiskey from Covington. Therefore I make a motion that hereafter this town be known as Covington."

The other story is that it was named for General Leonard Covington, the distinguished soldier who had stood with Claiborne in Baton Rouge at the demise of the West Florida Republic, and who died a hero's death during the War of 1812.

The first election of officials in Covington took place at William Bagley's house on June 2, 1817. Those elected were Thomas Tate, mayor, and John W. Collins, Jesse R. Jones, Dudley W. Packwood, and William Bagley, trustees.

In 1798, a Spanish grant was made to Juan Baham on the west bank of the Tchefuncta River, about two miles above its mouth. This grant included the site of Chifoncte. In 1814, a town, called Madisonville, was surveyed and formally dedicated by Baham. Madisonville was incorporated by legislative act, approved on February 18, 1817.

In 1813, a visitor to the area gave this description of the place and its people:

> Madisonville is handsomely situated on the west bank of the river Tchefonta, which rises and runs into lake Ponchartrain in

the parish of St. Tammany, in the state of Louisiana. At present this town has little more than the name, attached to an elegant, healthy, and eligible spot of ground for a seaport town. About half a dozen French built mud walled huts, and about as many log houses or cabins, and two or three small frames are all its present improvements. . . .

The Tchefonta is a wide and handsome little river, affording a safe harbor and navigation for any vessel that can be sailed through the Regulees. Schooner navigation extends several miles up the eastern branch, called Bouge Falia, on the west bank of which a town is laid off by the name of St. Jack; and several buildings are erected.

Madisonville is favorably situated for the coasting and West India trade, having about two days sail in going out, and about two weeks sail in coming in, the advantage of New Orleans: it lies more convenient to the necessary supplies for repairing and building vessels; it is believed to be a more healthy situation, less infested with musketoes, and furnished with good spring water.

Madisonville is situated two miles from the mouth of the river Tchefonta; about 30 miles N. of New Orleans; about 30 miles E. from Springfield; about 70 miles E. from Baton Rouge; and about 80 miles E. by S. from St. Francisville, at the mouth of the bayou Sarah, in the state of Louisiana. It lies about 80 miles E. S. E. from Woodville, the seat of justice in Wilkinson county; about 110 miles S. E. from the city of Natchez; about 60 miles S. E. from the seat of justice in Amite county; about 90 miles S. by W. from New London or Monticello, on Pearl river; about 65 miles S. W. from New Columbia, in Marion county; about 140 miles W. S. W. from fort Stoddert; and about 110 miles W. from Mobile town, in the Mississippi territory. These are the conjectured distances on rectalineal directions; for there are few or no roads leading towards Madisonville. The Old King's road, as it is called, leading in a direction from Baton Rouge to the bay of St. Lewis a few miles E. from the Regulees crossed the river Tchefonta about half a mile above the Cockle bank, now the site of Madisonville.

The United States' troops cut a road from the vicinity of

Tchefonta in a direction to fort Stoddert; but the water and the swamp obstructions on it rendered it almost useless, except in very dry weather; and the great hurricane of August last, has completely blocked it up as well as every other road approaching Madisonville; and the police laws, weak and unsettled in consequence of the many and recent changes of government, have not co-operated with public spirit to clear them out. . . .

Madisonville is understood to be chosen by the agents of the Navy Department for repairing, and even building of small vessels of war for the southern station; and it seems peculiarly adapted to these purposes: the vicinity abounds with oak, pine, and cypress: here also tar is made in abundance, with as great facility as in any part of the union: the spun hemp, or rope yarn of Kentucky, may be brought as cheap to this harbor as to any other, and the rigging may be laid in order at the navy yard with the greatest economy and advantage to the public service. Provisions will also be furnished here of as good a quality and as cheap as in any other seaport: the country between the Pearl and Mississippi rivers is extremely favorable to the growth of hogs: and cattle are reared to as great perfection, and perhaps to as great an extent, on the waters of Pearl river, and particularly in the Choctaw nation of Indians, as in any part of the U. States.

Why, it may be asked, have not the singular advantages of this place sooner manifested themselves? The French were the first, and for many years the only civilized inhabitants in the vicinity of Tchefonta. Enterprise is not one of the characteristic traits of the Louisiana French. A few small fields and mud wall houses, are the most of their improvements in this neighborhood. The burning of shell lime and charcoal, making tar and raising cattle, and carrying the product of their labor to the Orleans market, were generally the extent of their pursuits. Attempts at commerce must have proved futile, as there were no country settlements to support them; the neighboring country was still within a few years past inhabited only by Choctaw Indians.

By legislative act of March 25, 1813, Thomas Spell, Robert Badon, Benjamin Havard, Joseph Hertraise, and Benjamin Beakham (Bickham), who were the first police jurors of the parish, were appointed commissioners "to fix on the most convenient place not exceeding what they may perceive to be within three miles from the centre of said parish for the purpose of erecting a court house and jail; . . ." They selected a spot on the property of Judge Thomas C. Warner, near Enon on the Bogue Chitto River, and a court house was constructed there.

In 1817, an election was called to fix the seat of justice for the parish. The people must have voted to move the court house, because David B. Morgan, Jesse R. Jones, John Wright, James Tate, and Daniel Edwards were named by legislative act of March 16, 1818, as commissioners "to select the most proper site for a permanent seat of justice in or near the town of Covington."

The commission selected a site in the newly dedicated Town of Claiborne, which was located just across the Bogue Falaya River from Covington. This location was chosen because of the commitment of the Claiborne Company, which had laid out the new town, to build a courthouse and jail at its expense. The courthouse built by the Claiborne Company still stands, and is one of the oldest and most charming buildings in St. Tammany. Despite the presence of the courthouse, the town of Claiborne did not develop as expected, and, after a few years, the courthouse was moved to Covington, where it has since remained.

Shortly after Louisiana achieved statehood, the War of 1812, between the United States and England, broke out. Despite his otherwise low opinion of the people of St. Tammany, Governor Claiborne had no doubt as to their loyalty. Writing to Thomas Flournoy, Brigadier General of the Seventh Military District, he said: "The people of the several parishes of St. Tammany, S. Helena, Feliciana and Baton Rouge seem disposed to rally, *at the first call*, among the standard of their country. . . ."

At first, the theater of the war was confined to the east coast of the United States. However, by 1814, British strategy dictated an attack on New Orleans, and a powerful invasion force was assembled at Jamaica under Vice-Admiral Sir Alexander Cochrane. Major General Andrew Jackson, fresh from his victories over the Creek Indians and the capture of Pensacola, was appointed to command the defense of New Orleans.

Andrew Jackson ca. 1815 *(Courtesy The Historic New Orleans Collection)*

In early 1814, construction had begun at the Navy Yard near Madisonville on a large, shallow draft frigate, or block ship, called the *Tchifonta*. She was to be 153 feet long and rated at 22 guns. Construction was halted in March 1814, because the administration had decided that there was no danger of an attack on New Orleans. Consequently, the *Tchifonta*, which had been designed specifically to operate in the shallow waters of the approaches to New Orleans, was still in the stocks when the Battle of New Orleans took place. Some historians believe that the presence of the *Tchifonta* in Lake Borgne could have prevented the British from landing, and, consequently, the Battle of New Orleans would not have happened. A bomb ketch, the *Aetna,* was stationed in the Tchefuncta River to protect the *Tchifonta* from being attacked and burned.

On December 16, 1814, a general mobilization order for the Louisiana Militia was issued. The 13th Regiment, which was composed of men from St. Tammany Parish, was part of the 3rd Brigade, commanded by Brigadier General Robert McCausland. The 3rd Brigade was part of Major General Philemon Thomas's 2nd Division.

The commanding officer of the 13th Regiment was Colonel Thomas C. Warner, the parish judge. Officers serving under him were Captains William Watson, William George, and William Bickham and Lieutenant Elijah Harrell.

Elements of the 3rd Brigade were in the second line of defense at New Orleans, called Line Dupre, and were later transferred to the west bank of the Mississippi River to reinforce General David B. Morgan's forces. Shortly after January 12, 1815, McCausland's entire brigade was moved to Chef Menteur.

The 13th Regiment was later consolidated with the 12th Regiment from St. Helena Parish, and the muster rolls for those two regiments were kept as though they were one. After the British had withdrawn and the danger of invasion had passed, the Louisiana Militia was ordered mustered out and discharged without delay on March 7, 1815.

An affidavit made by Nathan Blackwell of Captain Bickham's company probably describes the typical military career of a St. Tammany volunteer in the War of 1812:

On this the Sixth day of November A. D., 1832, before me the undersigned a Justice of the Peace duly authorized by law

to administer Oaths within and for the Parish and State afore-
said Personally appeared Nathan Blackwell aged fifty five years
a resident of the Parish of Washington and State of Louisiana
who being first duly Sworn According to Law declares that he
is the identical Nathan Blackwell who was a late Private in the
Company commanded by Captain William Bickham in the
Thirteenth Regiment of Louisiana Militia Commanded by
General Morgan in the War between Great Britain and the
United States—that he volunteered into the United States Service at the Navy Yard on the Tchefoncta River in the Parish
of St. Tammany, State of Louisiana on or about the first day
of December 1814 to serve during the War or until Legally
discharged and Continued in active Service at the Navy Yard,
and from thence to New Orleans and was stationed six miles
below during said War for the term of Four Months received
from N. Y. paymaster (name not recollected) Eighteen dollars
pay and was on or about the first day of April 1815 at the
Navy Yard (the same place where I was mustered into service)
was Honorable discharged by being with the intire Company
of Captain William Bickham and of the Thirteenth Regiment
to which he was attached and was mustered out of service by
Captain William Bickham of the United States Army, all of
which will more fully appear by Reference to the Muster Rolls
of said Company. I was discharged by the Captain and of which
I took no certificate.

He makes this declaration for the purpose of obtaining the
Bounty Land to which he may be entitled.

It appears from available evidence that the St. Tammany contin-
gent did not directly participate in the fighting at the Battle of New
Orleans.

The same cannot be said of General David Bannister Morgan of
Madisonville, who commanded the American forces on the west
bank of the Mississippi River. He was charged with the primary task
of defending a battery of guns, commanded by Commodore Daniel
T. Patterson, which had been engaged in bombarding the British
troops attacking General Jackson's forces on the other side of the
river. Unfortunately, General Morgan's soldiers were routed by
British troops commanded by Lt. Col. William B. Thornton and the
battery was lost. Whether the defeat was due to the failure of the

Kentuckians under Colonel Davis, the failure of the Louisiana troops, or to faulty dispositions of his men by General Morgan is a moot point today. However, General Morgan's defense of his conduct and that of the Louisiana Militia, which was written from Madisonville on April 15, 1817, leaves no question as to his personal courage or his qualities of leadership.

When General Jackson came to New Orleans, he followed an overland route which led northwest from Mobile to the Pearl River, just above the Louisiana state line, and then southerly to Madisonville. His engineer, Major H. Tatum kept a diary, in which he details the route followed, and comments on the country through which they passed. The party spent the night of November 28, 1814, at Alston's place at Strawberry Bluff on the Bogue Chitto River. The journey through present day St. Tammany took one day:

Novr. 29th. (1814) Proceeded from Alston's and crossed the Creek, at 6 o'clock A. M. Passed over a good piece of Bottom Land and swam a Bayou at the extreme edge at William Rose's plantation at about ¾ miles. Passed the old cantonment on Little Feliah (or little Long Creek) at 11 miles. Near this place there is an excellent Saw-Mill on the same creek. Proceeded in all 16½ miles to the Town of Wharton on Bogue Feliah (or Big Long Creek) a fork of the Chefonta river. The Indians call both these creeks Bogue Feliah, and distinguish them by the Greater & Smaller, or Big & Little, and these names are still retained by the settlers.

Wharton is a small new Town containing but a few ordinary buildings. It is the seat of justice for the county in which it stands, and is situated at the head of navigation, on the bank of the creek. Sloops & Schooners ply between this place and the Bridge on The Bayou St. Johns, two miles distant from the Town of Orleans. It is said to be 30 miles by water, and not more than 10 miles by land, from hence to the entrance into the Lake Pontchartrain. It is 8 miles from Wharton to Maddisonville making in all 24½ miles from Alstons to the latter Town.

The lands from near Alston's (and from Rose's) are very poor and the growth altogether pine. About 5 miles of the distance between his residence and the Cantonment has been laid nearly bare of Timber by a severe Hurricane. The lands from Wharton to the Town of Maddisonville are a mixture of

Pine and Oak and contain several Tolerable farms & plantations.

The whole of this route contains excellent range for Black-Cattle which has become an object of primary Importance with the settlers in this quarter, cattle being considered as a species of circulating medium in most of their contracts. In fact, this currency circulates pretty generally from hence to, and on, the waters of Tombigby & Mobile Rivers.

From Wharton proceeded to Maddisonville & halted for the night, on the way crossed the Main Chefonta river (about 60 to 80 paces wide) at 3 miles.

It is estimated that the whole length of this river, on a direct line running from So. East to North West does not exceed 300 miles. The Course travelled this day was about So. So. West.

The Town of Maddisonville is situated on the West Bank of the Chefonta river about 2 miles from its junction with Lake Pontchartrain. This Town is small and indifferently improved. It lies about 2 miles, also, from the Navy-Yard. The only importance that can be attached to this place is, its advantageous situation as a depot for country produce destined for New Orleans distant about 30 miles, and also from its being the most advantageous place of landing, for all travellers from New Orleans, to Tennessee, Kentucky, Mobile & the back parts of Georgia. The distance from New Orleans, via Maddisonville, is now ascertained as not exceeding 200 miles, whereas by the way of the Levey road, Batton-Rouge, Natchez, Washington, &c. is, at least, 350 or 360 miles. This disproportion is much greater to those travellers that are bound for Mobile or the Tombigby settlements, Georgia, &c.

It is evident from this statement, that the growth & prosperity of this place must eventually depend upon the whims and caprices of mankind, when it is considered, in addition, that the country around will scarcely ever be able to produce more than the necessary provision for the support of life. Great quantities of Tar-Pitch and Turpentine might be prepared for use and exportation in the adjacent country, but, I apprehend a new supply of more industrious settlers must first inhabit this country.

Alston's is the property later sold to Richard S. Chappel, located at Strawberry Bluff on the Bogue Chitto River. It was here that Chappel later operated a ferry on the Military Road, and where the Military Road is shown by the old government surveys to cross the Bogue Chitto River. Since the route taken by Jackson also passes the old cantonment, which was located on the east side of the Little Bogue Falaya River, it seems almost certain that the route followed by Jackson was identical to the route later taken by the Military Road.

In the years following statehood, the growth of the parish continued slowly. One hundred and five land grants based on occupancy were made beginning in the years between 1813 and 1820. However, most of these were in the sections of St. Tammany Parish which are now parts of Washington and Tangipahoa Parishes.

In 1819, Washington Parish was created out of the northern section of St. Tammany. The new parish line was described as "beginning at David Robertson's on the Tanchipaho, thence a direct line to Daniel Edwards' on the Tchifoncta, thence a direct line to the Strawberry Bluffs on the Bogue-Chitto, and from thence a line on east until it strikes Pearl River. . . ."

In the next year, 1820, the first United States Census of St. Tammany Parish was taken, showing not too great a growth since 1812, despite the consistent immigration during the intervening years. The total population of the parish was 1,821. The white population included 338 men, 423 women, and 460 children. The free black population consisted of 10 men, 17 women, and 12 children. The slave population was 186 men, 177 women, and 198 children.

Of this population, 1,133 were engaged in agriculture, 11 in commerce, and four in manufacturing. Owners of the largest farms were Charles Parent—son of the former Spanish commandant, Terence Carriere, Bartholomew Martin, and David B. Morgan. Each of them had 28 or more people engaged in agricultural pursuits.

Individuals listed as working in commerce were D. W. Packwood, E. H. Hornsby, Robert Tait, Obed. Kirland, William Bagley, James Grant, and Jesse R. Jones. Those working in manufacturing were Daniel Searles, a gunsmith, and Samuel Edwards, as to whose product we are not enlightened. It would appear that the manufacture of tar and pitch had either died out by 1820 or was considered an agricultural pursuit. Apparently the manufacture of bricks had not

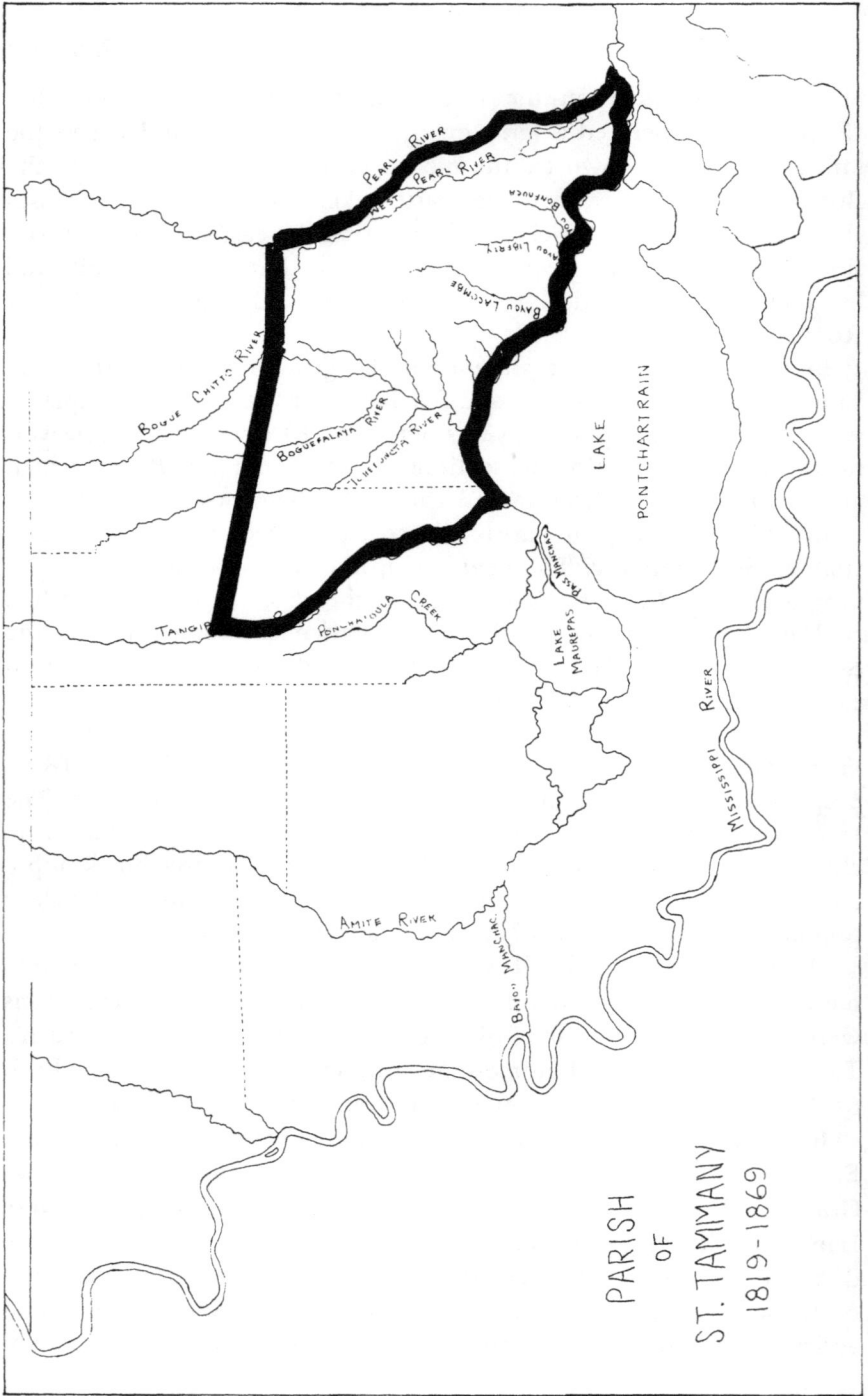

PARISH
OF
ST. TAMMANY
1819-1869

Pearl River
West Pearl River
Bayou Bonfouca
Bayou Liberty
Bayou Lacombe
Bogue Chitto River
Boquefalaya River
Abita River
Tangipahoa
Ponchatoula Creek
LAKE PONTCHARTRAIN
Bayou Manchac
LAKE MAUREPAS
Mississippi River
Amite River
Bayou Manchac

yet begun in 1820. On the other hand, a good lake trade would appear to have existed, judging by the number of people in commerce.

Boat building had not died out in St. Tammany. Between 1811 and 1820, 23 schooners were registered which had been built in the rivers and bayous of the north shore. Seven were built in the Tchefuncta River, six at Madisonville, and one at Covington; seven were built at Bayou Bonfouca, and the rest at Bayou Lacombe, Pearl River, and other places.

One last look at early St. Tammany Parish is afforded us by Charles S. Cosby, who was in charge of the land office for the Greensburg Land District:

> In the latter parish (St. Helena) the lands are uniformly level, and the soil, generally speaking, of very inferior quality. The only lands which are now cultivated lie on the margin of the different water courses bounding and running through the parish. The growth is almost entirely pine. The time may possibly arrive when those lands will sell. At present they are mostly unclaimed, and, we presume, will continue so for many years. Nothing but a monopoly of the rich territories of the United States can render them saleable. Stock, tar, and pitch are the only commodities which can be expected from pine woods. There are, probably, on the lake some eligible places, commanding an extensive range, and affording an easy communication with Orleans, which will be purchased. We speak of the lands generally. This parish is almost entirely inhabited by Americans: they are poor, but constitute a very valuable class of citizens.
>
> St. Tammany is bounded on the east by Pearl river; on the west by Tangipato, north by the line of demarcation, and south by the lakes Maurepas and Pontchartrain. The remarks made relatively to St. Helena, both as to the soil and inhabitants, are equally applicable to this parish. The only cultivable lands are situated on the different streams by which it is watered; the only principal streams are its eastern and western boundaries, and the rivers Bogue Chitto and Tchefonti. The latter is navigable fifteen or twenty miles from its confluence with lake Pontchartrain. The other, it is presumable, might be rendered so for small craft, if proper exertions were made for that

purpose. The lands lying on the margin of lake Pontchartrain, embracing Tchefonti as far as it is navigable, are generally covered by English and Spanish grants which have received the confirmation of the United States. The settlement claims are to be found wherever there are tillable lands. The section of the country, which we have thus attempted to describe, is probably as healthy as any part of Louisiana, or of the western country. The climate is equable and the atmosphere generally clear. Its humidity (occasioned, probably, by extensive swamps on the Mississippi,) is not sufficiently great to generate disease, except immediately on that river. After passing the Amite River, the boundary between the river and interior parishes, the inhabitants are scarcely acquainted with disease, except occasional intermittents of the mildest character.

CHAPTER XIII

Economic Development, 1820-1855

In about 1820, the early pioneer period in St. Tammany Parish came to an end, and a new phase of growth and development began, which was to last for over 30 years. It was a slow growth at first, but achieved almost boom proportions before it ended in about 1855.

Despite the somewhat pessimistic opinions of early observers as to the potential of St. Tammany Parish, all of the ingredients which were to contribute to its first period of growth and development were present. With the takeover of the Florida Parishes by the United States, the last international boundary was erased. Traffic down the Mississippi River increased, and so did the number of people who had to return north from New Orleans. The quickest route was across Lake Pontchartrain to Madisonville and Covington, and from thence north by road. There was a direct route to Nashville and short routes to both Baton Rouge and Natchez.

The direct route to Nashville was, of course, the Military Road, which was constructed by U. S. Army troops in the years 1817 through 1820. The idea for the road came from General Andrew Jackson, who recognized the necessity for quick military access to New Orleans in the event of war. Between Covington and the Mississippi state line, the Military Road probably followed the road down which Jackson and Major Tatum rode when going to the defense of New Orleans in 1814. The road was maintained by the residents of Washington and St. Tammany Parishes, who lived within five miles of it. They were relegated to this duty by an 1822 legislative act, which directed them to work on the "National Road" from Madisonville to Nashville, for 12 days a year, but not for more than six days at a time.

There must have been a lot of transient traffic through St. Tammany. In 1821, the legislature recognized this fact when it appropriated $800 to be used by the Police Jury for the support of "strangers" unable to support themselves. The preamble of the act says: "WHEREAS, it appears that the parishes of East Baton Rouge and St. Tammany, and the charity hospital of New Orleans, from their local situation, have incurred and must in future naturally incur heavy expense for the support of the sick and indigent stranger, therefore . . ."

An indication of heavy traffic on the Military Road was an exclusive franchise, granted by the legislature to Richard S. Chappell on January 13, 1821, to operate a ferry across the Bogue Chitto River on the main road from Covington to Jacksonville Springs, "at a place called the Strawberry Bluff." This, of course, was on the Military Road. He was authorized to charge 75 cents for a loaded wagon, 50 cents for a four-wheel carriage, 25 cents for a horse and cart, 12½ cents for a man and horse, and 6¼ cents for a foot passenger.

Traffic on the roads was not all to the north. Products of the country to the north of St. Tammany were naturally funnelled down the roads to Covington and Madisonville for shipment to New Orleans, as the nearest major trade center.

In those days, and up until the 20th century, roads were constructed and maintained by the people who lived in their vicinity. The Police Jury created road districts and appointed overseers in each, who had the right to call on the residents of the district for a certain number of days of work on the roads each year. People who lived in an area not served by a road could petition the Police Jury to have the road laid out and constructed. In this manner the local road system of the parish was gradually expanded.

In the middle 1820's, the first of the United States Government Surveys was made. The old land grants were delineated, and the remainder of the lands were surveyed according to the township system. Because of a number of inaccuracies in the work, the entire parish was later re-surveyed and that survey still stands as the basis of the title surveys made today.

This second survey, made in the late 1840's and early 1850's, shows that the major roads in the parish were established by that time. From Madisonville, the road to Springfield, the Turnpike Road, and the Covington road are shown. There is no direct road to Mandeville shown, although some 1833 Police Jury minutes indicate that such a road existed. From Covington, there is the Holmesville Road, now Highway 25; the River Road, which now goes out to St. Joseph's Abbey; the Lee Road, once referred to as the Lee Ferry Road or "the road leading to the ferry operated by a man named Lee"; the Military Road; the Columbia Highway, now Highway 21; the road running to Abita Springs, Talisheek, and thence down the West Pearl River; and the Mandeville Road. From Mandeville, the road continued east to Bayou Lacombe, and then on to the present location of Slidell. The Mandeville—Bayou Lacombe Road was there as early as 1820. From Slidell a road ran northeast to join the West Pearl River Road; and another ran southeast towards the Rigolets. Of course, at that time, Slidell, Abita Springs, and Talisheek did not exist.

The trade and the transient traffic which resulted from the roads into St. Tammany from the north stimulated the growth of both shipbuilding and the across-the-lake trade.

In the years 1821 through 1829, thirteen more schooners were registered as having been built in St. Tammany, five of them in the Tchefuncta River, two in Bayou Bonfouca, and the rest in Bayou Lacombe, Bayou Pacquet, Bayou Castein, and Pearl River. Many of the earlier-built boats were still engaged in the lake trade during this period.

The years 1830 to 1840 saw the construction of 27 boats in St. Tammany, including the *Pontchartrain*, first steamer to be built on the north shore. She was built at Mandeville in 1836, had a weight of 190 57/95 tons, was 129 feet 4 inches long, with a beam of 23 feet 7 inches and a draft of 6 feet 8 inches. She was described as having one deck, no masts, square stern, and two chimneys.

Of the vessels built in St. Tammany during the latter period, 11 were built in Bayou Bonfouca, six in the Tchefuncta River, three in the West Pearl River, and the rest in various other places.

The first steamboat recorded crossing the lake was the *Neptune*, which, in 1821, carried a letter from General Thomas Shields in New

Orleans to General David B. Morgan in Madisonville. Increasing trade and prosperity led to the introduction of other steamers into the lake trade. In 1832, William Bagley and Elijah Martin Terrell of Covington acquired the *Corsair*, which had been built in Elizabethtown, Pennsylvania, in 1829. She weighed 120 90/95 tons, was 97 feet long, 19 feet 10 inches in beam, with a six-foot draft, and was described as having one deck, no mast, a square stern, a figurehead, and a hurricane house on the deck. Mr. Bagley was the master. In 1834, she was thoroughly repaired and given a round stern which increased her length to 107 feet. Louis F. Knight became her master. Later in 1834, she was transferred to the ownership of the Lake Pontchartrain Steamboat Co., Inc.

In 1833, William Bagley, Jesse R. Jones, Elijah M. Terrell, Hezekiah Thompson, Martin G. Penn, Alexander G. Penn, and Sylvanus Parsons, of St. Tammany Parish, and others, acquired the *Planter*, a steamer weighing 145 58/95 tons. She was 112 feet 7 inches long, 21 feet in beam, with a draft of 6 feet 9 inches, and was described as having one deck, no mast, a square stern, and a hurricane house on deck.

Another steamboat was the *Blackhawk*, built in Portland, Kentucky, in 1833, weighing 137 17/95 tons, with a length of 113 feet, a beam of 20 feet 9 inches, and a draft of 7 feet 5½ inches. In 1835, she was acquired by a group composed of William Bagley, Jesse R. Jones, Elijah M. Terrell, Hezekiah Thompson, Martin G. Penn, and Alexander G. Penn, all of Covington, and others. The captain was J. W. Hoffman.

On Sunday morning, April 14, 1834, the following advertisement ran in *The Bee*, an early New Orleans newspaper:

For Madisonville, Fontainebleau and Mandeville

The Steamboat Blackhawk will commence running to Madisonville, Fontainebleau and Mandeville on Sunday the 12th April, and continue every Sunday throughout the season, leaving the railroad at half past 8 o'clock a.m., returning will leave Madisonville at half past 2 o'clock p.m., touching at the above places.

The same group of men who owned the *Blackhawk* also put in service in the lake five barges, which were large single-masted cargo vessels, sometimes propelled by rowing and sometimes by towing.

The increase in lake traffic was indicated by establishment of lighthouses at the mouth of the Tchefuncta River and at Bayou Bonfouca. Records show a lighthouse at the Tchefuncta River as early as 1826, and there is still a lighthouse in operation there today. The Bonfouca light was established in 1848, and was destroyed in 1862 during the Civil War. It was never replaced.

The keeper of the Tchefuncta lighthouse from 1837 until his death in 1845 was Benjamin Thurston. In 1842, he kept a diary of his everyday life, in which he mentioned the people he saw and the boats that came by, as well as listed his day to day activities. Some of the boats in the lake trade in that year were the sloop *Dart*, the *New Plan*, the *Sarah Bladen*, the sloop *Fanny*, the *Minerva*, the *Jane*, the *Esperance*, the *Pauline*, the *Maria*, the *Napoleon*, the *Train*, the steamboat *Dupre*, the *Walker*, the *Dream*, the steamer *Aynes*, and the *Mary*. Some of the captains were Howland, James Mortee, Watkinson, Newton, Kroger, Badon, Johnson, Wilson, Western Edgar, Perkins, Eddy, C. Robinson, Rodgers, Chesby, Ira Baker, U. Shinney, Hays, and Watkins. Mr. Thurston was a versatile man. In addition to his duties maintaining the lighthouse, he kept a garden, cattle, hogs, and chickens; maintained all of his implements; built, repaired, and maintained his boats; made lime from shells; built furniture; made lumber; cut and drove piling; made tubs; slaughtered his animals, picked moss, and kept nine pet alligators.

It has been estimated that during the peak of the boom, 40,000 to 50,000 bales of cotton per year were shipped through St. Tammany Parish ports to New Orleans. John M. Tate, writing his recollections of Covington in the *St. Tammany Farmer*, said that he could recall when the streets of Covington were blocked with loads of cotton extending from the graveyard to the river on Columbia Street.

The population of St. Tammany reflected the economic development which began, albeit slowly, in the 1820's. According to the 1830 census, there was a pronounced change in the character of the population of the parish. There was a decrease of 50 in the adult white population, although an increase in the number of white children brought the total white population to 1,318, almost 100 more than in 1820, but almost 80 less than in 1812. The number of free people of color increased to 186. The most significant change was in the slave population, which increased to 1,360, including 681 men, 378 women, and 301 children.

In 1820, Charles Parent, the largest slave owner, had 34 slaves. In 1830, 10 men owned more slaves than that, and one of these, Joseph Brana, owned 155. Other big slave owners were Cornelius Brown, 77; Terence Carriere, 69; David B. Morgan, 63; and Amos A. Johnson, 59. Joseph Soniat du Fossat, who was the owner of Desruissaux's Island, owned 40 slaves. John Gusman, heir of Bartholomew Martin, and owner of the former Rillieux property on Bayou Bonfouca, owned 35 slaves. Francois Carriere owned 39; Terence Cousin, 37; and Daniel Edwards, 35.

Of course, there had to be some economic reason for the sharp increase in number of the slaves. Unfortunately, the 1830 census does not give the occupations of the people enumerated, and the old records of the parish are of little help. One old document shows a brickyard on Bayou Bonfouca in 1826, so it is likely that Mr. Gusman, at least, and probably others, were starting out in the brick manufacturing business which was to be an economic mainstay of the parish for many years.

During the decade of the 1830's, the population had its first major increase since 1812. The 1840 census shows 802 white men, 517 white women, and 1,034 white children, for a total white population of 2,353. The free colored population increased to 305, with 114 men, 106 women, and 85 children under 10. The slave population increased to 1940, including 837 men, 513 women, and 590 children under 10.

The census also shows a decisive shift away from a primarily agricultural community. Of the labor force, 691 were engaged in agriculture, and 614 in manufacture and trades. There were 171 people engaged in navigation of lakes and rivers, 68 in commerce, and 15 in the learned professions.

Armand Marigny, who was a relative of Bernard, owned 153 slaves, and employed 18 men in agriculture, 20 in manufacturing, and 10 in navigation. What the other 105 slaves did is not stated. Marigny was probably starting up as a brickmaker, since this was given as his occupation in 1850. Other large slaveholders were Terence Carriere, who owned 66, employing 35 in manufacturing and three in navigation; and John Gusman, who owned 60, with 30 employed in manufacturing and five in navigation. Since Carriere, Morgan, and Gusman were all brickmakers in 1850, they were probably manufacturing bricks in 1840 as well.

Other men who were probably manufacturing bricks at that time were Francois Carriere, Terence Cousin, Francois Cousin, and Charles Parent.

Some who had large slave holdings were engaged entirely in agriculture. These included W. H. Ker, who owned 56 slaves, with 30 working in agriculture; Daniel Edwards, who owned 49 slaves, 20 in agriculture; and Alfred Hennen, who owned 46 slaves, employing 15 in agriculture. Mr. Hennen was a successful New Orleans lawyer who had served on General Jackson's staff at the Battle of New Orleans and had retired to St. Tammany. He bought a large tract of ground on Chappapela Creek, in what is now Tangipahoa Parish, and there constructed his famous "Retreat" as a home and summer resort for his family.

Over the years, Hennen continued to improve "Retreat" and, by 1860, had over 100 slaves working on the property. In 1870, after his death, the property was transferred to Mr. and Mrs. John A. Morris, Hennen's son-in-law and daughter. They fenced the entire tract and made a game preserve out of it, bringing in exotic animals and game birds. The property is still intact, and is now known as Zemurray Gardens.

The lumber industry was also getting a foothold in St. Tammany. Major Tatum mentioned a sawmill on the Little Bogue Falaya River in 1814. In 1821, Jeremiah Miller operated a sawmill on the Bogue Falaya River, at the present site of St. Joseph's Abbey. In that year he was authorized to clear logs and trees from the Bogue Falaya to give free navigation from Covington to Miller's Mills. Both of these early mills were water operated. Two other early sawmill operators were Moses Moore and Simon Gosseline, both of whom were located in the western section of the parish.

By 1850, the population had increased to 6,385, the major part of the increase having come from the white population, which went from 2,353 in 1840 to 3,663 in 1850. The free colored population went from 305 to 359, and the number of slaves increased from 1,940 to 2,363. The number of households increased from 435 to 786.

The major industries expanded, so that by 1850, there were 15 brickyards and 14 sawmills in operation. Only 192 persons identified themselves as farmers, contrasted with 339 laborers, indicating that more people earned a living working for others than by tilling the soil. There were 120 carpenters, indicating that the boat building and construction industries were flourishing.

The brickyard operators in 1850 were Terence Cousin, Terence Carriere, John Gusman, D. R. Morgan, W. Hutchinson, J. W. Goss, Anatole Cousin, Armand Marigny, Samuel Russ, L. Kelly, Charles Parent, Mandeville Marigny, I. Morgan, J. B. Baham, and Jules Le Blanc. It has been said that much of New Orleans was built with St. Tammany brick. Considering the number of brickyards in the parish, and the fact that New Orleans was the only nearby major market, there is probably more truth than fiction in that statement.

Among the sawmill operators were Jacob J. Ott, James Brown, Thomas Harper, Alexander G. Penn, A. Theriot, Moses Moore, and Simon Gosseline. It is likely that the products of these mills and the brickyards were a major factor in the increase in the lake trade.

St. Tammany's oldest industry seemed to be making a comeback by 1850, with 11 coal burners and one turpentine maker listed in the census.

The 1850 agricultural census gave the first clear look at St. Tammany Parish as an agricultural community. Although 192 farmers were counted in the population census, only 148 were included in the agricultural census. They were farming a total of 5,824 improved acres, which means the average farm was about 40 improved acres. The largest farm was owned by Armand Marigny, who had 800 improved acres. The same farmers owned 78,360 acres for an average of almost 530 total acres per farmer. The largest tract was that of A. W. Weems, who was the owner of Desruisseaux's Island, which was then called Weems' Island, containing 6,200 acres.

The farmers owned 461 horses, 132 asses and mules, 2,133 milk cows, 735 working oxen, 6,821 other cattle, 1,370 sheep, and 5,195 swine. In 1850, the major crops were corn, rice, and sweet potatoes. One hundred forty farmers produced 17,839 bushels of corn; 33 farmers produced 97,598 pounds of rice; and 103 farmers produced 22,352 bushels of sweet potatoes. Cotton, which was to become a staple crop, was raised by only three men, who produced 41 bales. Only one farmer, Armand Marigny, planted sugar cane, and he produced 20 hogsheads of sugar and 600 gallons of molasses. Other crops and produce were oats, 701 bushels by 12 farmers; wool, 1,458 pounds by 12 farmers; Irish potatoes, 310 bushels by 13 farmers; butter, 2,570 pounds by 22 farmers; and hay, 178 tons by 50 farmers. One man, Bill Levy, raised 54 pounds of tobacco.

An unusual crop which was important for a while in the parish was the growing of mulberry trees of the *Morus multicaulis* variety. In 1839, Pierre Lacroix of Mulberry Grove, about two and one-half miles north of Covington, advertised 100,000 young trees for sale, and there is a record of one sale by him of 1,000 trees in that year. These were sold to August Trois, Jean Aymard, and Jean Francois Buttiera, to be delivered to the plantation of Nathan Colder. Also in 1839, a piece of ground in Covington at the corner of Boston and New Hampshire, was leased for the purpose of growing mulberry trees. In 1850, Jules B. Maille gave his occupation as silk merchant, so it is likely that silk was being produced in St. Tammany in those days, even though it was not mentioned in the census.

Some of the larger farmers, after Marigny, were Terence Cousin, with 250 improved acres; Alfred N. Hennen, with 250; A. W. Weems and Daniel Edwards, with 200; Cornelius Cooper, with 150; and M. Wordsworth, T. Spell, J. B. Maille, Samuel Russ, Charles Parent, J. Cousin, Mary Carriere, Simon Ducre, and W. H. Martin, all with 100 acres of improved land.

All of this leads to the conclusion that perhaps Lt. Governor Browne and Major Tatum were justified in their somewhat pessimistic appraisals of the agricultural potential of St. Tammany Parish. Most of the owners of big farms were also big slave holders, and were in all likelihood planting large tracts just to support their establishments.

Although only three men identified themselves as stock raisers, cattle was still important to the economy, but not to the same extent as formerly.

All in all, the picture of economic development in St. Tammany between 1820 and the mid-1850's is one of constant growth and increasing prosperity. The trend of depleting the resources of the parish was accelerating, and the economic dependence on trade with New Orleans was becoming more pronounced. But things were looking good.

CHAPTER XIV

Effects of Growth

With the economic progress in the parish after 1820 and the population growth, came improvement in the way of life of the residents. There were no new land grants made in the 1820's, but during the 1830's, '40's, and '50's, settlers came in increasing numbers. Little land was left along the rivers, and, for the most part, the newcomers settled adjacent to the old land grants and along the roads.

Until 1834, Covington and Madisonville remained the only two towns in St. Tammany. During the mid-1820's, Bernard P. de Marigny de Mandeville, who was reputed to be, at that time, one of the richest men in the United States, bought the Antoine Bonnabel and Lewis Davis properties, on the east side of Bayou Castein. It was there that he built his famous Fontainebleau Plantation, the present site of Fontainebleau State Park. The ruins of his sugar mill can still be seen in the park. The stories that Marigny's father, Phillipe de Marigny, had entertained the Duc d'Orleans, who was to become King Louis Phillipe of France, at Fontainebleau Plantation in 1798, seem to be without foundation. There is no record that the Marigny family owned property in St. Tammany prior to the purchase of Fontainebleau by Bernard.

In the 1830's, however, he did become the first of St. Tammany's great real estate promoters. He acquired all the old English land grants along the lakeshore adjoining Fontainebleau Plantation on the west, and, in 1834, had this property subdivided into a town, to be called Mandeville. A great auction sale of lots and squares in the new town was held in New Orleans on February 24, 25, and 26, 1834, and Mandeville was an instant success. Eighty thousand dollars worth of lots were sold on those days. In short order, a gambling casino and hotel were built, and regular steamboat excursions were being run by the *Blackhawk*. In July 1837, the steamboat *Pontchartrain,* which was built in St. Tammany, began running to Mandeville, Lewisburg, Madisonville, and Covington landing three days per week, with regular Sunday excursions.

Lewisburg, which lies immediately to the west of Mandeville, was also laid out and dedicated in 1834. It was, and remains today, a lovely, quiet residential area. A number of fine old homes line the lakeshore. Fortunately for the residents of Lewisburg, it never became the commercial success that Mandeville was.

Another real estate promotion at about the same time was Jeffersonville, on the Tchefuncta River just above Madisonville. The property was purchased by Benjamin Hart and Jean Bernard Xavier de Marigny de Mandeville, one of Bernard's sons, but Hart later bought his partner out. The 1,600 arpent tract was subdivided into squares, which were put up for sale at public auction at the New Exchange Coffee House, on the corner of St. Louis and Chartres streets in New Orleans on November 7, 1836. Although many squares were sold, there was, apparently, never any further development of the property. The plan of subdivision, made by Jean Antoine Guerard, deputy surveyor general, has become lost, and there is no sign today that such a subdivision ever existed.

Another early attempt at development which has disappeared without a trace is Parsonsville, located in the fork of the Tchefuncta and Bogue Falaya Rivers, which was apparently subdivided by Sylvanus Parsons.

In 1819, the state legislature voted to appropriate money to the parishes to help finance "public" schools. The schools were not free schools, but were required to accept a small number of pupils who were unable to pay. The 1819 appropriation was $600.00. Probably in answer to this impetus, the first school in the parish made its appearance in 1820, when the Board of Trustees of Covington School bought two lots in Square 25 of the Division of Spring for a building site. Two years later, they bought the rest of the square, which is

The home of Judge Jesse Rubel Jones located at the corner of Portsmouth and New Hampshire ca. 1823-1830

Remains of sugar mill of Fontainebleau Plantation, Fontainebleau State Park

located at New Hampshire and Temperance streets, two blocks from the Episcopal Church. In 1823, the Reverend Timothy Flint had charge of a "seminary" (probably the original school) in Covington from March until October.

In 1820, the police juries were directed to appoint five trustees to administer the public schools, and the appropriation was increased to $800. The police juries were further authorized to levy a tax on land and slaves for the purpose of raising not more than $1,000 per annum for educational purposes. The act also directs the trustees to admit to the school "eight day scholars, from those families who are indigent—(who) shall receive instruction gratis, and be moreover furnished with classical books, quills, and paper, at the cost of said school—."

Then, by Act 10 of 1828, the Covington Academy was incorporated, the incorporators being Jonathan Gilmore, D. B. Morgan, James Hosmer, Joseph Laurent, Henry Tyson, William Bagley, Branch Miller, Moses Moore, Daniel Edwards, and others. The corporation was authorized to raise $25,000 through lotteries, to be held within three years. We do not know if these lotteries were held, or how successful they may have been.

Another step forward was taken in education with the foundation of the Covington Female Academy by Act 103 of 1837. An appropriation of $4,000 was made for the construction of suitable buildings for the school. Among the founders of the school were Jesse R. Jones, Robert McCay, Thomas J. Mortee, George F. Gilbert, Alexander G. Penn, John McDonald, and William Bagley. The school was located on Square 33 of the Division of Spring and Triangle 4 of the Division of St. John. Under Act 6 of 1839, an annual appropriation of $3,000 was made for the school.

Apparently, this school remained in continuous operation for many years after its founding, although not exclusively as a girls' school. Reverend S. B. Hall was operating the school in the 1850's under the name of Westminster Seminary, with a staff of twelve. He left in 1853, reportedly because of the yellow fever epidemic, and the school was then operated by a Mr. Hutchinson. It is now a part of the site of St. Scholastica's Academy, and it is possible that a school has been in continuous operation at that site for over 140 years.

Another school was incorporated in Covington in 1837. Fellenberg's Institute, a kind of vocational school, was established by Act 86 of 1837, at the behest of Thomas Kennedy, George Richardson, Joseph Walton, James C. Finley, Robert S. Finley, and others.

The 1840 census shows three schools in the parish: Robert Finley's academy, with 30 scholars; John Reid's academy, with 26 scholars; and William Blackwell's primary school, with 22 scholars, seven of whom attended at public expense. Unless there were other schools not listed, this means that 78 out of 1,034 white children were attending school in 1840. No provisions seem to have been made for the education of colored children at that time.

There is no way of identifying the schools in the 1840 census with the earlier schools mentioned above. Robert Finley's school could be Fellenberg's Institute, since he was one of its founders.

The school system seemed to improve during the years, since the 1850 census shows 13 school teachers and 583 children who had attended school during the past year. All of the teachers were men in 1850, and included J. B. Montgomery, Felin McManus, E. Lamulonsus, David Young, David Magee, George K. Spring, John Montgomery, Leon Lucas, A. Dorgate, M. H. Lippmins, John J. Wagner, Samuel Anderson, and George Miller.

The academy column of the 1850 census shows eight academies in St. Tammany, with 10 teachers and 170 pupils. These figures do not agree with an actual count of the census, but there does seem to be a substantial growth in the school system.

In 1844, Mandeville College was founded in Mandeville. James W. Mobley gives a brief history of it in his 1931 master's thesis, "The Academy Movement in Louisiana":

> Conditions in Mandeville in 1844 must have been vastly different from what they are today to have warranted the establishment of Mandeville College there. In the announcement concerning this school, it was stated that the plant consisted of three buildings with a combined length of more than 500 feet which furnished all space needed for activities of the College, together with ample boarding facilities.
>
> Lewis Elkins, formerly a teacher at Jefferson College, was president of this College, and he announced that physical development of boys had been neglected in schools heretofore,

but that this would be given special attention at Mandeville College. Assisting Mr. Elkins were Duncan Macauley, J. C. Porier, Felix Perin, J. Hazeldon, Zenon Goria, and Mrs. Macauley who had charge of the dormitories.

The course pursued appears to have been in line with those given by colleges of that day, and consisted of English, French, Spanish, Latin, Greek, mathematics, logic, rhetoric, history, geography, philosophy, drawing, astronomy and music. There is nothing to indicate the method of financing the school, but tuition charges were the usual method in those days.

The editor of the paper paid high tribute to the organizer of the school. He stated that no school in the country had a better location, and that there was no reason why the venture should not be a success. At this time about thirty students had enrolled, and there might have been promises of future support.

In 1846 a library was added to the school's facilities and the name was changed to St. Tammany College. However, something appeared to be amiss. James Whittaker was president and had eight instructors assisting in the work on September 5, but on September 20 Edward Barnwell was president and hope was expressed that changes which had been necessary would bring harmony, and with this would come success for the institution. It is not known what effect the housecleaning had, as reports cease at this point. Many things might have worked toward the dissolution of the school, none of which could be of any importance now.

In 1853, records show that there were 15 public school districts in St. Tammany Parish, with 818 children in attendance. These were probably three-month schools located around the parish, and had most likely been in existence for some time, although there are no early records to substantiate this supposition. In any event, the school system reached a peak at about the same time as the economy of the parish.

The earliest formal religious observances of which there is a record took place in the north end of St. Tammany, in what is now Washington Parish, when the early Methodist circuit-riding ministers visited the settlements along the Bogue Chitto.

In 1823, Reverend Timothy Flint, a Presbyterian minister, came to St. Tammany "to take charge of a seminary there, and to supply, as a minister, the two villages of Madisonville and Covington." He described his visit:

Y ou enter over a bar with only five feet water, a broad placid stream called Chiffuncta, and you sail up this stream, still bounded by a dead swamp, two miles to Madisonville, a small village, to which the citizens repair for health, in the summer months, from New Orleans. There is one large hotel, and a number of neat and comfortable houses for entertainment, which in the sickly months are generally full. Some cotton is shipped from this village, and a number of packet schooners ply between it and New Orleans. The sailors employed in this desultory and slavish trade are generally of that class, that have been sifted out of all better employment, and are the most abandoned and blasphemous of the profession. The rivers that run through these level and swampy pine forests, are called, in the Indian language, "Bogue," with some attribute denoting the character of the stream; for instance, "Bogue Chitto," "Bogue Falaya," denoting the river of laurels, or chincopins. The people are a peculiar race of "petits paysans," small planters, engaged in the lumber trade, in making tar and charcoal, or shepherds engaged in raising cattle. The wealth of a young lady about to be married is measured by the number of her cows, as in the planting part of the state, it is by her negroes. Some have two thousand cattle; and the swamps afford ample winter range, while the pine woods furnish grass in the summer.

There are a number of Bogues that are navigable by schooners for some distance into the country. The most considerable village is Covington, the seat of justice for the country of St. Tammany. You ascend the Bogue Falaya, twenty miles by water, and six by land, from Madisonville to this village. It contains about a hundred houses, employs a considerable number of schooners, and as it is the head of navigation on the river, ships very considerable quantities of cotton, from Pearl River, Florida, and the lower part of the state of Mississippi. Goods in return from New Orleans are deposited here, to be conveyed to their destination in the country by waggons. There is a navy-yard between Madisonville and this place, where it was proposed to build gunboats. Much money was expended here, and the place is now abandoned. There is nothing worthy of notice in the village of Covington, except that, contrary to the common practice, they have a burial-ground substantially and handsomely enclosed; and that, equally out of the fashion of the country, the people were united and punctual in their attention to religious worship.

All that part of Florida that I have seen, has one aspect, and from information I judge that to be a fair sample of all the rest. It is divided into savannas, or low grass prairies, pine woods, or inundated swamps on the margins of the rivers. The soil is nowhere beyond second rate, and, even in the richest alluvions, pine trees make their appearance among the laurels, beeches, and oaks that compose the mass of the timber on the lands capable of cultivation. The swamps, as every where in this country, are occupied by the cypress, and loblolly pine, and for animal life, by alligators, moccasin snakes, and musquitoes. Nine tenths of the country are covered with the long-leaved pitch pine, which rises before you, as you ride along, in countless millions, as straight and as uniform as a file of soldiers. The country is so level, and every where so exactly uniform, that I have never been in a region where it was so easy to get lost, and so difficult to find your way again. "Haud inexpertus loquor." This I have found to my cost. Thirty miles from the sea, which is every where bounded by white sand beaches, the pine lands become rolling and dry.

Such is the general face of the country in West Florida. It possesses in its swamps a considerable quantity of live oak, and masts and spars enough for all the navies in the world. It is capable of furnishing inexhaustible supplies of pitch, tar, &c. The high grass, which grows every where among the pine trees, opens an immense range for cattle. There are some tolerable tracts of land along the rivers; but generally the land is low, swampy, and extremely poor. The people, too, are poor and indolent, devoted to raising cattle, hunting, and drinking whiskey. They are a wild race, with but little order or morals among them; they are generally denominated "Bogues," and call themselves "rosin heels." The chief town is Pensacola, which grew rapidly, and received an increase of many inhabitants and handsome houses, until the fatal summer of 1822, when it suffered so severely from yellow fever, since which it has declined. It has a fine harbour, and the government has made it a naval depot, which will probably raise it once more.

We passed a tranquil and pleasant summer at Covington, in the discharge of duties so uniform in character as to furnish nothing of interest for relation.

The present Presbyterian congregation in Covington traces its origin to 1850, when the Reverend S. B. Hall was in Covington. The Presbyterian church in Madisonville is even older, having celebrated its 100th anniversary in 1944.

The Methodist church in Covington was chartered on August 29, 1834, when it was founded by Lyman Briggs, John McDonald, John Bickham, Ezekiel Parke Ellis, Hezekiah Thompson, and John Jay Mortee.

Christ Episcopal Church was founded in 1846. The original church, which was consecrated on April 11, 1847, still stands on New Hampshire Street near the entrance to the Bogue Falaya Park. The first pastor was Wiley Peck.

St. Peter's Catholic Church was founded about 1843 in Covington, and, by 1850, there were Catholic churches in Madisonville and Mandeville. There were also missions at Bonfouca, Bayou Lacombe, and Chinchuba, which were served by Father Adrien Rouquette.

In the census of 1850, we find the major religious denominations represented by resident priests and ministers. The Roman Catholic priests were Joseph Ondenuch and the famous Adrien Rouquette; the Episcopal minister was A. Smith; the Presbyterian minister was S. B. Hall; the Methodist preachers were John Lusk and W. Wordsworth; and the Baptist preachers were Richard Lyntall and Elliott W. Moore. The distinction among priest, minister, and preacher was made by the census takers, but it is not known if that represented official government policy.

In 1832, the first newspaper in St. Tammany made its appearance, when the *Palladium* began publication, probably in June. Unfortunately, no copies of this paper survive, although there are a few clippings of stories and articles written by James Rees, a frequent contributor.

The original agreement relative to the operation of the paper, which is in the handwriting of Jesse Jones, gives us the names of the men responsible:

Be it remembered that the *Press Types* and *apparatus* belonging to the Office of the Covington *Palladium* belongs as follows:

To Joseph D. Davenport the value of		$ 600
"	Jessie R. Jones the value of	100
"	E. M. Terrell & Co the value of	150
"	T & J Mortee the value of	100
"	M. G. Penn the value of	100
"	A. G. Penn the value of	50
"	C. R. Hyde the value of	50
"	Wesley Mallory the value of	25
"	Isaac Lazarus the value of	25
	making the Total value of	$1200

The said Joseph D. Davenport agrees to conduct the said Establishment to the best of his ability for the space of one year from the 23rd of December last to devote the whole of his personal attention to the Same, as well as the personal services of his apprentice Charles F. Oldecop; . . .

Mr. Rees, who boarded with a Mr. Hamilton, was apparently not employed except in his writing. He was an observer of his scene, had an eye for the ladies, a tendency to disputation, and a taste for the grape. On July 21, 1832, he wrote:

My usual walk of a morning and evening is down through the romantic glade leading to the school house. There is something pleasing in the situation of the rural building, presenting the appearance of Goldsmith's scene in the "Deserted Village," it leads, however, to a delightful spring, the resort of all the little boys and girls of Covington, as well (my own eyes can bear witness) as many a blushing modest lass, whose rosy look, gives blooming proof, that health is here, the presiding goddess. Connected with the spring there is many a meandering path, leading through a truly romantic wood; where the classic scholar can recall the many oft told tales of "Crete" and his celebrated labyrinth; or the lover mourn over "love departed," and sigh amid the sombre shade of wiry vines and tall stately trees.

Rees's "Journal of a Week in Covington" contains the following extracts:

Sunday.—Rose at 7, being awoke by the ringing of a bell, sounded very much like a Steam Boat just about leaving the wharf—breakfasted, look'd up one street, then down another, groaned in spirit, and wondered how people could live in a place so retired . . . drank two mint juleps and walked down to the village school, heard one of Blair's Sermons read by a young man with great perspicuity, and much feeling . . . Saw a beautiful girl, and that is all, umph, no society here. Monday—Rose at 6, took a walk down to McCay's spring; delicious water . . . Tuesday—After breakfast, walked down to the Labyrinth, had a propensity to climb a tree, done so, and fell to the ground—broke no bones, but fell very flat, no person saw me, however—went down to the Bogue Falia, curious kind of name, means Bog Trotter, I suppose, tried to fish, got five hundred nibbles, and caught a snapper, stole a man's boat and rowed down the river— came home late to dinner . . . amused by the whole town of Covington working on the roads, all things in common, curious law this, don't understand it, asked Judge _____ about it, cautious man that Judge, expressed himself in limited terms, admire him for it: ladies very fond of riding horseback; delighted with several pretty faces. Wednesday . . . took a more full view of Covington, astonishing place; more goods sold here than in a northern town of three times its size . . . met several ladies on horseback, envied them much, umph!! can't ride myself, never could . . . Thursday.—Took a book with me down to the Labyrinth, Irvine's Sketches; was followed by a genius I do not like, who talked so much about his wife, that I strongly suspect he whips her, was pleased when he left, only staid with us three days . . . ladies on horseback again, fine recreation, umph, wished I could ride, got drunk and went to bed; dreamt of wild horses and beautiful women . . . Friday . . . met our evening coterie under Hamilton's Piazza; much pleased with the conversation of my new friends; getting more fond of Covington; moon light nights are sublime; drank two bottles of claret, and washed it down with a glass of brandy; the only fault I have is drinking; it will keep off Cholera; I can prove it, went up to my room and

finished the essay on Dyspepsia; dreamt of swallowing an ox . . .
Saturday.—Rose at 8 o'clock, did not go to bed until one on the
evening previous, had a very interesting conversation with a very
intelligent gentleman already mentioned, about Bonaparte,
Aaron Burr, &c.,; like to talk about Aaron, can't give any definite reason . . . After this I went to the school house, and placed
up a placard "beware of false Prophets." The man calling himself
"Christian" is going to preach there to-morrow: returned home,
went to my chamber, called for a bottle of wine, drank it all
myself; if I have a propensity in the world it is to drink wine,
umph! like to get drunk every saturday; can't account for the
passion; intend to quit it as soon as I can . . .

We also learn from the *Palladium* that the business of the Post
Office in Madisonville is poorly conducted; and that, despite the
existence of the School House, there is a need for a good school.

The want of a good school in this place is most sensibly felt.
There seems to be a carelessness on the part of parents respecting
the education of their children, which amounts to a fault. The
advantages of well regulated schools are so universally exper-
ienced in every place where they are located, that it would be
an insult to the good sense of our citizens to reiterate them
here.

The *Palladium* tells us that there was, in October 1832, a yellow
fever epidemic in New Orleans, "as fatal and extensive in 1822."
It states that many people from New Orleans "have sought refuge in
Covington, which for salubrity of air, goodness of the water, and
many of the luxuries of the season, is not surpassed by any place of
known resort in the State." The article continues:

And we are confident that if it was better known as a summer
retreat, we should have the pleasure of welcoming among us
many who otherwise go farther and fare worse. We shall probably
renew this subject again, and hope to be in part, the humble instrument of making known the many advantages strangers
would have in selecting out the pine woods as their home, for
a short season.

The *Palladium* of November 3, 1832, announces that cholera had
broken out in New Orleans, "even while the yellow fever is raging,"
with death running from 100 to 113 per day. However, the *Palladium*

was "pleased to inform distant friends, that our town is perfectly healthy, not one case of sickness of any kind within our knowledge exists here."

These comments are the first of many on the desirability of St. Tammany Parish as a resort area, and on the healthy nature of its climate and its waters.

In 1833, Joseph D. Davenport sold his interest in the press, type, and other equipment of the *Palladium* to John J. Mortee, who began the publication of the *Louisiana Advocate*, which was to last up until the time of the Civil War. By 1839, Mr. Davenport was once again the publisher.

The 1850 census indicates how much the opportunities for St. Tammany's citizens had expanded. For instance, there were 26 merchants, 13 shop keepers, 12 bakers, eight butchers, six shoemakers, six grocers, three coffeehouse keepers, and two fruit sellers, indicating a substantial service industry. The 1850 census also reveals that there were six hotel keepers, six barkeepers, a tobacco seller, a cigar maker, a barber, a restaurant operator, and a confectioner, which would indicate that St. Tammany Parish had become a resort area.

There were also seven lawyers, seven engineers, four doctors, nine tailors, four gunsmiths, three captains, two fishermen, two lighthouse keepers, a clock maker, a music teacher, a ginwright, a pilot, an artist, a cotton broker, a potter, a silk manufacturer, a midwife, a machinist, and a speculator.

One business that did not do so well was a pottery established in Mandeville by Emile Lamuloniere and Charles Jacques Arme de la Bretonne, under the name of C. de la Bretonne & Co. in 1847. The pottery was located on the banks of Bayou Castein on property leased from Louis Coquillon, and consisted of several buildings, two kilns, four potters' wheels, and a complete line of necessary equipment. In February 1848, the business failed, and after all the property was sold there was enough left to pay the court costs, leaving the creditors holding the bag to the tune of over $11,000. A survey of property on Bayou Castein in 1895 shows a "potter's landing" two bends above Atalin Street, or just above Prieto's Marina.

In 1853, another yellow fever epidemic struck New Orleans, and once again, refugees flocked to St. Tammany Parish. This time, however, some of the local people contracted the disease. Five members of the Smith family of Covington died, and so did the Methodist minister, and others. Most of the victims were from New Orleans, however. Every boarding house was full, and many private families took in the stricken people from New Orleans. This humanitarian attitude by Covingtonians was to be repeated again and again, even in times when all other places were quarantined against New Orleans.

Sunday excursions to the north shore were increasing in popularity among the city dwellers in New Orleans. In 1850, two more steamers, the *Lenora* and the *Jenny Lind*, began running regular excursions to Covington, Madisonville, Lewisburg, and Mandeville, for 25 cents per passenger, stopping at Mandeville first on the way over and last on the way back. One visitor described a day in Mandeville in 1855:

> Those of our good citizens who have not visited this charming village, know not what a pleasant retreat it is, nor how delightful and invigorating is the trip across Lake Pontchartrain.
>
> A day or two since we found ourselves with a small party of particular friends, on board the good steamboat Lenora, Capt. Dunnica, at the lake end of the Pontchartrain Railroad, and in some two hours and a half were safely landed on the picturesque beach at Mandeville. Although the boat was crowded, the trip was most agreeable, the morning breeze being just fresh and cool enough to make one feel like nodding, and forget the heat of the city. There was also a capital fish breakfast on board, at which all varieties of the "finny tribe," and cooked in every style, were bountifully served out.
>
> Arrived at Mandeville, our little party took up its march for the hospitable mansion of one of our fellow citizens, which was christened "Free and Easy Hall," and where the day was passed only as days should be passed in this hot weather, in lounging with coats, vests and cravats off, reading, bathing, fishing, sailing, eating and drinking. We had the blessing of a charming breeze all the while, and there was not a fly or mosquito near to "disturb or make us afraid."
>
> Ample justice was done to our host's fine oysters, courtbouillion, shrimps, fried croakers, trout and red fish omelettes, spring chickens and delicious fresh butter—all of which were well washed down with the purest of old Sauterne.
>
> There was another dish of fish, not enumerated above, be-

cause it deserves separate mention and a most capital dish it was. The reader need not start when we say it was sturgeon! We vouch for the truth of what we say, and there are scores of witnesses to support us. His sturgeonship was taken by the seine in front of Mr. W. A. Nott's presence and we saw him dragged from the water alive and fluttering. His length was four feet nine inches and a half. How this stranger got into Lake Pontchartrain, or where he came from, we cannot conjecture. We only know he was there, and probably 'his mother don't know he was out.' He was served up in two ways—by boiling and broiling—and it is long since we have eaten anything more delicious in the fish line.

We met with another curiosity also at Mandeville in the person of a Choctaw Indian—a regular 'native'; not that a Choctaw Indian is a curiosity, but this fellow's intelligence—not to say accomplishments—makes him one. He speaks English, French and Spanish, besides his own vernacular, and as a matter of course drinks "whiskey heap." The case of this "child of the forest" proves that much may be done by tutoring the savage mind.

Mandeville has grown very considerably within a year or two past and now boasts a large number of inhabitants, much increased just now by many of our most refined Creole families, who are passing the summer there.

Having passed several hours in the most agreeable manner with our friends at Mandeville, the Lenora returned to the wharf from Madisonville, we placed ourselves once more on board, and by 8 o'clock, P. M., were comfortably walking up Royal Street, greatly refreshed and invigorated by a trip on and over beautiful Pontchartrain.

By the mid-1850's, St. Tammany had reached the apex of its first burst of prosperity. A number of men contributed to this growth.

Probably foremost among the early leaders was Jesse R. Jones, who came to Covington in 1813, and who achieved great success both politically and financially in Covington and New Orleans. His original homestead lay on the west bank of the Bogue Falaya River, just north of Covington, but his principal residence was a beautiful old Georgian house, which stood on the now empty lot near the entrance to Bogue Falaya Park and across the street from the new Episcopal Church.

Judge Jones was on the first town council elected in Covington, and served as the third parish judge of St. Tammany, his term beginning in 1819. As such he served as ex-officio president of the police jury, in addition to handling his usual judicial chores. He was relieved of his duties as presiding officer of the police jury by a change in the law in 1830. His letter to the police jury at that time has survived:

According to an act of the Legislature passed at last session the Parish Judge is no longer President of the Police Jury. Could I have been at home during your session although not a member of your body I would take pleasure in assisting you in your deliberations—as many of you may be new members, and as I have for a long time been President of the Police Jury and consequently made myself acquainted with the laws on the subject, I have thought that it would not be improper for me to mention to you some of the most prominent subjects which will require your deliberation—In the *first* place previous to organizing yourselves you will *take the oath before any Justice* of the peace—according to existing laws assessors are to be appointed on the first Monday of June; also five persons to serve as *administrators of Schools* for the next two years, a parish Tax is to be laid sufficient to pay the ordinary expenses of the parish and *one thousand dollars* of the *price of the Court House*—I will remark that by the 5th Section of an act to amend the act entitled an act further defining the organization authority and functions of Police Jury papers at last session you are authorized to *Tax Grog Shops* to any amount you may think proper, it is a subject worthy of your deliberation, whether it would not be advisable to lay such a Tax on Grog Shops as would lessen the number of them—

These are the subjects of the most importance—I am gentlemen with much respect & esteem your

Humble Servant
Jesse R. Jones

Judge Jones also served as judge of the 8th Judicial District Court from April 1835, until November 1846, and as judge of the 6th Judicial District Court from May 1865, until May 1866. In addition, he served in the state legislature as representative from St. Tammany Parish.

Judge Jones operated a brickyard south of Covington on the Bogue Falaya River, where the lovely home of Walker Percy now stands. He also operated a saw mill, was a successful merchant in association with James Gilmore of Covington, and operated a number of schooners and steamboats in the lake trade. He owned a great deal of property, having bought the Town of Covington from the Collins family, and owning much other property both in St. Tammany Parish and in New Orleans.

Another important early figure was Thomas Cargill Warner, who was the first parish judge of St. Tammany Parish. Judge Warner was also the Colonel of the 13th Regiment of the Louisiana Militia, which participated in the Battle of New Orleans. It is not certain when he came to the area, but it might have been as early as 1802. He was certainly here in 1806, when he was acting as a surveyor in establishing the boundary between the two early Spanish grants. He was succeeded as parish judge by James Tate in 1813, but, when Washington Parish was established, he became parish judge of that parish, and served as such until his death in 1833. Judge Warner had 13 children, six sons and seven daughters, and through them, almost everybody in Washington and St. Tammany Parishes can claim kin.

His daughter, Tabitha Emily Warner, married Ezekiel Parke Ellis, and they settled in Covington. Ellis was elected Clerk of Court in 1834 and served until 1839. He was also one of the founders of the Methodist Church in Covington. Ellis practiced law in St. Tammany for a number of years, but moved to Clinton so as to be near Centenary College, where his sons were to be educated. Family legend says that the real reason he left Covington was because it was "the wickedest place on the face of the earth." Although not then a resident of St. Tammany, he served as judge of the 6th Judicial District Court, succeeding Jesse Jones in 1866, and, therefore, presided over court in St. Tammany.

His sons, Thomas C. W. Ellis and Stephen Dudley Ellis, each served as District Attorney of the district including St. Tammany Parish, and Stephen later became one of the first judges of the First Circuit Court of Appeal.

The Penn family was also prominent in the early days. Martin G. Penn served as District Attorney in 1831, and as District Judge from 1846 until 1852. Alexander G. Penn was Sheriff from 1824 until 1829, and later served as Congressman from the 4th Congressional District from 1850 to 1853. Abraham G. Penn served as Sheriff from 1843 through 1848.

Penn's Mills, one of the early water mills in the parish, was located on the Tchefuncta River, west of Covington, and was owned by Abraham Penn. He sold the property to Alexander, who built a fine home there, which he unfortunately burned to the ground while trying to get rid of an infestation of fleas, a somewhat extreme remedy.

David B. Morgan, the War of 1812 general, was another influential early settler. He was successful both as a brickmaker and planter, and was active in parish affairs, holding office as justice of the peace and as police juror. He served as president of that body from 1842 until 1845. His many descendants include Charles Morgan, who served as Sheriff from 1854 to 1856; Lewis L. Morgan, who was Sheriff from 1856 to 1857; William C. Morgan, who was Clerk of Court from 1876 until 1890; Lewis L. Morgan who served as District Attorney from 1908 to 1912 and as a member of Congress from 1912 to 1917; and James L. Morgan, who was president of the Police Jury from 1960 to 1962.

Other men whose names appear often in the early days were James Tate, the first parish judge; William Bagley who was a merchant, a member of the first town council of Covington, president of the police jury from 1850 to 1851, and a member of the commission which prepared the post-Civil War resolutions; and Elijah M. Terrell, a Covington merchant, and police juror, having served as president from 1846 to 1847.

The pattern of the early development of St. Tammany was just about complete. Her prosperity came from her geographic situation and her natural resources. Natural deposits of clay adjacent to navigable streams created the brick industry. The seemingly limitless forests of yellow pine led to the sawmills and the manufacture of turpentine, pitch, tar, resin, and charcoal. The highways leading into the interior giving the quickest access from New Orleans to Baton Rouge, Natchez, Nashville, Mobile, and points east, west, and north, coupled with the convenient ports at Covington and Madisonville, led to the development of the area as a trade and transportation center. The quiet beauty, clean air, and sparkling waters of the river and springs led to the development of the area as a summer and health resort. Of course, none of the development would have been possible without New Orleans, which was the market to which the trade goods were shipped, and the major source of the people who enjoyed, on a temporary basis, the beauties of St. Tammany.

CHAPTER XV

The Beginning of Decline

The *Louisiana Advocate* of June 11, 1851, carried a story that a railroad from New Orleans to Jackson, Mississippi, via Madisonville, was contemplated. It was reporting the beginning of the economic downfall of St. Tammany.

In 1851, a movement was started to subscribe money for a railroad from New Orleans to Jackson, then known as the Jackson Road. Although some consideration was given to building the line through Madisonville, the decision was made to build it around the west end of Lake Pontchartrain through the swamps and marshes bordering the lake. This was quite a feat of engineering for that day, but work proceeded expeditiously, and the road, known as the Orleans, Jackson, and Great Northern Railroad, was opened for business on August 23, 1854.

Almost immediately the trade through Covington and Madisonville began to dry up because the railroad was closer, faster, and more convenient for shipping cotton, farm products, and other goods to New Orleans from the areas which had formerly used the St. Tammany Parish route. Neither the bricks, lumber, and sand of St. Tammany, nor the tourist industry were enough to sustain the prosperity which had been enjoyed.

The Panic of 1857, which had a profound effect on the economy of the country as a whole, also contributed to the economic downfall of the parish. The census of 1860 tells the sad story. The total population of the parish fell from 6,385 to 5,406, according to the official count. The white population fell from 3,663 to 3,332; and the slave population fell off to 1,836 from 2,363. Only the free colored population increased, from 359 to 408. The number of households fell off from 786 to 635.

The number of brickyards went from 15 to 8 and there were only 11 sawmills, down from 14 in 1850. The number of farmers increased to 288 from 192, which indicates that men who had formerly made their living at a job were forced back to the land in order to get by. The area must have continued to function well as a resort; since there are six hotel keepers and four bar keepers tabulated.

There were still some large slave holders and some wealthy men in the parish. Alfred Hennen now owned 117 slaves, and property valued at $100,000. All of his slaves were engaged in maintaining his "Retreat," but, according to one observer, the property was not even productive enough to maintain the slaves because the soil was so poor. "Retreat" was an expensive luxury. Other large slave owners were Peter Poutz, owner of Fontainebleau Plantation, with 78; J. W. Cutrer, 83; A. Baham, 70; Daniel Edwards, 58; Jesse R. Jones, 56; and Alexander G. Penn, 53.

Some of the more affluent citizens were Hennen, who describes himself as a farmer; Poutz, a planter, worth $100,000; Terence Cousin, brickyard owner, worth $95,000; T. W. Crawford, merchant, worth $87,500; S. C. Bankston, a farmer, worth $66,000; and W. McGay, a retired merchant, worth $64,000.

Not surprisingly, considering the increase in the number of farmers, farm production increased between 1850 and 1860, but not greatly. The two major crops continued to be corn and sweet potatoes, with 41,390 bushels of corn raised by 189 farmers, and 31,443 bushels of sweet potatoes raised by 143 farmers. Other crops included 3,334 bushels of peas and beans raised by 80 farmers, 251 tons of hay, by 57 farmers; 22,049 pounds of rice, by 41 farmers; and 200 bales of cotton, by 18 farmers. Rye and oats which were each grown by only one farmer, were minor crops, as was honey, of which 160 pounds were produced by four farmers. There was a small wool clip of 1,450 pounds, from 12 farmers; and 22 farmers produced 7,979 pounds of butter.

The farmers owned 448 horses, 99 asses and mules, 1,638 milk cows, 755 working oxen, 5,823 cattle, 2,247 sheep, and 6,793 swine, all valued at $108,955.99. The average farm size was 32.41 acres, and the largest was Hennen's farm, with 800 acres under cultivation.

Other owners of large farms were Daniel Edwards and Peter Poutz, who had 300 acres improved; A. W. Weems, with 180; H. Cooper, with 125; and L. Thomas, L. Bell, and L. C. Bankston, all with 100 improved acres.

Despite the existence of these large and, in most cases, successful farmers, it seems apparent that most of the farm products were grown for consumption rather than for sale, and that there was, therefore, a good bit of subsistence farming in St. Tammany.

Before there was any opportunity for the area to recover from its financial reverses, another event took place which was to result in destitution for St. Tammany.

On a national level, the great political differences between North and South began to come to a head in the late 1850's. In 1860, the election of a Republican president, Abraham Lincoln, brought about the final rupture.

On December 20, 1860, the Louisiana Legislature issued a call for a convention to decide on the question of secession. The election of delegates was held on January 7, 1861, at which time 19 parishes elected delegates for secession and 9 elected delegates opposed to leaving the union. In accord with its tradition of being out of step, St. Tammany Parish, which had voted for the Unionists in the 1860 presidential election, instructed its delegates to vote against secession.

As was preordained by the election, the convention voted for secession, and, for the fourth time in its history, the people of St. Tammany found themselves unable to control their own destiny. On February 12, 1861, the National Flag of Louisiana was adopted, becoming the seventh flag to fly over St. Tammany. On March 21, 1861, the convention ratified the Constitution of the Confederate States of America, the Confederate flag became St. Tammany's eighth national flag, and the Civil War was on.

CHAPTER XVI

The Civil War

In spite of the Unionist leanings of its people, St. Tammany was soon swept into the Confederate war effort. Many of the local men volunteered into various companies and saw action throughout the war. Probably the most popular of these was Miles Legion, commanded by Colonel William R. Miles. Other companies which came out of the parish were the St. Tammany Greys, commanded by Captain C. Crosby; the St. Tammany Artillery, under Captain J. A. Turner; and the Mandeville Rifles, commanded by Captain Charles Morgan.

Another company which was popular with St. Tammany Parish men was Hardy H. Richardson's company, which was organized by Captain Richardson in Washington Parish in June 1861, as the Washington Rifles. It fought in many of the big battles of the Civil War from 1862 through 1865. Among the St. Tammany Parish men who were killed or wounded while fighting with this company were Daniel Fendlason, Jacob Bruhl, G. M. Penn, L. L. Morgan, J. C. Blackwell, and St. Ange Bossier.

The St. Tammany Regiment of the Louisiana Militia which was to include all able-bodied white men between the ages of 18 and 45, was organized in June 1861, when elections for company officers were held. It was commanded by Colonel George H. Penn, with William B. Hosmer as Adjutant. Company A was commanded by Captain Andrew J. Edwards. His officers were P. H. Baham, First Lieutenant, Samuel B. Cooper, Second Lieutenant, and Theodule Sharp, Third Lieutenant. Company B was commanded by Captain George B. Miller, with John G. Carpenter, First Lieutenant, E.

Grantham, Second Lieutenant, and John Edwards, Third Lieutenant. Other officers were captains Matthew Dicks, Emile Laurent, Alfred Hennen, and A. J. Morgan; and lieutenants M. Sharp, Lewis Joyner, and F. Bustillo. These latter officers were relieved from duty because there were only a few men in their companies. On August 19, 1862, of the 98 privates in the regiment, only 43 were present for duty, the other 55 being absent, most of them in New Orleans, which was then in Union hands.

Another company stationed in Covington was Captain M. G. Mullins' Company of Scouts and Sharpshooters. Louis S. Greenlee, one of the lieutenants, proved himself to be a first class provider for the Confederacy during the latter part of 1863. Court records show that he was sued five different times by people trying to recover property which he had taken from them on behalf of the military. Among the property he seized was Joseph Cousin's schooner *Rosa* and Raymond Carriere's schooner *Perserverence*. He also pressed a number of horses in St. Helena and Washington Parishes.

By April 1862, it was estimated that some 400 St. Tammany men had enlisted and gone off to war. In many, if not most cases, their families were left without support, and the Police Jury had to assume that burden. An appropriation of $20,000 for the purpose of furnishing this support was made in early 1862, which subjected the parish treasury to unaccustomed strain. In 1863, the state assumed the burden of supporting the families of the soldiers, appropriating $5,000,000 for the purpose. The wife, father, and mother of the soldier were to receive $10 per month, and each child, brother, or sister under twelve was to receive $5 per month, as were any other dependent relatives.

Unionist sentiment in the parish did not subside entirely after secession was a fact. In March 1862, Colonel Penn ordered the arrest of Samuel and Jacob Loyd who were charged with organizing a Union company in St. Tammany. We do not know how successful they may have been.

In 1862, the Union forces under Admiral David G. Farragut began their drive to take control of the Mississippi River. Farragut brought his forces up the river, fought his way past Forts Jackson and St. Philip at English Turn, and on April 29, 1862, New Orleans surrendered without a fight.

Only a week later, on May 5th, the first naval action in Lake Pontchartrain took place, when the U.S.S. *Calhoun* captured the schooner *Rover*. The next day, the *Calhoun* took the Confederate steamer *Whiteman* in the lake. On May 13, 1862, the first military action of the war in St. Tammany Parish took place, when a small party from the *Calhoun* captured the Confederate gunboat *Corypheus* in Bayou Bonfouca. The *Corypheus*, a small sailing vessel, armed with only one brass four pounder, was guarded by Confederate soldiers who offered no resistance when the cutting out party arrived from the *Calhoun*. The *Corypheus* was taken over by the Federals, and served most of the rest of the war as a United States gunboat in the lake, coming back to haunt the Southerners on more than one occasion.

With New Orleans in Federal hands, and St. Tammany in Confederate territory, trade with the city, which was the economic life-blood of St. Tammany came to an abrupt stop. A number of local citizens then petitioned the Confederate Army for permission to continue trade with New Orleans. They received this reply:

Gentlemen:

Your petition, asking permission to open trade with the Enemies of your country, who now occupy New Orleans and Baton Rouge, the Commercial and Political Capitols of your State; has been received by General Ruggles, and I am directed by him to reply. In doing so, I beg leave to call your attention to General Order No. 2 from these Headquarters, and to paragraph II of General Order No. 9, from Department Headquarters, which prohibit all intercourse or traffic with the enemy or persons within his lines, and denounce the penalty of death against persons engaged in it. Copies of these are herewith enclosed for your information.

These orders have been called for by the stern necessities of the times, and it is believed, have met the almost universal approval of the loyal citizens of the Country. Nor is there anything novel in the regulations they prescribe, or the penalties they announce. They but declare, and clothe with penal sanctions, doctrines long established, and universally recognised. Even in your communication, while seeking to be exempt from their provisions you recognise their justice, for you say, "We are aware that in time of war there should be no trade between belligerents." But you urge that yours is an exceptional case, and that to enforce the rule would subject you to great hardships.

For now more than twelve months your country has been engaged in a gigantic struggle for existence. Her noble people have poured out their treasures as water, and like the ancient Patriarch have not even withheld their children from the sacrifice; but have cheerfully sent them forth to encounter the toils of the massacre, the diseases of the camp, and the perils of the Battle Field. Hundreds of them have fallen by the wayside; thousands have lingered and died in the Hospitals, many of them for want of medicines that could not be obtained; and thousands more have perished on the field of Battle. But their thinner and wasted ranks have been filled by others eagerly pressing forward to take the places of the fallen, and to day your Flag is proudly borne in the face of, and *behind* the foe by men half clothed, half fed, and who for months have not known even the rude comforts of a soldiers tent. Nor has the Army been alone in this respect; every class of society has, to a greater or less extent, been subjected to hardships and privations, which, to their lasting honor be it said, have been firmly, and even cheerfully borne. And if, Gentlemen the time has come when you are called upon to take your share of this wide spread suffering, the General commanding hopes and believes, that you will not be found wanting in courage and fortitude to bear it like Men, and Patriots.

You say that if not permitted to dispose of your Bricks, Lumber &c. they will be "mere rubbish on your hands." You cannot be ignorant Gentlemen, that in this you but share the common fate of your fellow citizens. There is now held by the Patriotic planters of the Confederate States, more than two hundred millions of dollars worth of produce which, so far from seeking to sell or barter, they stand ready to destroy, and have in many instances, with their own hands voluntarily applied the torch, and with a self sacrificing devotion worthy of men who aspire to be free, calmly seen it reduced to ashes rather than sell, even at the most exhorbitant rates to the Enemies of their Country. And you have only to turn your eyes to a neighboring parish to see the very materials which you fear will become "rubbish" on your hands—though but recently formed into comfortable dwellings, and sheltering helpless women and children—reduced to heaps of "rubbish" and ashes; while the occupants have been driven forth into the woods, and deprived of all means of subsistence. And this has been done by the very men with whom you would now open commercial intercourse; to whose avarice you would minister, and whose wants you would supply.

The General commanding directs me in conclusion to say: That regarding these prohibitions of traffic with the Enemy, as essential to the successful defence of the country, he is determined rigidly to enforce them; and that any one who may be detected in an attempt to evade or violate them, will be promptly brought to condign punishment.

Very Respectfully
James O. Fuqua
District Provost Marshal Genl

The citizens of St. Tammany responded to this stern letter as they had to similar prohibitions in the past. Smuggling across the lake was carried on briskly for the duration of the war, despite the effort of both United States and Confederate forces to stop it.

When New Orleans was evacuated by the Confederates, there were three Southern gunboats in Bayou St. John, the *Oregon*, the *Carondelet*, and the *Bienville*. The officer in charge of these vessels was told to take them to Mobile, but, instead, he brought them to the Bogue Falaya River, where they were stripped of their armament and burned and sunk in the river.

The *Oregon* was sunk across the channel near the present location of the boat launch at the foot of Second Avenue in Covington. The *Carondelet* was sunk in an inlet called Caesar's Bayou, on the east side of the river, a short distance above. The *Bienville* was sunk against the right descending bank of the river, near the property presently owned by the Favrot family.

Later in 1862, the first expedition into St. Tammany by Federal troops took place. On July 27th, the *Grey Cloud*, commanded by Lt. Buchanan of the United States Navy sailed into the Tchefuncta River. She was carrying five companies of the 12th Connecticut

Volunteer Regiment, and a section of Captain P. E. Holcombe's Second Vermont Battery, all under the command of Major Frank H. Peck.

As she passed Madisonville, the *Grey Cloud* was fired on, and responded with a shot from one of her 32 pounders. No one was hit on board the ship, but, according to one Confederate report, a woman and child were killed by the *Grey Cloud*'s shot. She continued up the river until her further progress was obstructed by the wreck of the *Oregon*. At that point, the men on the *Grey Cloud* heard the shots of pickets in the woods, and the roll of drums, but saw no Confederate troops.

Since further progress up the river was obstructed, the soldiers landed and proceeded to Covington on foot. The advance party saw five armed and mounted men and fired on them without result. In Covington they were told that a number of bands of Confederate troops of from six to 50 men, had passed near Covington, meaning to concentrate at some point to meet the Federal troops. The Federals marched the American flag through the principal streets of Covington, noticing as they did that white flags were hung from many of the houses in the town. They then returned to the *Grey Cloud*. Two of the men died of sunstroke during the return to the boat.

As the *Grey Cloud* prepared to leave, she was again fired on from the banks of the river, one soldier and two sailors suffering wounds. The fire was returned as she departed and there were no further incidents as she descended the river to Lake Pontchartrain, although they did spot a number of Confederate soldiers.

The *Grey Cloud* returned to St. Tammany on July 29th, and "by one of the bayous went some distance into the country." They heard reports of Confederate troops everywhere, but did not see any of them. The next day, they went up the Pearl River as far as Pearlington, where they "found the people in great destitution and beset by plunderers on every side."

On August 1st, the expedition visited Lewisburg, where it found that all the docks and landings, both at Lewisburg and Mandeville, had been burned two weeks before by the Confederates. A company of troops was landed in small boats, and marched back into the woods, looking for a Confederate camp. According to Major Peck, "they found it deserted, as about this region too there was nothing left to plunder."

The expedition then returned to Madisonville, where they found the troops gone, the town deserted, and nearly every public and private building closed. Major Peck's evaluation of the expedition was uncomplimentary to the Confederate forces in St. Tammany:

> Though the tangible results of our expedition may seem small I have no doubts of its good effect. For more than a week we have hunted guerrillas at every point where we could hear of them. Nearly every day we have invited them to a fair engagement distant from our support. On each occasion we obtained only dissolving views of them. Authorized and commissioned as they are, they are actuated by no motive but plunder. They fight only from ambuscade, and war indiscriminately upon friend and foe. The conduct of officers and men during the whole expedition has been most creditable.

Actually, there were no Confederate forces in St. Tammany which could have effectively stood up to the United States troops. Captain John J. Slocum's Company of Mounted Rangers, which was stationed near Covington, had about 90 men. Major J. De Baun reported that his men were so scattered in picket duty that he was unable to mount an effective force. In addition, the Confederate intelligence was bad. Estimates of the Federal force varied from 200 to 4,000 men, and the naval vessels from one boat to four large transports. In any event, before there was a chance to react, the *Grey Cloud* was gone. We do not know what the Confederate reaction was to the later forays made by the expedition.

Martial law had been declared in Military District No. 1 on July 2, 1862, by the Confederate authorities, but was later abolished. In September 1862, Jules LeBlanc was appointed provost marshal for St. Tammany Parish. His duties were "to preserve order among military persons and to prevent improper intercourse with the enemy, by either citizens or soldiers . . . ."

The *New Orleans Daily Delta* of September 2, 1862, carried a story that a Mr. Ricard "a loyal citizen of the United States, was hanged by the rebels on his arrival in Covington," where he had gone with provisions for his wife and family. There are no other sources to confirm this somewhat grim story.

Two shiploads of paroled Confederate sympathizers deported from New Orleans for refusal to sign a loyalty oath to the Union depart for Madisonville on February 20, 1863 (*Courtesy The Historic New Orleans Collection*)

By October 22, 1862, there were three companies of mounted rangers stationed at Covington at what was known as Camp Slocum: Norman's company, with 25 men; Terrell's company with 48 men; and Slocum's company, which had 91 men.

The only other action in 1862 was on November 21st, when 25 men of Captain Bredow's company of Partisan Rangers, under Lieutenant Evans, attacked a Federal steamboat, the *G. Brown*, in Bayou Bonfouca, killing three men, and forcing her to back out of the bayou.

In December 1862, people in New Orleans who had applied to go to Confederate territory were permitted to leave. The first group, consisting of those whose names began with the letters "A" to "H" were transported to Madisonville by steamer on December 18, 1862. Later, the people of New Orleans were required to take an oath of allegiance or else register as "enemies of the United States." Many of those who refused to take the oath were deported from New Orleans on February 2, 1863, by the steamer, *J. D. Brown* to Madisonville. The journey across the lake was covered by a correspondent from *Harper's Weekly*, and the magazine carried the story, with pictures.

By December 10, 1862, smuggling in Lake Pontchartrain had achieved such magnitude as to attract the attention of Admiral Farragut. Apparently, many vessels from New Orleans would be given passes to leave the city for ports outside of the lake, and would then immediately cross the lake with cargoes of salt, blankets, shoes, and other articles which were sold to the Confederates and other residents of the north shore.

The U.S.S. *New London* had been in Lake Pontchartrain, but was ordered out in January 1863. Although U. S. Brigadier General Weitzel had emphasized the importance of maintaining navy patrols in the lake, Admiral Farragut reported that there were no naval vessels in the lake as late as January 27th.

Shortly thereafter, the *Corypheus*, now under the command of Acting Volunteer Lieutenant A. T. Spear was on duty in the lake, and in August she captured a boat and recovered a number of letters which had been thrown overboard, including one for General Robert E. Lee.

On August 26, 1863, Acting Master Francis M. Green received the following orders:

You will proceed with the U.S.S. *Commodore* into Lake Pontchartrain, via Ship Island, for the purpose of breaking up the blockade runners in the form of boats of 5 tons and upwards, which run to and fro between New Orleans, the bayous, and adjacent coasts.

Allow nothing to pass to or from the insurrectionary districts unless they have the pass of the senior officer in command of the naval forces here.

Pursue them into the rivers and bayous whenever you hear of them but I wish you to be on your guard against ambuscades in the rivers, which they often establish in the tops of trees, commanding your decks. The U.S. schooner *Corypheus,* commanded by Acting Master Grove, is employed on the same service and you may require his cooperation whensoever it may be desirable.

Keep me informed of your proceedings by official reports, and you will be careful to keep a record of all the captures you may make, noting their place, circumstances, cargoes, tonnage, and names of vessels.

There is no record of any capture made by the *Commodore* during 1863, so the blockade runners must have been doing all right.

The Confederates were also trying to break up the smuggling. On December 10 and 11, 1863, a party under the command of Captain Greenlee captured and burned four vessels which were engaged in that nefarious activity. There were the schooner *Josephine Truxillo*, owned by Joseph Lewis, which had come to St. Tammany for a load of wood and charcoal; the barge *Stepheny*, 26 tons, owned by Hypolite Cousin, which had come for a load of cattle and wood; the barge *Helena*, owned by George Bernes, which had come for a load of spars and wood; and the schooner *Sarah Bladen*, of 43 tons, owned by Warren Sanchez, which was to take a load of bricks to Ship Island. The *Truxillo* and the *Stepheny* were burned in Bayou Lacombe on December 10th, and the other two boats in Bayou Bonfouca on the next day.

On December 28, 1863, the *Commodore* was ordered to report to Colonel W. K. Kimball of the 12th Maine Volunteers, to accompany him across the lake and assist him in any military enterprises in which he might engage. The enterprise proved to be the occupation of Madisonville by a substantial Federal force. The objectives of the occupation were to obtain timber, lumber, tar, turpentine, bricks, and wood, and to attempt to break up the smuggling and the running of Confederate mail across the lake.

The force, which consisted of over a thousand men under the command of Colonel Kimball, left New Orleans on January 3, 1864, and occupied Madisonville that same day without incident.

The occupation lasted for over a month, during which time a number of expeditions were sent out into the surrounding country. One of these left Madisonville on February 1, 1864, rode to Franklinton, and occupied that town for about an hour. On the next day, they went over to the Tchefuncta River, where they met another party which had come up the Tangipahoa River and cut over to the Tchefuncta. The two parties returned to Madisonville and, during their march, chased several Confederate patrols and captured one Confederate officer.

They arrived at Madisonville on February 3rd, bringing in 12 mules, 3 yoke of oxen, 15 horses, 157 cattle, 76 sheep, 9 shotguns, and 1,000 rounds of ammunition, all of which they had confiscated during their patrol. The cattle were in such poor condition that they turned most of them loose outside of Madisonville. They reported "no enemy within our reach except small roving parties."

A second expedition from Madisonville departed on February 11, 1864, heading west on the Ponchatoula Road. Captain Adolph Bery was in command, with First Lieutenant Henry P. Anderson, four sergeants, two corporals, and 23 privates of Squadron C; and with Lieutenant Moore and 20 men and non-commissioned officers of Squadron D. There was also Dr. Stephenson, an ambulance and driver, and a guide named Bailey.

When the expedition reached the Tangipahoa River, it was fired upon and Captain Bery decided to retire along the road leading north to Hennen's farm. Lieutenant Moore, who had been wounded, was placed in the ambulance. After they had proceeded about a quarter mile, they were attacked by a force estimated at 70 to 100 men. Captain Bery's horse was shot from under him, and he was captured. When his men saw that, they became panic-stricken and fled. The doctor abandoned the ambulance, and the entire force ran all the way to the Turnpike Road.

In all, the expedition lost Captain Bery, who was reported as missing; Lieutenant Moore, Corporal John C. Klinke, and Private Wilhelm Engel, reported wounded and missing; and Private B. K. Jones, the driver of the ambulance, missing. Of course, they also lost the ambulance, its two horses, and a lot of miscellaneous equipment. This appears to be the only Confederate military success in St. Tammany Parish during the Civil War.

The occupation of Madisonville was a hard time for its citizens, since the Union soldiers foraged for much of their food and took whatever they could lay their hands on. One resident described what their life was like:

My father had some money, but could buy nothing except some corn in the ear, which was old and musty, paying as high as $10.00 a barrel, and hauling it forty miles. When cornmeal could be found in the village, it was sold at the enormous price of $40.00 a bushel. The corn we ground by hand in a small steel burr mill, thereby getting meal, grits, and husk. Coffee could not be had at any price, although a few families had it all the time. We used sweet potatoes as a substitute. They had to be cut in small pieces and then dried in the sun, then dried again in an oven or stove, then roasted and ground the same as genuine coffee, and it was hard to detect the difference. A great many parched meal, and others used the seed from our coffee weed, I suppose owing the name coffee being attached to it. Father was very fortunate in finding an opportunity to purchase a barrel of molasses, although it was 40 miles from home. He paid $110.00 for it. Would not our planters of today be glad to obtain such a price for one barrel of molasses? We had mush and molasses for dinner and supper, and in the morning would partake of molasses and mush, for a change. In the country of piny woods they fared some better, having their hogs and chickens, corn and sweet potatoes to fall back on. To get salt to cook with, many had to dig the ground floor up in their smoke houses and put it in water and boil it down. Burnt corn cobs served us as soda, a very good substitute. Tallow was used to cook with instead of lard, as it was so scarce. Our ladies became shoe makers. They would save all the soles of their shoes, and make new uppers of cloth or canvas, and sew them onto the soles, making a very soft and elastic shoe.

The *Louisiana Advocate* ceased publication, probably shortly after the war started. In December 1863, *The Wanderer* appeared, edited by James Bowie and published by M. J. Scott. Business was probably not too good, considering the economic condition of the parish. The edition of March 26, 1864, the only surviving issue, had a notice in it that the paper was for sale, after only 15 issues. The conditions in the parish are graphically illustrated by this item:

Mile's cavalry, formerly Mile's Legion, paid this part of the country a visit the past week, gathering up the command, conscripting all of the available age, recruiting, etc. We are sorry to say the impression left behind is none to the credit of the command; however, they may have been acting under orders; and in that case, are excusable. A more persecuted people never existed, than those of St. Tammany. The Yankees come along and destroy and plunder everything in their reach; next in turn comes the Confederates, in whose strong arm all think themselves secure, with orders of impressment for horses, mules, wagons, etc., and yet, the citizens are not subjected to punishment and miseries enough. Jayhawkers come in and take the very bread out of our mouths and that of our children. How long such things are to be God only knows, but this we do know it is not safe for a man to have two days' provisions ahead, and let it be known.

On the other hand, the following advertisement appeared in the same issue:

NOTICE TO THE PUBLIC.

It is with great pleasure that I announce to the public the largest stock of Dry Goods that has been in Covington since the war, for which I will receive Country Produce, such as Corn, Chickens, Bacon, Lard, Turkeys, Ducks, Geese, Sheep, Beef, Hogs, Eggs, and Confederate Money.

My stock comprises, in part, mourning calicos, calicos of all pat, alpaccas, flannels, sewing thread, shoe thread, ribbons, toilet soap, matches, segars, smoking tobacco, chewing tobacco, pins, combs, buttons, corsetts, skirts, playing cards, pipes, candles, coffee, letter paper, drop shot, varnish, and gentlemen's ladies and misses' shoes, and whiskey without end &c, &c, &c. Cheap.

C. G. Cousins

Between April 1st and April 10, 1864, another Federal expedition operated in St. Tammany Parish. Major Martin M. Pulver and Companies C, D, E, and F of the 20th Infantry Corps d'Afrique, aboard the steamer *Lizzie Davis*, made a reconnaissance up the West Pearl River. They ascended the river as far as Holmes Bayou, spent the night of April 3rd tied up near Indian Bayou, and on the 4th landed three companies of men on Honey Island. These men crossed the Island to the Pearl River, where they got possession of the ferry. They crossed over to Mississippi, and in McCall's River found the hulk of the *J. D. Swain* afloat. They captured her and floated her down the Pearl River to Fort Pike.

On May 3, 1864, Admiral Farragut's report reveals three vessels operating in Lake Pontchartrain: the *Commodore*, the *Corypheus*, and the *Stockdale*, a steam powered, tinclad gunboat, commanded by Lieutenant Thomas Edwards. She was involved in one of the better documented incidents of the Civil War in St. Tammany. Lieutenant Edwards' report of the incident follows:

U.S.S. Stockdale

Lake Pontchartrain, May 17, 1864.

Sir: It becomes my painful duty to respectfully report to you the loss of three of my officers, Acting Ensign John Lowrie and Acting Third Assistant Engineer Samuel (James?) Lockwood, taken prisoners, and Acting Master's Mate Gilbert H. Moore, severely wounded and since died.

The circumstances of the capture are the following: On Monday morning, May 16, about 6 o'clock a.m., I went into the mouth of the Tchefuncta River, where the smugglers make it a practice of running whenever the opportunity affords. After I came to anchor the executive officer, Mr. Lowrie, reported to me he would like to go on the point at the mouth of the river and get some sand. I gave him the order to go and sent Mr. Moore as officer of the boat, with five men well armed, and to have the bow gun trained upon the point. The boat went to the point and got the sand and came on board. Not having enough sand, Mr. Lowrie said he would like to go himself this time. I told him to go and be (back) as soon as possible, as I was going to get underway. He went, but instead of going to the point after the sand, he went about 400 yards up river from the point into the mouth of a small bayou, where it was thickly wooded, and the moment the boat struck the shore a whole company fired into them. The men immediately jumped overboard (three colored men and one white man) and the officers, by their staying in the boat, stopped to fight them, I think. I immediately commenced firing my bow guns (30-pounder Parrotts) with 5-second shell, and they left, but taking Mr. Lowrie and Mr. Lockwood with them, leaving Mr. Moore overboard wounded. As I was lying about 400 (yards) from where the boat landed, I immediately steamed up to where my men were and got them and the boat, still shelling the woods, but wounding only two or three, which I have since learned. I then went to Mandeville; sent on shore by flag of truce to get my officers, if killed. I was informed that Mr. Lowrie was wounded in the shoulder and Mr. Lockwood in the hand. I also gained intelligence that this was an expedition of cavalry, commanded by a Lieutenant-Colonel Hill, for the purpose of capturing the *Stockdale*, should she go into the Tchefuncta River on Sunday night. For this purpose they had six boats at Lewisburg, but on Sunday afternoon I went and took them all and did not go into the Tchefuncta River on Sunday night. They also had a man in a small boat to make a signal should I come in the river; him I took as a prisoner. I also have learned since that they have three companies of cavalry about 3 miles back of Lewisburg (La.), I also respectfully report the capture of a man in a small boat running the blockade on Sunday morning; he threw everything overboard before I reached him.

I have the honor to be, sir, very respectfully, your obedient servant,

Thomas Edwards,
Acting Volunteer Lieutenant

Commodore James S. Palmer
Commanding Naval Forces, New Orleans, La.

Other correspondence shows that Lieutenant Edwards, after arriving off Mandeville, demanded the return of Acting Ensign John Lowrie and Acting 3d Assistant Engineer Samuel Lockwood by 12 o'clock, "or I will shell the Town of Mandeville." At the request of Lieutenant Bouny, who was in command of the Confederate Lake Shore Headquarters, Edwards granted a three hour delay, but repeated his threat to fire on Mandeville. Lieutenant Bouny replied: "In response to your threat of firing on the town of Mandeville the L. C. comdg. has to say that the prisoners mentioned in your communication will suffer death by hanging when such fire commences."

The *Stockdale* departed without further demands, and without firing on Mandeville. There is more to the story of the man in a small boat, who was alleged by Lieutenant Edwards to have been part of the plan to capture the *Stockdale*.

Matt M. Morgan, writing in the *Farmer*, says that he was fishing with his father and his step-brother in the Tchefuncta River at the time the *Stockdale* put the party ashore. After the skirmish, they and their pirogue were taken on board the *Stockdale*, which then proceeded to Fort Pike. The two boys were held on board ship there for two weeks, and then were taken out into the lake and set adrift in the pirogue. With evident relish, Morgan writes:

> They put us over about two miles out from Mandeville, while the wind blew a gale from the southwest, the whitecaps ran high. Now imagine two lads of 9 and 14, in an open boat, fifteen feet long and three feet beam, and twelve inches deep, battling with the waves. But if those cruel Yankees could have thrown a rabbit in a briar thicket, they would have harmed it just as much as they did us by placing us in a boat in the water.

The boys were soon safely at home, bringing with them a fine mess of crabs which they caught on the way.

Matt's father was held by the Yankees for eight weeks, accused of waving his paddle as a signal for the skirmish to begin. However, Mr. Morgan was able to demonstrate that he was not in sight of the *Stockdale*, and General Butler, who tried the case, set him free.

Smuggling continued to be a problem. On April 23, 1864, Confederate Brigadier General Taylor addressed a letter to Messrs. F. Cousin, L. Cousin, Jos. Cousin, and John Cousin of Bayou Lacombe; and T. Cousin, A. Cousin, A. Cousin, and Mr. Jones, overseer for J. A. Blanc at Bayou Bonfouca:

> I have been informed that you are the owner of a number of boats which are engaged in running the blockade with passengers and property, and thus carrying on an illicit business. Such being contrary to law, I order that it be immediately stopped.

For any violation of this, you will be held responsible, your boats and cargoes seized and confiscated or destroyed. All permits for the shipment of articles into or out of the Confederate lines must come from these or higher Hd. Qrts.

On October 13, 1864, Lieutenant Commander J. C. P. de Krafft, United States Navy, in command of the gunboats *Elk* and *Fort Gaines* carrying a detachment of troops, went to the north shore of Lake Pontchartrain. At daylight on the 14th they ascended the Tchefuncta River "several miles above Madisonville touching at the town on their return without finding any indications of refugees, rebel pickets or cavalry, or any means of transportation which could be available to the enemy."

After visiting the Tangipahoa River, they then reconnoitered the north shore of Lake Pontchartrain examining the villages of Lewisburg and Mandeville without seeing any activity. On the 15th, both vessels went up Bayou Bonfouca, and the *Fort Gaines* went several miles up Bayou Vincent, without seeing anything which could be used for transportation except a few small skiffs which "being necessary for the use of the wretchedly poor families living on the bayous, were not molested, as they could be of no service to the enemy." Commander de Krafft's report concludes as follows:

In all, we did not see over a dozen men on these bayous, and they were nearly all old persons, but few negroes, and, except at Madisonville and Mandeville, not more than six or eight families of women and children.

Madisonville appears to be nearly deserted, and the inhabitants of this whole region painfully destitute and needy, with scarcely clothing. The appearance of the whole country is that of a silent wilderness, in which no laborers could be found to build launches for offensive purposes if any such project had ever been entertained.

In the next month, on November 29th, the *Elk,* commanded by Lieutenant N. Kirby, spotted a boat running into Mandeville, which was caught by her gig within one mile of the Mandeville piers. It proved to be a blockade runner manned by George Arlick and George Cranford, carrying a cargo of whiskey, coffee, hams, woolen clothing, opium, and quinine, a peculiar cargo to be carrying to a destitute area. It was confiscated.

parish as the war wound down, but the end of the war did not end the tribulations of St. Tammany.

CHAPTER XVII

Reconstruction and the End
of the Decline

With the surrender of General Kirby Smith's troops on May 26, 1865, the Civil War in Louisiana came to an end. As a result of the depredations of federal troops and Confederate deserters, St. Tammany Parish lay depleted and exhausted. On June 2, 1865, Henry W. Allen, Confederate Governor of Louisiana, issued a proclamation advising the people to cease all resistance and to rebuild the state within the United States. J. Madison Wells, the federally appointed Governor, issued a proclamation of his own on June 10, 1865:

To the People of the Parishes of Saint Tammany, Washington, Saint Helena, Livingston, West Baton Rouge, Point Coupee, Saint Martin, Concordia, Madison, Carroll, Franklin, Saint Mary, East Feliciana, West Feliciana, Tensas, Vermillion, Saint Landry, Lafayette, Calcasieu, Avoyelles, Natchitoches, Sabine, Caddo, Ouachita, De Soto, Rapides, Morehouse, Union, Jackson, Caldwell, Catahoula, Claiborne, Bossier, Bienville, and Winn.

I extend to you my heartfelt congratulations on your being restored to the protection of the flag of our country, the symbol of law, order and freedom, and which now waves in majestic power over an undivided nation. Our once wealthy and fertile State, now bankrupt and desolate from the ravages of intestine war, resumes her natural relations (which have been temporarily disrupted) within the glorious Union of the States, united by the bonds of universal freedom and ties that can never be disserved. It is not my purpose to rake up the ashes of the past, by enquiring who has erred and who has not erred, in the fearful

The James R. Hosmer plantation house is among the oldest continuously occupied homes in St. Tammany Parish

Side view of the James R. Hosmer plantation house

struggle the nation has just passed through. Whatever may have been the causes of the outbreak, and however bitter may have been the feelings engendered in the hearts of some, it is better that all such matters be buried out of sight forever. It is not the past, but the present and future, we have to deal with. Great and responsible duties rest upon every citizen at this crisis, to manfully go to work and assist in the re-establishment of civil government. In that connection it is a most cheering sign to see the spirit of submission to the laws and willingness to acquiesce in the result manifested by those so recently engaged in hostility to the Government. Even the soldiers return to their homes, wiser and better men, frankly owning to the failure of their experiment, and all expressing a desire to atone for the errors of the past, by cheerful obedience to the Government, and glad again to enjoy its beneficent rule. You my friends and fellow citizens, for I esteem it a privilege to call you so, must follow in the footsteps of so good an example. You must go to work to organize civil government in your respective Parishes. Sheriffs, Recorders, Clerks of Courts, and Police Jurors, will have to be appointed provisionally, until elections can be held, to fill these offices as provided by law. You must confer among yourselves, and select men of integrity and capacity to fill these positions. I will act on your recommendations by appointing the persons named by you, if they are men of proper character, and have taken the oath prescribed in the President's Proclamation of the 8th of December, 1863, or that of the 29th of May, 1864. This will be pre-requisite in all cases, the original or certified copy of which oath, must be transmitted with the application for appointment. It is also my intention to organize the Judiciary throughout the State by appointing provisionally Judges of the District Courts and District Attorneys, as soon as practicable. The former class of officers are made appointive by the Executive under the new Constitution for a term of six years, and I invite recommendations from you as to who shall fill those offices, as also District Attorneys.

I cannot urge upon you too strongly the importance of your acting promptly and with unanimity in the matters herein brought to your notice. If you neglect to avail yourselves of the opportunity offered you, I shall be compelled to make appointments to office for your section, from the best information in my possession and you cannot blame me, if they are not acceptable to you. Important elections will be held this fall. Members of Congress and a Legislature will have to be elected, and if each parish is provided with proper offices to open the polls, an election for Governor and other state officers according to the new Constitution will take place at the same time.

While the population of that portion of the State which has been so fortunate as to enjoy the protection of the strong arm of the General Government, sooner than other sections (and for which they are not entitled to any merit of their own) in order to hasten the restoration of civil government in the State, have adopted a new Constitution and elected a Legislature which has passed laws, yet I feel authorized to say, that it was with no intention of forestalling or denying your rights, to participate in the making of the fundamental, as well as all other laws.

In conclusion, I assure you that no one is more anxious to have the whole State represented in all general elections, and particularly for the office of Governor, than myself.

St. Tammany Parish responded, apparently in keeping with their former Unionist sympathies, by holding an assembly at the courthouse on August 2, 1865. The presiding officer was Alfred Hennen then in his 80's and the secretary was James R. Hosmer. "Boy" Hosmer was a grandson of Judge Jesse R. Jones, and was to become a powerful figure in St. Tammany Parish politics, although not a seeker of political office. At that time, however, he was just out of the Confederate Army, in which he had served with distinction. A committee, composed of John A. Burns, William Bagley, Sr., Duncan N. Hennen, and George H. Penn was appointed to draft resolutions expressing the sentiments of the assembly, which were adopted.

The citizens of the Parish of St. Tammany, La., assembled today at the Court House, when the venerable and patriotic Alfred Hennen, Sr., called to the chair, and Jas. R. Hosmer, Esq., was named Secretary; whereupon the President, in his usual terse and eloquent style, announced the object of the meeting, and concluded by appointing John A. Burn, Wm. Bagley, Sr., Duncan N. Hennen, and Geo. H. Penn, a committee to draft resolutions expressive of the sentiments of this assembly.

The committee withdrew, and afterwards, through their chairman, Mr. Duncan N. Hennen, reported the following resolutions, which were adopted unanimously:

1.   Resolved, As citizens of Louisiana, we welcome the return of peace, and believe all will cordially unite in restoring order and submission to the laws and Constitution of the United States.

2.   Resolved, That the sudden emancipation of the slaves without preparation for the change, was a grievous injury done to both master and slave, but, as a necessity, we accept the situation, and will use our best endeavors to lessen the evils which the change is liable to produce.

3.   Resolved, That we believe that in this district there exists a prevailing feeling which induces the freedman to look to his former master for advice and protection, and that the former master views the emancipated slave as a being to whom he owes advice and protection, and that if this relation is not disturbed by the interference of designing meddlers, the freedmen will soon be induced to go to work for reasonable wages, and the two classes of society will mutually benefit each other.

4.   Resolved, That we consider the laws of the State, if properly administered by the civil authority, amply sufficient to protect the colored population in their rights as freedmen, and to keep them in subordination to the laws.

5.   Resolved, That we highly approve of the course of Andrew Johnson as President of the United States in relation to the question of State suffrage and State rights.

6.   Resolved, That the conduct of J. Madison Wells, as Governor of the State of Louisiana, has met our entire approbation, and we earnestly trust he will not only be continued as Provisional Governor but that he will be elected as permanent Governor for the first term under the Constitution.

7.   Resolved, That we view, in the selection of J. Madison Wells as civil Governor of the State, a wise and discriminating choice, and in his after confirmation as Provisional Governor by President Johnson, we discern the act of a patriot and a statesman.

8. Resolved, That we cordially endorse the civil and provisional administration of Governor Wells, and regard his official path as one not strewn with roses, but encumbered and encompassed with difficulties demanding the highest qualification and combination of heart and mind to surmount.

9. Resolved, That in his appointees to office in this parish we recognize a strict adherence to the time honored, loyal and purely American criterion of qualification, and in every instance the honest, capable and loyal man, under his benign selection, has become the incumbent of office.

10. Resolved, That a copy of these resolutions be forwarded to Gov. Wells, and that copies be furnished the New Orleans Times and the Picayune, with request to publish.

Whereupon the meeting adjourned.

Reports in the *New Orleans Tribune*, which was the official organ of the Republican Party, and which might be suspected of some bias, indicated that all was not so peaceful in St. Tammany as the above resolution might indicate. In August, it reported that one of the German farmers in St. Tammany had been imprisoned for enticing a slave to abscond, although slavery had, of course, been abolished. Another story in September 1865, states that in St. Tammany Parish, slavery still existed in full force, and that the slaves were being kept "in perfect ignorance of their rights" and that, on many plantations, were still unaware that they had been set free.

In November 1865, the *Tribune* reported that the gubernatorial election had not been held in St. Tammany because of intimidation. However, it also reported that the polls were open in Madisonville, and that H. C. Warmoth, the Republican candidate, received 136 votes.

St. Tammany lost a large piece of its territory in 1869, when Tangipahoa Parish was created out of parts of Livingston, St. Helena, Washington, and St. Tammany Parishes, reducing St. Tammany to its present borders. The west line was moved from the Tangipahoa River to the line between Ranges 9 and 10 East and the Tchefuncta River.

The 1870 census tells just how badly the parish was hurt by the Civil War: the population had increased slightly, from 5406 to 5586, according to the official census figures. There were 11 brickmakers and 6 sawmill operators enumerated, indicating that the major industries of the parish were still functioning. However, there were only 28 house carpenters and 22 ship carpenters, a sharp decrease from 49 and 56, respectively in 1860, indicating that both the construction and boat building businesses had fallen off. Only one hotel keeper is listed, along with three boarding house keepers and three bar keepers, which tells us that the resort business was, for all practical purposes, nonexistent. However, the oldest industry in the parish was on the increase, with 24 charcoal burners and eight tar burners enumerated.

The most telling statistic on the economic condition of the parish is the wealth of its more affluent citizens. In 1860, there were 27 men in the parish who reported owning property valued at $10,000.00 or more, including two who were worth $100,000.00. In 1870, the wealthiest citizen in St. Tammany was F. V. De Gruy, who owned a sawmill, and who was worth only $8,000.00. Terence Cousin, a brick-yard operator, who reported himself to be worth $95,000.00 in 1860, was worth only $6,000.00 in 1870. Other affluent citizens were S. C. Thompson, a brickyard operator; James Duncan, who had a sawmill; G. A. Fosdick, a commission merchant; and Alexander Chevallon, the tax collector.

The school system appeared slightly improved by 1870, with 13 school teachers and 313 children who attended school during that year. Five clergymen were listed: J. A. Maneratta, a Roman Catholic; James H. Harper and G. T. Vickers of Covington, both Methodist; Levy Johnson of Mandeville, one of the first two black clergymen listed, a Methodist; and Henderson Parker, of Madisonville, also black, with no denomination given.

There were seven physicians and two lawyers, up two from 1860. One of the lawyers, James M. Thompson, son of Dr. J. W. Thompson, was to become one of St. Tammany's most distinguished sons. He served as District Judge and Court of Appeal Judge, and was a leader in nearly every important enterprise in the Covington area for the rest of the 19th century.

The only hotel in the parish was operated by Henry Earl, in Madisonville. Mandeville boasted three restaurants, run by Francois Colomes, Jean F. Jean, and B. Philibert. There must have been some trade across the lake, since there was one steamboat captain, Elijah Miller; one schooner captain, Paul L. Gusman; and 58 sailors enumerated.

The agricultural census for 1870 also shows a depressed economy. Only 121 men were actively engaged in farming, and only two had 100 acres or more under cultivation, Peter Poutz with 130 and E. Grantham with 100. The staple crops were once again Indian corn and sweet potatoes. Only 6,140 bushels of corn were produced by 70 farmers, and 12,316 bushels of sweet potatoes by 114 farmers. Rice production was 21,698 pounds by 13 farmers, and seven farmers produced 660 gallons of molasses. Two of these produced 36 hogsheads of sugar. Other crops produced were cotton (22 bales), peas, beans, Irish potatoes, and hay. Farm products also included butter, wool, milk, beeswax, and honey. For the first time, orchard products appear as having been grown in St. Tammany. The value of all farm products was $79,670, including livestock. There were 155 horses, 41 mules and asses, 610 milk cows, 309 working oxen, 935 cattle, 586 sheep, and 1,630 swine, valued at $25,345.

The 1870 census also includes, for the first time, the population of the towns: Covington was the largest with 579 people; Mandeville had 537; Madisonville, 400, and Lewisburg had a population of 110.

In 1868, the Republican Party, backed by the authority of the United States Army troops who occupied Louisiana, took control of the state government. During the next ten years, Louisiana was subject to what was probably the most corrupt administration in its history. During this time the economy of the state remained depressed, and St. Tammany Parish was no exception. In 1877, as a result of the deal which put Rutherford B. Hayes in the White House, the federal troops were withdrawn from Louisiana, and the control of the Republicans over the election machinery was ended.

With the great virgin pine forest virtually untouched, it is not surprising that the lumber companies began to move into St. Tammany. Poitevent & Favre Lumber Company of Pearlington, Mississippi, acquired thousands of acres of untouched pine and cypress lands in the east-central part of the parish in the 1880's and others were not far behind.

In the decade between 1870 and 1880, the population increased from 5,586 to 6,887. Farming and livestock raising were approaching their pre-war levels by 1880, and appeared to be in a healthy condition. Covington boasted four hotels, but there was only one in Mandeville.

Not everything was so good, however. Between 1870 and 1880,

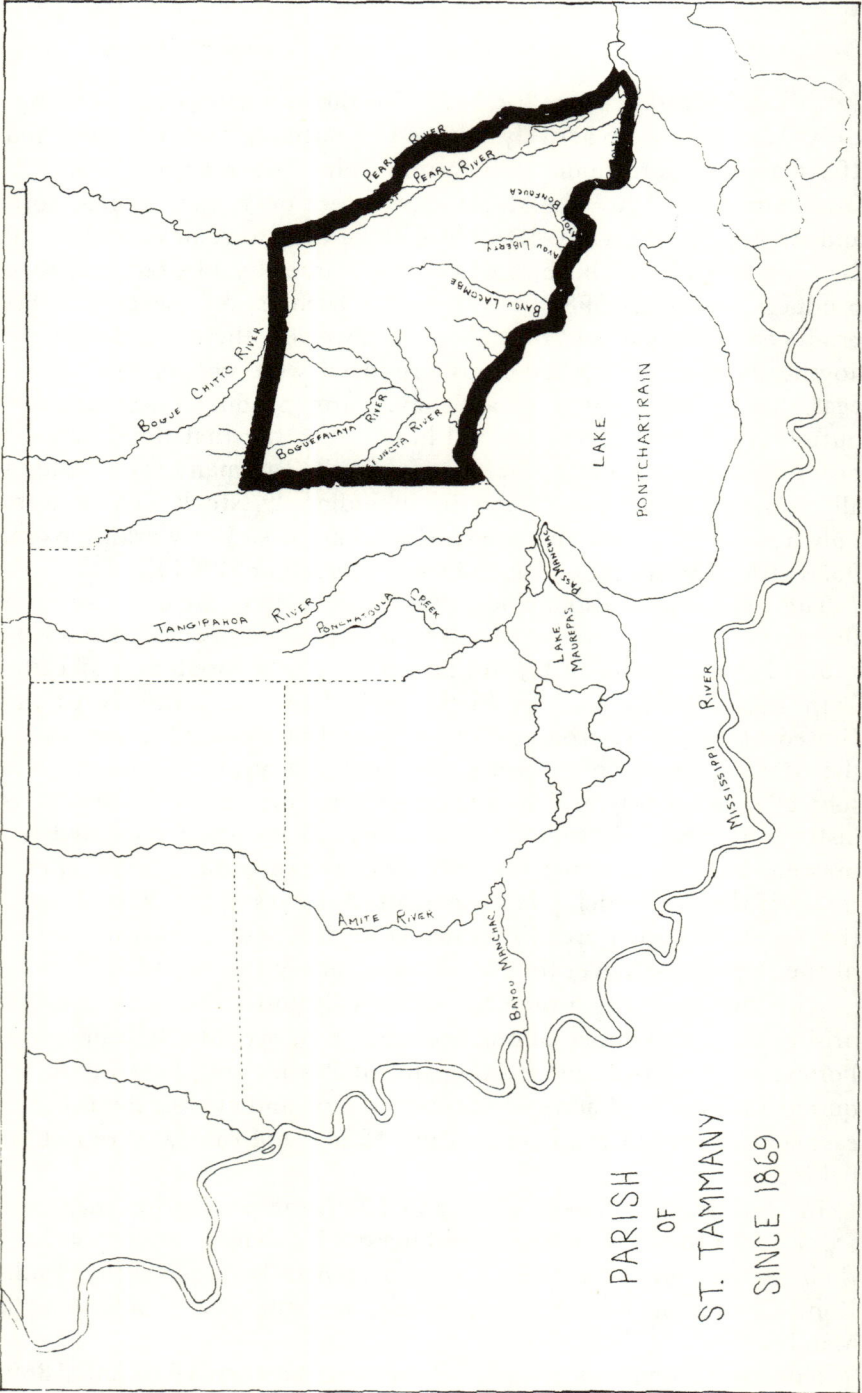

PARISH
OF
ST. TAMMANY
SINCE 1869

LAKE PONTCHARTRAIN

Pearl River
Pearl River
Bayou Bonfouca
Bayou Liberty
Bayou Lacombe
Bogue Chitto River
Boquefalaya River
Lunta River

Tangipahoa River
Ponchatoula Creek
Lake Maurepas
Mississippi River
Mississippi River

Amite River
Bayou Manchac

the number of brickyards decreased from 11 to five. One of these is particularly worthy of note, because it was owned and operated by a black man, Gabriel "Gib" Parker, who must have been an exceptional person to achieve the success he did during post-Reconstruction times. The *Farmer* had this to say:

> To show that it is not necessary for a black man to go to Kansas to get rich, we refer to Gabe Parker, a freedman of this parish, and an example of honesty and industry, worth of commendation. Gabe Parker is, in appearance a genuine specimen of the African race. He was born and raised a slave, and freed with the balance of his race in the South. He is now the owner of a fine farm and brickyard on the Abita river, and two schooners, one of which carries wood, brick and sand to New Orleans, and the other is in the trade from New Orleans to Mobile. On a recent visit to his place, we were surprised at his crop of rice and cotton, especially the latter, which can hardly be excelled in the parish. He is out of debt, is reputed honest, and known as a man of wealth.

The Parker property, which later was the Alexius brickyard, is today the site of the Delta Regional Primate Center. Others operating brickyards in 1880 were Frank Jackson, Peter Vagen, Max Cousin, and Hypolite Cousin.

Sawmill operators decreased from six to three between 1870 and 1880, possibly because accessible timber was becoming harder to find. The sawmill operators in 1880 were James Blackwell, Nathan Page, and Henry Heisser.

Education continued to be a less than universally supported enterprise. In 1870, in addition to the public schools, there was a Covington Peabody Institute, operated by Reverend Clute Barron assisted by Mmes. V. Pritchard and A. Morto, which received aid from the Peabody fund. None of those names appear in the 1870 census as teachers or preachers, however.

In 1875, the Report of the State Superintendent of Education gives a fairly complete picture of the public school system in St. Tammany, which was guided by six directors: A. A. Annas, president; George Ingram, treasurer, M. L. LeBlanc, Robert Williams, Nic Claudel, and William Bosque. There were nine school districts, probably one in each ward, with a total of 1,333 educable youths between six and 21 years of age. The state contributed $133.30 to the parish or ten cents per student. Of these, 370 attended public schools and 175 went to private schools. The public school system employed nine teachers, four male and five female, and the private schools six, making a grand total of 15 teachers, who were paid an average of $40.00 per month. There were two frame school houses, valued at $1,433.00, which were pronounced to be in good shape. All of the public schools were primary schools, there being no intermediate or high schools in the parish. There were 39 whole months of school taught in public school for an average of just over four months per year per school. The private schools were usually conducted by the public school teachers when the public schools were not in session, and attended by children of the more affluent citizens who could afford the $2.00 per month tuition.

The 1880 census shows 15 teachers in the parish including the first two black teachers, Israel Jones and Israel Young. Education was on the rise, however. In 1882, Covington had two white public schools, one for black students, and one white private school. The private school was probably the one operated by the Covington School Association, the officers of which were: William C. Warren, president; W. B. Cook, vice president; J. M. Abney, secretary; and C. G. Joyner, treasurer. The teacher was Reverend G. T. Vickers, and he had 33 pupils who were paying $2.00 per month.

By this time, St. Tammany Parish had hit bottom in the long decline which had started in 1853, and was beginning what was to be a long upswing.

CHAPTER XVIII

Recovery and the Railroads

As the Reconstruction period came to an end, and the 1880's began, the long economic decline stopped, and a period of growth began which lasted until the end of World War I. During this period, St. Tammany Parish would emerge into the modern age.

In 1880, however, St. Tammany was substantially as she had been since 1820 in a number of respects. The population was larger, of course, but more than two-thirds of the land was public, and the privately owned properties still clustered along the streams and in the vicinity of the towns. The major center of population remained in the southwest section of the parish, where the three incorporated towns of Covington, Mandeville, and Madisonville were located.

Although the sawmills and the loggers had been operating for 75 years, and the tar burners for about 150 years, they had barely scratched the surface of the timber resources of the parish, probably because the primitive technology of the day limited the area in which timber could be cut. Generally speaking, timber was cut only in the vicinity of the rivers, which were necessary for the transport of the logs. In those days the logs, after being cut, would be branded by the owners and rolled into the rivers to await the next high water, when, hopefully, they would float down to deeper water. Needless to say, the logs constituted a constant hazard to navigation and were occasionally responsible for washing out a bridge. Some of the logs can still be seen embedded in the banks along the upper reaches of the Bogue Falaya and Little Bogue Falaya Rivers.

The main roads remained as they had been in 1850, and the favorite mode of land transportation was still the horse and the ox

The *Camelia* on Lake Pontchartrain *(Courtesy The Historic New Orleans Collection)*

Ferry on Lake Pontchartrain in 1909; President William Howard Taft is aboard

wagon. After the Civil War, shipping remained depressed, along with everything else, but began to recover as the economy slowly came to life. As early as the late 1870's, a few boats began to make regular runs, both for trade and for excursions.

Probably the most famous of the lake boats was the *New Camelia*, which was crossing the lake on a regular basis in 1878. Originally built in 1863 on the east coast of the United States as the *Zephyr*, she was brought to the Gulf Coast in the late 1860's, and put in the trade between New Orleans, Mobile, and Pensacola. When the construction of the Morgan Railroad, now the L & N, made this impracticable, she was put in the lake trade, first as the *Camelia* and then as the *New Camelia*. She was still at it in 1916, and finally sank at her moorings in Madisonville in 1920. Her captains, William Hanover, H. T. G. Weaver, and Jim Dandy were well known and popular figures on the north shore.

Another well known boat in the early days was the schooner *F. M. Pippo*, owned by the lake captain of the same name. In 1878, she was making one round trip per week, carrying cotton at 25 cents per bale, dry barrels at 25 cents each, and sacks for 15 cents each. Captain Pippo also operated the schooner *Dorio and Doria*, and in 1879, he put the steamer *Alice* in the lake trade.

In July 1879, six steamers were making excursion trips across the lake on Wednesdays and Sundays. They were the *New Camelia*, *Abita*, *Alice*, *Georgia Muncy*, *Heroine*, and *Henry Wright*. This brisk business gave rise to Robert Badon's Hack Line, which connected with the *New Camelia* at Mandeville, Madisonville, and Old Landing. Shortly after, W. H. Davenport's Omnibus Line, which connected with the *New Camelia* at Old Landing on the Tchefuncta River, south of Covington, and took passengers to any part of St. Tammany and adjoining parishes, started up. Charles Frederick's Stage Line also went into business in 1879, connecting with steamers at Mandeville, Madisonville, and Covington.

Apparently the principal beneficiary of the lake traffic was Mandeville, the population of which increased from 541 to 753 between 1870 and 1880, making it the largest town in the parish. In contrast, Covington lost slightly from 585 to 567, and Madisonville increased slightly from 400 to 441.

The early 1880's brought the beginnings of the two major influences which were to carry St. Tammany Parish, kicking and screaming, from the depths of economic despair into a prosperous modern world. These were the population boom and the railroads, the former resulting from the vast public lands there for the taking, and the latter from the great pine forests which were growing on the lands.

The lands were available at $1.25 per acre to those who were willing to homestead the property by living on it and cultivating and improving it for a period of five years. Hundreds of families took advantage of the opportunity. In addition, the railroads and the large lumber companies, particularly Poitevent and Favre, were able to acquire thousands of acres of timber land from the State of Louisiana. Such was the appetite for land that by 1910, there was virtually no public land left in the parish.

The population figures for the parish jumped from 6,911 in 1880, to 13,335 in 1900, and 20,645 in 1920. One visitor painted this picture of the parish and its people during the early part of the period of expansion:

It is now 10 years since I left Racine County—since then I have lived in the Gulf States. This must be the Eutopia of Henry George, for, by common consent of all, land is of no value, and there are to-day, within 40 miles of New Orleans, hundreds of thousands of acres of public lands that no person will accept as a gift. The forest primeval which covers this land is almost valueless. The pine forest extends over a large portion of the Gulf States and the traveler in this forest will find himself surrounded by much natural beauty. The trees are straight and 100 feet high, with branches and leaves at the top only. They sway back and forth like masts of ships, and their continual whisperings sound somewhat similar to sea waves, and remind one of the spirit land. These pine lands produce little or no underbrush, and objects at a distance are visible. There is no frontier. A home may be found every two miles, which means a clearing of about one acre, surrounded by a zigzag fence; the trees have not been removed, some have simply been deadened (girdled), and still stand; they have lost their leaves, twigs and bark, and their white trunks and large branches resemble ghosts with arms extended to heaven. In this clearing may be found a log house, consisting of one room, balconies on the front and sides, and a kitchen in the rear; also a stable and cow-pen in front of the house (to be handy). In this house 12 children have their existence, and there they will remain until each seeks a similar home of his own. These houses I refer to are occupied by white people. The negro cannot endure isolated country life, he is too sociable for that, and remains in the towns.

The country is slightly undulating, and the swells, or slight ridges, are dry; and although the soil is naturally poor, it will produce abundantly if fertilized. This last item is hardly worth considering, however, as the planter can pen his cows or sheep, a few nights in his one-acre field, then turn his ridges up with a plow made at the nearest blacksmith shop, and set out the sweet potato vines. In the fall he will point with pride to his potato patch, roasting ears and razor back hogs, and exclaim, "Look! we raise our own bread and meat!"

The climate is very healthful and sickness is unknown. The Abita Springs, in St. Tammany parish, La. is supposed to be the fountain for which Ponce de Leon sought in vain.

Sheep are valued at $2 per head, goats and hogs at 25 cents, and cattle at $8, though sometimes the latter sell for $5.50.

School houses are found every ten miles, and are kept open three months in the year. The children don't care to attend school, and their parents don't encourage them, for they say, "Our children have all got plenty mammy wit, and that is a heap better than the learning taught in school." Calligraphy is an accomplishment the native does not possess, but he is a natural arithmetician. Every cracker-boy knows how many 5 times 15 are, and if asked, "What is the half of 35?" he will reply, "One-half is 17 and the other half is 18."

When I first taught school I was loth to leave my dictionary in an open school house during the night, but a visiting clergyman assured me there was no danger, as its use was unknown. The few settlers are perfectly happy, and earth has no further gifts they want.

Whatever the qualities of the settlers and other people of St. Tammany might have been in those days, theirs were the hands that built the parish during its entry into the modern era. And it rode into the modern era on the railroads. As early as 1868, George Ingram organized the Mandeville and Sulphur Springs Railroad Company. In 1870, the name was changed to New Orleans and Northeastern Railroad Company, and it was authorized "to locate, construct, maintain and operate a line of steamboats, barges, or other means of conveyance from their depot now established and hereby fixed at or near the dividing line between the Towns of Mandeville and Lewisburg, in St. Tammany Parish, to one or more points within the corporate limits of the City of New Orleans . . . ."

A pier was built out into the lake at Lewisburg and a right-of-way was cleared from Lewisburg to several miles past Sulphur Springs, just outside of Covington. Unfortunately, Mr. Ingram's untimely death brought the operation to an end.

In 1880, however, interest in the railroad was revived. The St. Tammany *Farmer* reported: "Able engineers have pronounced it practicable to build a line directly across Lake Pontchartrain, about 22 miles, and greatest depth of water about 22 feet."

The road was to run from New Orleans, across the lake to Lewisburg, and from thence via Sulphur Springs and Bogue Chitto to Meridian, Mississippi. In May 1881, the *Farmer* reported the preliminary survey complete, and that the road would cross Lake Pontchartrain to Mandeville on a trestle. However, a major change in plans was made, and the decision was made to build the New Orleans and Northeastern Railroad through the eastern part of the parish. It was scheduled to be completed by December 31, 1882.

The road was not completed by the scheduled date, but in March 1883, the *Farmer* reported that it should be running by September 1st. Finally, on October 15, 1883, the "first train ever" on the New Orleans and Northeastern passed W. B. Porter's store at Halloo, now Pearl River, at 11:30 a.m., headed south. It arrived in New Orleans at 6:00 p.m. the same day. On board were G. Bouscaren, the chief engineer, R. Carroll, the general superintendent, S. Whinnery, the division engineer, and H. Colbran, general freight agent of the Alabama and Great Southern Road.

The railroad fever was catching. In October of 1884, a road from Slidell to Covington via Bonfouca was proposed, and by August of the next year, the St. Tammany, Lakeshore, and New Orleans Railroad Company was chartered. Apparently, that is as far as it ever got.

The New Orleans and Northeastern Railroad was to open up the east end of the parish for the first time, although the primary purpose of the road was communication to the northeastern part of the United States. However, the next railroad to come was planned primarily because of the timber reserves of the parish.

In 1885, the Poitevent & Favre Lumber Company began the construction of a road from Pearl River to Abita Springs, called the East Louisiana Railroad. The road was probably intended primarily as a logging road, to be used in transporting timber from the vast Poitevent & Favre properties in central St. Tammany Parish to their mill in Pearlington. However, the people of the west end of the parish looked forward anxiously to the completion of the road.

On June 26, 1887, the first excursion train arrived in Abita, with 500 people aboard. Other visitors swelled the crowd to 1,000. The train came in at 10:37, after a two and one-half hour trip from New Orleans, with the band playing "Goodbye, My Honey, I'm Gone." Unfortunately, the pavilion was not quite complete, so that the dancing planned there could not take place.

Finally, on May 16, 1888, the East Louisiana Railroad reached Covington, when a passenger train operated by Conductor F. Ladner and Engineer Moody, crossed over the new iron bridge and entered the town, carrying a party of ladies and gentlemen who got on at Claiborne Station and rode into Covington.

The next step was the construction of a branch line to Mandeville by the East Louisiana Railroad, which left the main line about eight miles east of Abita and ran southwest to Mandeville. This line was completed and in use by May 22, 1892, when the first excursion train arrived in Mandeville.

It was from these lines that the first great incursions into the timber of the parish were made. Not only was the timber on the vast properties of Poitevent & Favre cut and transported out of the parish, but the new settlers who wanted their lands cleared were happy to sell to the timber buyers who flourished in St. Tammany.

There was a pause in railroad construction until about 1902, probably because there was so much timber to be cut along the existing lines. Then in 1902, the Greenlaw Lumber Company began construction of a branch line from Covington to its sawmill located four miles to the north on the Holmesville Road. It was completed to that point in June 1903, and construction was continued to the north. By December 1903, the track was complete to Red Bluff, about seven miles north of Covington, where a depot was constructed. Sometime during the next year the track was taken over by the East Louisiana Railroad, which had secured right-of-way to a point 16 miles north of Covington where a 25-acre site had been secured for a depot and town site.

Meanwhile, the Salmen Brothers of Slidell had commenced construction of a new railroad from Slidell to Mandeville. The road was to be completed during the winter of 1904-1905. It was in operation to Bayou Lacombe in 1905.

In 1904, the East Louisiana was sold by Poitevent & Favre to the Great Southern Lumber Company, which changed the name of the line to New Orleans Great Northern Railroad Company. They proposed to extend the line from Slidell through Florenville and on through Washington Parish to a point in Mississippi known as China Grove. Another line was proposed from Pearsall Junction to join with the extension running north from Covington, which by then had been extended to a point 12 miles north of Covington. By August 1, 1906, the trains were no longer running to Covington via Pearl River, but were going direct to Florenville from Slidell. The line from Pearl River to Florenville was abandoned.

In September 1906, the N.O.G.N. decided to build its main line from Slidell to Abita Springs via Mandeville. On January 17, 1909, the railroad began running over the new lakeshore line, as it was called, and the line from Florenville to Abita Springs was abandoned shortly thereafter. At about the same time, the Great Southern Lumber Company completed building its great mill and the new town of Bogalusa, and moved the general office of the N.O.G.N. from Covington to the new town. The main yard was moved from Florenville to Bogalusa, and that town then ceased to exist. Today the highway from Abita Springs to Hickory runs along the right-of-way of the old line. Florenville was located where the highway passes over the railroad, now part of the Illinois Central system. The Mandeville branch line, which was also abandoned, now forms the roadbed of State Highway 1088.

The lakeshore line is, of course, still in use, furnishing a greatly reduced rail service from Slidell to Covington, via Mandeville and

Advertisement for the East Louisiana Railroad Company (Courtesy The Historic New Orleans Collection)

A typical Lake Pontchartrain schooner *(Courtesy The Louisiana State Museum)*

An electric railroad car at Abita Springs

Abita Springs. The line running north from Covington, which had its eventual terminus in Folsom, has long since been abandoned and its right-of-way is almost undetectable. It was the instrument for logging all of the lands between Covington and Folsom.

The next construction took place in 1907 and 1908. In February 1908, the Baton Rouge, Hammond, and Eastern Railroad, which ran west from Covington, and which was financed in part by a tax millage in St. Tammany was completed and in operation. It was never a commercial success, and its tracks were recently taken up between Covington and Hammond.

The last attempt made at rail travel in St. Tammany was the electric train line of the St. Tammany and New Orleans Railway and Ferry Company. This company ran electric cars from Covington to Abita Springs and then to Mandeville, where the cars ran out on a long pier into the lake. At the pier, the line connected with steamers which crossed the lake on a regular schedule to New Orleans. Along the right-of-way, the property was laid off in lots and squares, and it was anticipated that a community of commuters would build up along the line. In January 1909, the first trial run over the new track was made by Joseph Birg, president of the company, and Clay Riggs, the manager.

Despite the revenues from a tax voted by the Third Ward to help finance the operation of the line, it was not a success, and it went out of business in June 1918. Its assets were sold off for $86,900. The old right-of-way can still be seen. Where the Helenbirg Road, which was named for Joe Birg's niece, makes its first sharp turn to the left, it then runs along the old roadbed of the electric train line.

Today, only the Slidell-Bogalusa and Slidell-Covington lines remain of the East Louisiana and New Orleans Great Northern roads. The New Orleans and Northeastern line, now part of the Southern system, is one of the two main lines from New Orleans to the northeast. The Illinois Central is presently seeking a curtailment or discontinuance of its rail service, and that line may soon be no more in St. Tammany.

So let us not forget those exciting days when the first train passed through Halloo; or came into Abita to the strains of "Goodbye, My Honey, I'm Gone"; or entered Covington with a party of ladies and gentlemen who had boarded at Claiborne Station; or came into

Folsom. Or that glorious day when the first fully vestibuled com-
muter train in the world rolled from New Orleans to Covington in
the record time of one hour and 24 minutes.

CHAPTER XIX

Post Reconstruction Economy

That part of the economic life of St. Tammany most immediately affected by the railroads was the logging and sawmill industry. As pointed out, the railroads gave access to the great untouched timberlands of the central section of the parish. Dummy lines, built into the forest on either side of the main lines opened up even more country to the loggers.

And did they cut timber, and cut and cut until, by the early 1920's, it was all gone. The rolling hills of northwest St. Tammany and the flats of the south presented the same unbroken vista of stumps, as far as the eye could see. In 1908, when John A. Todd moved his mill from Bayou Lacombe to Bonfouca, the *Farmer* reported that he had bought the last stand of yellow pine in the area. The only notice taken of this wholesale destruction of the beauty and the economy of the parish was by the *Farmer* in April 1906, when it said: "The timber lands are rapidly being denuded by the saw mills, and it will not be long before the 'piney woods attractions' and the 'ozone belt' will be a thing of the past, if this practice is not regulated by legislative authorities."

Of course, this wholesale destruction of the forests had its immediate return to the people of the parish, who were enjoying an economic resurgence. Those people, who did not have the benefit of historic hindsight, saw, for the most part, only the economic good which flowed from the timber industry. It was not until the juggernaut ground to a halt that they realized the timber was not an inexhaustible resource.

The 1880 census shows that there were only three sawmills in the

Charcoal or tar kiln *(Courtesy The Louisiana State Museum)*

parish in that year, operated by James Blackwell, Nathan Page, and Henry Heisser. Another early mill, not mentioned in the census, was the Bordeaux Saw Mill, near Covington, owned and operated by Captain W. H. Toomer and his son, J. R. Toomer. The Messrs. Hamlet, Bliss, and Elliot had a mill in Slidell in 1882, and the Salmen Brothers' mill was established there shortly after. W. T. Jay had a large mill on Ponchitolawa Creek in 1881, which was destroyed by fire. By 1885, he had relocated to a spot across the Tchefuncta River from Madisonville. The Sunnyside Sawmill, which was located on the Abita River and Fly Branch, was being operated by Keen and Jay in 1886.

A few small sawmills started business during the 1890's, although most of the cutting was still being done along the railroad tracks and being shipped to the big mills. In 1891, J. H. Miller established a complete saw and planing mill at Old Landing, below Covington and a new sawmill was built at Chubby Hill Plantation that same year. In 1893, the Depre Brothers built a 40-horsepower steam sawmill at the mouth of Bayou Castein. In 1894, the Alton Lumber Company was established at Alton, on the N. O. & N. E. Railroad north of Slidell, where there were 100 inhabitants living in 12 or 15 houses. J. A. Barker had a mill on Simalusa Creek about eight miles north of Covington in 1895.

W. T. Jay built his large mill across the Tchefuncta River from Madisonville in the early 1890's, and, in 1895, built a logging railroad from Madisonville to Tangipahoa Parish. The area around the mill where many of its employees lived became known as Jaysville. In 1906, the mill was sold to Houlton Lumber Company and Jaysville became known as Houltonville, the name by which the area is still known today.

Another early mill was located on Honey Island in 1893, where F. M. White had a sawmill, a spoke factory, and a logging railroad which ran across the center of the island.

In 1913, Poitevent and Favre Lumber Company moved its mill to Mandeville. It was located at a site just to the east of the causeway toll plaza, where Mariner's Village is now located.

Another well-known mill was that of John H. Davis at Lacombe, which later became better known as the Davis-Wood Lumber Compamy.

In the years since the yellow pine was cut the forests have come back in many areas, although there is little of the slow growing, long leaf yellow pine. A number of other sawmills, large and small, have come and gone in those years, subsisting on the second and third growth timber which the parish has produced. Today, there are only one or two sawmills in the entire parish, and most of the building materials sold here today are imported from far away.

The brick-making industry was also enhanced by the railroads, although not to the extent that the lumber industry was. Prior to the railroads, brickyards had to be located on navigable water in order to get their product to New Orleans and other more distant markets.

Two major new brick yards were located on the New Orleans and Northeastern line shortly after its completion in 1883. The largest of these was the yard of the Salmen Brick and Lumber Company in Slidell, which was to become an economic mainstay of that town during its early years. The other was the St. Joe Brickyard, operated by Colonel Peter W. Schneider at St. Joe station, a few miles above Slidell. This yard, still controlled by the Schneider family, is still in business and is the only major brickyard still in production in St. Tammany.

In addition to the Salmen and St. Joe brickyards, there were seven others in production in 1891. These included W. B. Lancaster's yard, near Madisonville in the First Ward; the G. C. Alexius yard, formerly Gib Parker's, on the Abita River; the Demoruelle brickyard, formerly Alfred LeBlanc's on Ponchitolawa Creek and the Tchefuncta River; the three Cousin brickyards on Bayou Lacombe; and the W. J. Tracy yard, formerly Webber's, on the Tchefuncta River in Ward Four. It was estimated that these yards would produce 20 million bricks that year.

In 1893, Southern Brick and Tile Manufacturing Company was in business, making 25,000 bricks per day. In 1899, when its facilities were leased to Kern, Moyse, and Co. of New Orleans, its "immense kilns" were said to have a capacity of 350,000 to 400,000 bricks at a time.

Two brickyards were established along the line of the New Orleans Great Northern north of Covington. The St. Tammany Brick Company was operated by Samuel Cole at Ramsay, in 1907, and the Fendlason and Son Brick Company was in business in Folsom in 1908, making fire bricks.

In addition to the local brick industry, there were a few instances when the clay was used to make pottery, terra cotta, and charcoal furnaces. These enterprises were all short-lived. St. Tammany clay was, at one time, shipped out in carload lots to other parts of the country. In addition, much of the famous Newcomb pottery was made from St. Tammany Parish clay.

As in the case of the lumber industry, the brickyards slowly disappeared after 1900, probably more because of lack of demand than lack of raw material, since suitable clay beds still abound throughout the parish. Some of the old clay pits and ruins of the kilns are still in evidence in some places.

The boat building business and the lake trade were hard hit by the railroads, but both persisted for years and, at times, flourished.

Of course, much of the produce of the parish formerly carried by the boats was transported by rail after the trains came. However, some of the boats managed to stay in business. As late as November 1899, there were four schooners which made regular weekly runs to New Orleans. In one week, the *Josie Weaver* carried 52 bales of cotton, 126 barrels of rosin, six barrels of turpentine, 250 barrels of sand, and 25 barrels of clay. The *Rosa A.* carried 50 bales of cotton, 200 barrels of rosin, and six barrels of turpentine. The *J. R. O'Roark* carried 18 bales of cotton, 250 barrels of sand, six barrels of rosin, eight of turpentine, and five of tar. The *John F. Popp* was loaded with 25 bales of cotton, 400 barrels of sand, and six bales of moss.

After the turn of the century, the lake steamers seemed to do better, particularly in the excursion business. Foremost among these was the *New Camelia*, which was joined by the steamer *Sarah* in 1906. In July 1906, the steamer *Pineland*, built in Marblehead, Massachusetts, was brought to Madisonville by the Tchefuncta River Packet Company. She was designed to carry 250 passengers at 20 miles per hour, but proved to be too heavy for the shallow waters of Lake Pontchartrain. In 1909, after being rebuilt, she did enter the lake trade as the *Ozone*.

In 1907, four schooners were still running across the lake on a regular basis. These were the *Josie Weaver*, *Rosa A.*, *Eunice Hawkins*, and *Anita D.* Captain Weaver put his new steamer, the *Josie*, in commission in 1908. The *Margaret*, which could hold 2000 passengers, began regular runs in connection with the electric train line on Easter Sunday, 1909. A second *Pineland*, owned by the Houlton Brothers of Madisonville, began regular runs in April 1909.

Two more boats came into the lake in 1910. The sidewheel excursion steamer *St. Tammany*, a former revenue cutter capable of holding 1,000 passengers, was bought by the St. Tammany Steamship Co., of Covington. A second steamer, a new steel hull boat called the *Dolive*, was bought by the same company for regular runs between Covington, Houltonville, and Mandeville. She could carry 250 passengers and 35 tons of freight at 12 miles per hour, and took the place of the *Minnie B.* The same company also acquired the *Ossinning* for the lake trade in late 1910, but withdrew her in April 1911.

Daily boat service between Covington, Houltonville, Madisonville, and way points was instituted on February 25, 1912, on the gasoline launch *Belle Isle*. In 1913, the steamer *Fairhope* was only charging 35 cents for a New Orleans to Mandeville round trip.

In June 1914, the new steamer *Hanover*, 205 feet long with a capacity of 2,000 passengers, began in the lake trade. Renamed the *Mandeville* in 1916, she took the place of the *New Camelia*, and was to continue to operate on Lake Pontchartrain for many years.

As late as March 1920, Captain Victor LeBlanc was still operating a schooner, the *Margaret L. P.*, between New Orleans and Covington. She sank that year, and may have been the last of the schooners to operate commercially in the lake.

The last of the excursion steamers operated in the 1930's, the business having been extinguished by the depression and by the increased utility of the automobile. There is virtually no commercial lake traffic out of St. Tammany today.

The boat building business also had its ups and downs during this period. In the late 1880's there were two shipyards in Madisonville, one operated by Oulliber and Baham at the lower end of town, and the Cardone Brothers' yard at the upper end. By 1895, there were four: Charles Oulliber's, V. P. Baham's, F. Cardone's and Louis Baham's. Louis Baham had taken over the Cardone Brothers' yard, and V. P. Baham was operating the old Drinkwater Shipyard.

In 1907, Charles Oulliber and V. P. Baham were still in business, and Ernest Lee Jahncke had started his shipyard just below Madisonville.

In 1913, A. D. Canulette announced plans for the construction of a large drydock in Madisonville. World War I brought a boom to the town, as the Jahncke shipyard, now called the St. Tammany Shipbuilding Company, got government contracts for two subchasers and two 3000-ton vessels. The Baham shipyard was bought out by Southern Oil and Transportation Company and became the Gulf Shipbuilding Company. In March 1918, it launched the largest ocean-going tug ever built in the South. Another shipyard was built in Pineland Park, just upstream from Madisonville.

The end of the war in November 1918, was the end of the boom, however. The big government contracts were cancelled, and by early 1919, 400 workers were laid off. During the war five large wooden ships had been built at the Jahncke yard, including the *S. S. Pontchartrain* and the *S. S. Tchefuncta*. Unfortunately, no more wooden ships were to be built.

Slidell also shared in the World War I boom. In August 1914, the Slidell Shipbuilding Corporation, F. W. Salmen, President, began business. In January 1917, a 229-foot wooden ship was launched at that yard. Slidell's shipyards were extremely busy during the war, but they suffered the same fate as those in Madisonville when the war ended. The government contracts were cancelled and hundreds of employees were laid off.

Today, Equitable Equipment Company of Madisonville and Southern Shipbuilding Corporation of Slidell carry on the tradition of shipbuilding in St. Tammany. And members of old St. Tammany families such as the Galatases and the Bahams, who have been ship carpenters and shipbuilders for well over a century, are still plying their trades.

However, lumber, bricks, and transportation, the three most important economic influences in the early history of the parish, are no longer major factors in its development.

CHAPTER XX

Post Reconstruction Agriculture

One important part of the life of the parish not affected by the railroads was agriculture, which continued to follow the same erratic course as it had in the past. Corn and sweet potatoes continued to be the major crops, although Irish potatoes became more popular during the 1890's. Other major crops were oats, rice, cotton, and molasses.

Statistics for 1891 show that St. Tammany farmers were average or slightly below average in yield per acre for corn, cotton, sweet potatoes, and oats, and well below average for rice and Irish potatoes. By 1899, they were well below average for all of the above crops. However, the farmers and the parish were getting good publicity, whatever their actual performance might have been. The *Times-Democrat* had an article on farming in St. Tammany in 1891:

No better location for immigrants can be found in the world over than in the pine land region of the parish of St. Tammany. The East Louisiana Railroad joins it by a few hours ride to the City of New Orleans, and gives the farmer living there a rapid outlet for his crops, whatever they might be. The climate of this portion of the State of Louisiana is beyond compare for health. The country is slightly rolling, and is intersected by streams and springs of mineral water, which in part account for the extreme salubrity of that whole region.

. . . .

The infinite resources of the parish of St. Tammany have not yet been appreciated by outsiders, nor have they begun to be utilized, except superficially.

It has been ascertained—and this by the most crude methods of culture—that cane, rice, cotton, corn and fodder are crops which can be grown there with a good profit to the farmer. The soil being light, the cultivation of cane there requires one-tenth of the amount of labor and number of hands requisite on the heavy rich alluvial lands bordering the Mississippi. The use of a moderate amount of fertilizers will produce admirable results without detracting from the farmer's profit.

On January 6, 1892, the *Times-Democrat* reported that the rice crop in 1891 was 50,000 barrels, as opposed to the 32,000 pounds reported by the State Department of Agriculture. It also reported herds of cattle from 500 to 1,500 and flocks of sheep running from 200 to 3,000. The report tells us that St. Tammany Parish wool is quoted higher than any other in the state because it is free from dirt and burrs. On June 18, 1892, the *Farmer* reported that the wool clip in St. Tammany would exceed 100,000 pounds, with an average price of 21 cents per pound.

Farming in St. Tammany was as erratic as ever in the first 20 years of the century. By 1910 there were 626 farmers and by 1919, 672. Corn was still the major crop. In 1901, 58,605 bushels were produced; in 1904, 154,170; and in 1919, 86,029. Sweet potatoes were also a big favorite. In 1901, 119,175 bushels were grown, highest in the state. However, by 1919, the total was down to 89,632. Cotton growers produced 1,485 bales in 1901, 1,688 bales in 1904, and only 531 in 1919. Of course, the boll weevil had made its appearance in the meanwhile. Other crops were oats, Irish potatoes, hay, and sugar cane, none of which were grown in significant quantities.

Livestock production was up from the 1890's. In 1901, there were 14,875 cattle, which declined to 11,702 by 1920, including working oxen and milk cows. Sheep increased from 8,022 in 1901 to 12,038 in 1920; swine went up from 1,260 in 1901 to 13,378 in 1910, and down to 9,357 in 1920. In 1920, poultry in the parish totalled 23,449.

There were a few exotic crops grown during the latter part of the 19th century which are of greater interest than the ordinary agricultural pursuits.

Grape culture became popular as early as 1879, when Mrs.

Burns, of Chubby Hill Plantation, Mr. Norman, who lived 10 miles from Covington, and Christian Schultz, who lived five miles from Covington all were raising Concord grapes. In 1884, John T. Munsch, whose "Live Oak Place" was located on the Bogue Falaya River near Red Bluff, was raising grapes and making red and white wines in commercial quantities, the red from Concord grapes and the white from Herbemont. Another wine maker was Louis Mathieu of Hickory Grove Place, who also made both red and white wines, as well as grape vinegar. Other varieties of grapes which were successfully grown at that time were Ives, Delaware, Lenoir, Norton's Virginia, Cynthiana, and Cruchine.

Munsch, who also produced a claret wine, was apparently a remarkable farmer. He was a Civil War veteran, having fought for the Confederacy. His farm was described in an article in the *Farmer*.

We paid a visit, last Sunday, to the Live Oak Place Vineyard, owned and managed by John T. Munsch, one of our most enterprising and progressing planters. Mr. Munsch has thousands of hardy vines, mostly of the Concord and Herbemont varieties, which appear to be the best adapted to our soil and climate. He kindly showed us over the place, first taking us to the wine cellar, where we found a number of barrels of white and red wine, which we sampled several times, trying to decide which kind was the best, and finally concluded that it was all of the best quality. In another building we saw the wine press, and several barrels of fine grape vinegar. From there we proceeded to the smithy and workshop which is well filled with all the necessary tools for repairing or making plantation implements. We then took a stroll through the vineyard, and were surprised at their extensiveness. We had no idea there were so many grape vines in the parish. After our walk we partook of "a little more Herbemont," and returned well pleased with our visit, and fully convinced that our parish is especially adapted to the grape and wine industry. All we lack is the "men and muscle, men who understand the business, and are not afraid of work."

Another wine grape grower was Alphonse Dutruch, whose Caverne Vineyard was located about eight miles from Covington. He was raised in the Bordeaux region of France, and said that he found the growth of the vine here to be remarkable, and that no finer grape and wine country could be found anywhere. Mr. Dutruch attempted to encourage others to start vineyards by offering to give away 30,000 cuttings, in lots of 2,000 each, to anyone with a knowledge of wine making who would pay attention to the business.

It was mainly through the efforts of these three men that St. Tammany became known as a grape and wine producing area. However, there did not seem to be any other men "with a knowledge of wine making" who were prepared to carry on. Although grapes were grown well into the twentieth century, commercial wine production in St. Tammany stopped with Munsch, Mathieu, and Dutruch.

The silk industry also got a little boost during the 1880's. In 1881, the versatile Jules Maille, then managing Sulphur Springs Plantation, had a large number of silk worms. The *Farmer* ran a number of articles in 1883 and the following years on silk raising, and mentioned a John Rocchi of St. Tammany Parish, who made $10,000 in one year selling silk worm eggs which he raised in St. Tammany, to Italy, where the entire crop had been lost due to disease. The records show that Mr. Rocchi bought property in Covington in 1859, so he probably made his killing either immediately before or after the Civil War.

In 1884, Mr. Charles Thiery was raising silk cocoons at Mulberry Grove which were pronounced as fine as any in Europe and worth $1.40 per ounce. In 1885, Mr. Thiery received 40 ounces of silk worm eggs, which came to 160,000 eggs. According to a story in the *Farmer*, one ounce of eggs, fed on the leaves from one acre of mulberry trees (200 trees), would produce 120 ounces of eggs in six weeks, for a profit of $360 per acre.

As early as 1883, Jules Herbelin was growing mulberry trees in Lewisburg and had constructed a silk factory, which was surrounded by 7,000 young mulberry trees. In 1884, he announced plans to plant 25,000 more. Then in November 1885, the following article from the *New Orleans Bee* appeared in the *Farmer*:

> The United States Silk Filature and Lewisburg Colony, lately known in New Orleans under the name of the New Orleans Experimental Filature, has just been transferred to Lewisburg, Parish of St. Tammany, La.

The establishment is managed by Mr. Jules B. Herbelin, commercial agent of the Department of Agriculture in Washington, under the auspices of the federal government.

The transfer took place because Lewisburg offers more facilities with regard to the purity of the air and the properties of the water.

The families (in preference those who have daughters, and women of all ages, able to work at the Filature), will find there lodging and fuel, several arpents of land, and the necessary seeds, all furnished gratuitiously. They will have the privilege of raising, for their own account, poultry and cattle.

The wages of the female spinners vary from forty to seventy-five cents per day, payable monthly. Several families are already at work.

Lewisburg, which is situated on the shore of Lake Pontchartrain, is in communication by steamer and telephone with New Orleans. A postoffice will soon be established there; also, a school and a grocery store, which will sell goods to the employees of the Filature at city prices.

Lewisburg is two miles from Mandeville, which possesses a College, churches, a doctor, drug store, several groceries, hotels, and all necessary comforts.

A hotel will soon be opened on the Lake shore, and the colonists will have an opportunity of selling their products as advantageously as in New Orleans.

Apparently, Mr. Herbelin was not moving so much as he was fleeing, since in January 1886, he was being sold out and his property was in the hands of his creditors. After the sheriff's sale in August 1886, Mr. Herbelin wrote a long letter, blaming his failure on governmental inconsistency. Except for one brief mention in 1887 and a short burst of interest about ten years later, the silk industry was dead in St. Tammany, despite its promise of quick riches.

Some of the farmers of that period deserve mention. Mrs. John A. Burns, of Chubby Hill Plantation, assisted by her oldest sons, Milton and Preston, had an extensive operation on the upper reaches of the Bogue Falaya River. In 1880, they were operating a sugar house and a steam cotton gin, the first in the parish. The *Farmer* described the plantation:

We took a little ride in the country last Sunday, as far as "Chubby Hill Plantation," where we found our friend Milton "at home." After resting a while, we proceeded to inspect the new steam cotton gin which he has recently erected. The gin is one of the celebrated "Eagle" gins, and has all the latest improvements. Judging from the large pile of well cleaned seed and the fine appearance of the lint cotton, we should say that Milton is doing excellent work. A short distance from the cotton gin stands the sugar mill, quietly waiting for the "rolling season" to begin. Everything about "Chubby Hill" bears a prosperous and businesslike appearance, which is no doubt owing to the fact that Milton and Preston go about things systematically and in the right way, and there are no drones in the hive. The large new residence of Mrs. Burns is nearly completed, and will be an ornament to that portion of the parish. The corn crop is unusually fine this year and sugar cane is looking well. All it needs is a few weeks of seasonable weather, when it will be ready for business. We were surprised at the large amount of cane being grown in that neighborhood. The fields of Messrs. Theobald, Munsch and Mathieu, on the right side of the road, and Mr. Allison, on the left, all looked well. The yield of sugar and molasses will no doubt be greater this year than ever before if we have a few weeks of the right kind of weather. The acreage in that section is being increased every year, and we hope the results will amply repay the efforts of our enterprising friends, whose success thus far is sufficient proof of the fact that St. Tammany parish is rich in agricultural resources, if they were only properly developed.

Harry Dutsch of the German Settlement was also an extremely active farmer. In 1883, his place had a steam sawmill, a cotton gin, a sugar mill, and a blacksmith shop. He raised cotton, corn, sugar cane, and other crops.

Jules Cahier's Pecan Grove Plantation, on the Lee Road about two miles from Covington, had 250 bearing pecan trees plus a large number of younger trees, a vineyard, from which he made wine, and a steam sugar mill.

In 1894, there was a report that a few people were experimenting with tobacco in the St. Joe area. The crop was reported to average about four feet high, with very large leaves. In Covington, Havana tobacco had been grown successfully by one man for over 30 years, and he was reported to have a very high grade leaf.

The only commercial production of tobacco, however, was by John H. Davis at Bayou Lacombe, who produced cigars from locally grown tobacco—the St. Tammany Special, a ten-cent cigar, the St. Tammany Maid, and the Ozone, which sold for a nickel.

Despite these exotica, however, agriculture in St. Tammany remained of minimal importance to the overall economy of the parish, but of great importance to the subsistence of a substantial segment of the population. There were a few exceptional farmers, but for the most part, farming techniques were primitive and production was low. The publicity which farming in St. Tammany received was always far more optimistic than the reality would seem to justify. Nevertheless, the agricultural potential of the parish continued to be described in glowing terms.

CHAPTER XXI

Population Growth and New Towns

The population increase brought about a number of new settlements, usually built up around a post office.

Some early post offices were Violin, located in the Evans Creek area, and Sun, where the present town is located, and which was so called as early as 1886. In 1894, Matthew Mizell was postmaster there, and by 1900, Sun had two stores and a hotel, in addition to its post office. Talisheek was originally located 14 miles north of Covington on the Columbia Road, a post office having been established there in 1880, with J. M. Abney as postmaster. Because of a confusion of names, a new post office at the Talisheek Crossing of the N. O. G. N. Railroad was given the name Talisheek in 1907, and the old Talisheek Post Office had its name changed to Waldheim. If that is not confusing enough, the present Waldheim settlement is located only about seven miles north of Covington on the Columbia Highway.

Many new place names came into being during the decade of the 1890's, as new post offices and businesses were established. Chinchuba, between Covington and Mandeville, became a post office in 1892. It was the site of the St. Clair Plantation of Father Hyacinth Mignot, on which he established, in 1890, the famous Chinchuba Deaf Mute Institute.

On September 24, 1890, the Dominican Sisters arrived in Chinchuba to prepare for the opening of the Institute on October 1st of that year. For the first few years of its existence, it was supported almost entirely out of Father Mignot's personal means, but later an association of Catholic laymen took over that responsibility. In 1900, there were 49 children in residence, who were taught by 14 Sisters of Notre Dame.

Another place of interest in Chinchuba was the Kneipp Institute, Maurice Lafargue, Director. This Institute administered a famous "water cure" of which, regrettably, no details are available.

There were post offices established at Delph, on the Bogue Chitto, Henry Shaw, postmaster, and Theodore Talley, assistant, in 1890; and at English Lookout, near the mouth of the Pearl River, S. A. Wilkins, postmaster, in 1895.

Honey Island, which is today largely unpopulated, has a colorful history. In the 1840's it was a hideout for the notorious Copeland-McGrath gang, which operated from Alabama to East Texas, robbing and murdering. During the Civil War it was largely populated by Confederate deserters and draft dodgers, and generally had a disreputable name. However, by 1893, it was a different place, according to a letter in the *Farmer*:

> Your correspondent was in Honey Island last week, and I find the Baton Rouge *Truth* was mistaken all the way through, from beginning to end. First, the editor of *Truth* states that a part of Honey Island lies in Mississippi. The Island all belongs to St. Tammany Parish, and is filled up with good citizens who own large stocks of hogs and cattle. The Baton Rouge *Truth* says they have no roads. This is another mistake. They have a public road and numerous other roads, and the New Orleans and Northeastern Railroad runs across the Island, and has two stations within its limits.

> There are two saw mills. Mr. F. M. White owns one mill and a log railroad which runs through the center of the Island.

> The people who live on the Island are not thieves and robbers, they are law-abiding citizens and taxpayers, and they are not descendants of the old Copeland and McGrath gangs, that at one time (forty or fifty years ago) inhabited the Island. During the war it was a hard place, where deserters hid themselves away in the canebrakes, but the old gang is all gone, and people from all parts of the country have settled on the Island, as it is very rich land, and they can raise more corn and potatoes to the acre, without fertilizing, than they can in the piney woods; and sugar cane, rice, tobacco and all kinds of vegetables and fruits do well on the Island. In fact, Honey Island is as rich as any land in Louisiana. The only drawback is the high water.

They have a church and school house, and one preacher, but strange to say, they have no public school. Their school director lives at Pearlville, and has turned a deaf ear to their cries for a public school, which they are entitled to as taxpayers. They hire their teacher and go down in their pockets to pay for having their children educated. They would like to know, through your valuable paper, if there is any remedy, by calling on the President of the School Board.

Dr. John Mars is a resident of the Island, and is worth considerable in the way of live stock.

Mr. Adolph Frederick, of Covington, familiarly known as "Man," was down on the Island on a hunt. He had a good time, and bagged quite a lot of game, including two bronze cranes. Come again, "Man."

The United States snag-boat is doing good work in West Pearl River. The boat is commanded by Capt. Monday, and he is the right man in the right place.

In 1894, F. M. White was operating a spoke factory in conjunction with his lumber mill, and was shipping his product as far as New Jersey. In 1879, Honey Island was made the 10th Ward by the Police Jury, and in 1895, it had its own post office, H. S. Monroe, postmaster. However, disastrous flooding forced the inhabitants to leave, and in 1902, the post office was closed.

Thomasville, which was on the Bogue Chitto River, 18 miles from Covington, received a post office in 1892, and in 1893, had two schools, the Cooper School, taught by Professor W. M. Alford, and the Jenkins School, taught by Mrs. A. M. Bowman of Madisonville. It also boasted of having some 200 inhabitants within a radius of four miles.

In 1892, a post office was established at the 11-mile house on the Holmesville Road, called Verger, with Paul Verger as postmaster. This would be approximately where Folsom is located today.

The railroads had yet another effect on St. Tammany Parish. They opened up thousands of acres of land which had been inaccessible. The settlers flowed into the new territories, and new towns and settlements came into being. The advent of the first of these was announced on March 8, 1882, in a letter to the *Farmer*:

Thinking that a few notes from the New Orleans and Northeastern Railroad might prove interesting to your many readers, I send you the following items:

A large mill, owned by Messrs. Hamlet, Bliss and Elliot, enterprising young men from Alabama, situated at this place, formerly known as the "Robert brick house," is now in full operation, and employing as many hands as will apply. The brick house itself has been turned into a lodging house, by the enterprising merchant, Mr. Beer, of Tallulah, who also owns the grocery store situated a few feet from it.

The name of Slidell Station is very properly given to this place in honor of our distinguished diplomatist, whose daughter married, in Europe, Mr. Erlanger, of syndicate repute, who, with the lash of his many millions, led this formidable enterprise to a sure and speedy success. I say speedy, because the railroad must be completed by the 31st of December next.

The creosote works, being permanently established here, are rapidly progressing, under the direction of Mr. Tobias, an excellent gentleman.

In the midst of the whir of machinery and the excitement created by the arrival of all the contractors and their employees, clearing the right of way, our minds were agreeably relieved in our weekly labor by the soothing influence of Right Rev. Bishop Xavier Leroy, coadjutor of our venerable and honored Archbishop. Scientific and learned beyond the power of my feeble pen to describe, Bishop Leroy sits highly on the rock of eloquence, possessing the natural sublime Ciceronian simplicity of language so unsuccessfully studied by orators, combined with the eloquence of his Virgilian poetical expressions. If Demosthenes, practicing the power of his voice over the waves of the sea, did not succeed in arresting them from dying on the shore, surely will the powerful eloquence of our beloved Bishop rescue many a soul from the shores of eternal death.

In my next letter I will furnish you with full particulars of the progress made in clearing the roadway, building the bridge across the Lake, and other matters of general interest.

Another new town was building at Pearl River Station on the New Orleans and Northeastern and Poitevent & Favre's East Louisiana Railroad. In August 1886, a depot was being built there by the two railroads, and excursions were being run to the new pavilion built nearby. Samuel R. Poitevent, who was in charge of the East Louisiana Railroad, had a house and store there. In 1888, the name of the post office was changed from Halloo to Pearl and then to Pearlville. Eventually both the town and the post office took the name of the station.

About five and one-half miles northwest of Pearl River was situated the town of Florenville, where the yards and stores of the East Louisiana Railroad and the houses of the railroad logging employees were located. A post office was established there in May 1888, with John A. Orr as postmaster. A Catholic church was built in 1891, with funds supplied by M. Florenville, the French nobleman for whom the town was named. In 1892 there was a school taught by a Mrs. Wilson of Bayou Lacombe. Florenville declined in importance after the territory between there and Abita Springs was logged out and the main line of the railroad was moved to the present lakeshore route. The post office was discontinued in 1904, and there is nothing there now except a cord wood yard and scale.

St. Joe Station, on the New Orleans and Northeastern Railroad north of Slidell, became the site of a brick works in 1889, and by 1894, boasted 200 inhabitants, two stores, one barroom, a wheelwright, one blacksmith, and the brick manufacturing plant, owned and operated by Colonel P. W. Schneider.

The Town of Guthrie, on the New Orleans and Northeastern Railroad, had a post office in 1891, with John J. McCarron as postmaster. St. Peter and Paul's Catholic Church was built there in 1904 and 1905.

Along the N. O. G. N. tracks from Slidell to Bogalusa, we find the towns of Audubon, Maud, Talisheek, and Bush. Maud, which was also called Pineacre, was seven miles north of Slidell, and in 1908, had a hotel, a store, H. S. Hutchison's shingle mill and creosote works, and was applying for a post office.

Probably the most spectacular attempt at a real estate development which resulted from the railroads took place in August 1900, when plans were announced for a new town in St. Tammany Parish, two and one-half miles east of the Mandeville Junction on the East Louisiana Railroad, between Florenville and Abita. The town was to be called St. Tammany. On Saturday, March 2, 1901, the Louisiana

The Folsom depot in 1905

The Fendlason family farmhouse in Alma, Louisiana, in 1895

Colonization and Land Company, Limited, held a big auction sale of 3000 lots in the new town, which was reported to have been a big success. How big is not said, but in April 1901, lots in St. Tammany were being offered for $5.00 each.

In December 1901, it was announced that a new company was taking over the development of St. Tammany. St. Tammany Health Homes Co., Ltd., which had offices in New Orleans and New York, advertised the new town extensively in the best magazines and newspapers in the country. It was predicted that within two years, 5000 people would be in residence in St. Tammany. A large two-story building was built with Henry Keller's store in the ground floor and a boarding house on the second, operated by Mrs. Briggs of Poplarville, Mississippi. On April 26, 1902, it was reported that there were five houses at St. Tammany, all built within the past 30 days.

A big pavilion in the shape of a maltese cross, with 2,000 square feet of floor space, was built in June 1902, when another great auction sale was held. Two excursion trains brought 1000 people to St. Tammany for the sale. In October 1902, a depot and post office were opened at St. Tammany, but the town was in trouble.

In 1905, St. Tammany Health Homes went under, and Poitevent & Favre took back the land. In November, plans were announced for a big hotel in St. Tammany, to cost $400,000.00, but this project went the way of all the big hotel proposals. In 1907, the Louisiana Anti-Tuberculosis League built its sanitarium near St. Tammany in the piney woods. However, the relocation of the main line of the N.O.G.N. to the lakeshore line was the death of the town.

The town of Ramsay, which was built in connection with the Greenlaw Lumber Company sawmill, was located about where St. Gertrude's Convent now stands on the Folsom Road. Originally known as Blair, the post office was established there in July 1903, at which time there were about 30 houses in the town. The name of the town was later changed to Ramsay, after James Ramsay of the Greenlaw Lumber Company, who was the postmaster. After the lumber company went into receivership in 1904, there was some difficulty, but operations continued. The Village of Ramsay was incorporated in 1906. In 1907, the Greenlaw Mercantile Company was established, and Samuel Cole established the St. Tammany Brick Company near Ramsay the same year. In 1908, there was a

Hotel St. Joseph in the town as well as a library. By 1910, Ramsay had a population of 425, larger than both Abita Springs and Pearl River. In 1912, however, the Greenlaw Company failed, and its property, valued at $400,000.00 was sold to Lampton Realty Company for $66,000.00. The mill was back in operation in the latter part of 1912, but apparently not for long, there being no further mention of the mill or the town, as such, after that year. The old Greenlaw Company store was still standing in the 1950's but has been demolished, and there is now nothing to remind one of the mill or the town which once stood there.

A somewhat more successful town was Folsom, which was established at Alma post office, 12 miles north of Covington at the terminus of the Greenlaw Railroad in 1904. George N. Fendlason was the founder of the town. A depot was built there in 1905, and by 1908, the town had progressed to the point where a movement was started to have it incorporated. In June 1908, the *Farmer* reported that Folsom had several general merchandise stores doing a nice business, a drug store, operated by Dr. Charles J. May, a barbershop, a meat market and "one of the best hotels you can find anywhere," called the Pine Grove. There was even a Folsom Debating Society. In addition, the Fendlason and Son Brick Company was turning out fire bricks and the Folsom Gin Company made 63 bales of cotton in 1908.

On May 14, 1913, there was a "Grand Auction Lot Sale" in Folsom, to sell off 300 choice vacant lots in the town, the auction scheduled to start at 10:00 a.m., on the arrival of the New Orleans train. In May 1916, the *Farmer* reported that Folsom had forgotten to hold its municipal election. Up until that time George N. Fendlason had been the mayor. Today, of course, Folsom is a prosperous commercial center for the rapidly growing Second Ward.

CHAPTER XXII

Approaching the Twentieth Century

In the latter part of the 19th century, as the parish began to expand, education finally began to get a little attention.

In September 1882, the Covington High School for Boys and Girls was established by the Covington School Association, under the direction of W. W. Dunbracco. This school lasted for two years, and then in September 1884 Mr. Dunbracco opened his own school, Covington Academy, in the same building. In the same month, the St. Tammany Association School, J. M. Abney, principal, opened in Covington, with primary, secondary, and grammar departments. Mr. Dunbracco's school had 1st, 2nd, 3rd, and 4th Departments, so it was probably a little more advanced. There were also two private schools in Madisonville in 1884, Mr. Smith's, which opened on September 21st, fairly attended; and Miss Amanda Clark's.

The public school system in 1884 showed a substantial advance over that of 1875. There were 23 schools in operation for white children in the nine wards, and nine for black children. All were for three months, except for six-month schools in the 4th, 5th, and 6th wards, and three one-month schools in the 8th Ward for white children and in the 1st and 2nd Wards for black children. There were 583 white students and 310 black students.

It was during the 1880's that the Catholic schools first appeared. In 1886, St. Eugene College in Mandeville, run by Father E. Aveilhe is first mentioned in the *Farmer*. Its grounds were apparently quite extensive:

> The gardens and grounds of St. Eugene College are the prettiest and best laid out of the town, the most beautiful feature of

which is one of the best vineyards in the parish, the pride of Father Aveilhe's heart, and justly so. The scholars are not allowed to handle the fruit or grapes, and are commendably obedient, and so are all who visit the grounds. But last Wednesday a party of ladies and gentlemen from one of the New Orleans churches, accompanied by the priest of the Church, called at the College to pay their respects to Father Aveilhe, and while the gentlemen, except one, were conversing, the young ladies and gent pitched into the grapes, without permission, and literally destroyed the early grapes that were not quite ripe. Such behavior, from ladies and gentlemen who are permitted to walk in a fruit garden, needs a thorough reprimand, which they would have received, had Father Aveilhe discovered the disgraceful mischief before they left.

Other private schools during the 1880's were operated by Miss Kate McDougall, Mrs. L. M. Cloud, and Reverend L. W. Wood, and there was Jules B. Maille's school at Claiborne Cottage.

The 1890's brought about a public demand for better schools. Up until that time, the public schools, with few exceptions had been taught only three months per year. In 1890, one Slidell resident publicly bewailed the fact that there were only three months of school per year, but in 1891 there was not enough money to support even one school there. Citizens in Madisonville and at Sandy Hill in the First Ward petitioned the school board for schools in their area. In February 1891, the Second Ward claimed the only public school then operating in the parish, taught by J. Keller.

Mandeville in that year had two private schools, a Catholic school, run by Father Lavaquery and taught by Professor Cooley, and Harvey's Academy, for girls and young lads, operated by Widow C. Harvey Roame. Mrs. Roame had 27 scholars in attendance.

In April 1891, the Covington Normal Institute, Professor J. N. Silbert, principal, began operations in Covington, and in August of that year, Reverend J. E. Smith opened a private school for black children in Covington.

Other private schools were opened by Miss Maloney in Abita Springs in 1891; Mrs. Wilson in Florenville in 1892; and Miss Josie Bechtel in Abita Springs in 1892. There was also a parochial school in Covington in 1892, which held classes in the old Catholic Church, built in 1842. This was probably St. Peter's School, which was operated by the Benedictine Sisters, possibly as early as 1875. St. Francis Xavier School was in operation in Madisonville in July 1893, when its commencement exercises were held.

By 1893, the school board had so expanded its operations that there was school for nine months of the year in all wards except the third, where Covington was located. It does not appear, however, that the schools were graded, or that there was any high school level work given. This was soon to follow, however.

Private schools continued to come and go in Covington. In 1897, Misses Emma and Josie Whelpley taught and operated the Covington Select School. In September 1898, the Covington Graded and High School opened its doors with 75 pupils. It was operated by Professor Charles E. Hill, with the assistance of Mrs. M. B. Miller and Mrs. Hill, who handled the grammar grades. Miss Eva Ward had a school in the cottage of W. W. Ward on the Roche place in 1899, and Professor P. L. Mitchell opened a private school in the Episcopal parsonage the same year. In November, that school, which was known as Covington Academy, moved to the former Bank Hotel on the corner of Rutland and New Hampshire streets.

The most important private school opening of 1899 was that of Professor W. A. Dixon, who, assisted by Mr. Harry Kopman, opened his school in the Dowling cottage on October 2, 1899. In 1900, Dixon Academy opened in its new building on Jahncke Avenue with 200 day students and 35 to 40 boarders. About ten years later, it was to become St. Paul's College, which, as the St. Paul School, is still in existence. The original building still stands.

At about the same time, the Benedictines acquired Cedar Hill, the old James R. Hosmer plantation, and founded St. Joseph's Abbey. In conjunction with the Abbey, they started St. Joseph's College, a boarding school for boys.

The public school system of the parish was placed on a modern footing shortly after 1900, under the inspired leadership of Joseph B. Lancaster, the Superintendent of Schools. Mr. Lancaster, a member of an old St. Tammany family, was later to serve the parish as representative, district attorney, and district judge.

Other changes were in store as St. Tammany moved into the 20th century. There could be no surer sign of the entrance of St. Tam-

A Jackson automobile ca. 1910 (*Photograph from the collection of J. Louis Smith, Jr.*)

many Parish into the modern age than the formation of the forerun-
ners of the Chambers of Commerce. In May 1900, a Businessmen's
Progressive League was formed in Covington, which was followed by
the Slidell Progressive League in 1905. From 1900 on, these two
towns were to be the principal business centers of the parish.

Another indication of modern times was the formation of the St.
Tammany Protective Labor Union No. 1 in Covington on March 16,
1901. A. O. Pons was named president; Frank P. Biery, vice president;
Christian Beck, financial secretary; Joseph C. Beck, recording secretary; George Mehrhoff, treasurer, and Toulis DePriest, sergeant-at-
arms. There was a Socialist ticket in the Covington municipal elections of 1903, headed by Christian Beck, running for Mayor. The
Socialists only pulled five votes in the election, despite the fact that
there were seven men on the ticket. The conservatism that was evident in 1779, 1810, and 1860 was still holding firm.

In 1904, the *Farmer* mentioned in passing that automobiles were
becoming numerous in Covington and would soon cease to be a
novelty. The first reported automobile accident did not take place
until 1910, when W. A. Hood's automobile, driven by Arthur de
Labreton, with Marshal Loyd as a passenger, blew out a tire and hit
a telephone pole.

By 1910, there were two automobile agencies in Covington.
George E. Sears was agent for the Ford Automobile Company, and
J. Louis (Deed) Smith had the agencies for the Flanders and Brush
automobiles. In 1911, Deed Smith accomplished the feat of driving
his new EMF 30 from Detroit where he picked it up to Covington,
a distance of 1431 miles, in only 11 days. He used $4.35 worth of
lubricating oil and $16.75 worth of gasoline on the trip, using 103
gallons of the latter. Mr. Smith, something of a daredevil, also
brought his gasoline launch, the *Jeanette D.*, from Davenport, Iowa,
to Covington via the Mississippi River.

Mr. Sears made an auto trip around the parish in June 1910, driving from Covington to Slidell, via Abita, Talisheek, Pearl River, and
Alton, and returning via Bayou Lacombe and Mandeville. He was accompanied by E. J. Domergue, who drove his own automobile on
the trip. Mr. Sears had also driven to such distant spots as Madisonville, Ponchatoula, and Hammond.

It was the advent of the automobile, the good roads which it required, and the mobility which it provided, that tolled the death knell of the excursion business, both by train and steamer.

On July 7, 1907, the *Farmer* reported that the "five cent show, or electric theater" was well patronized. In May 1908, there were two moving picture theaters in Covington, the Covington Electric Theater, Pape and Bourgeois, proprietors, showing "the finest animated pictures"; and the New Rink Electric Theater, "the largest moving picture theater outside of New Orleans." The New Rink was probably operated by George Sears. Victor H. Frederick opened the Air Dome, a 500-seat theater, on Boston Street soon after. On September 7, 1912, a Mr. Ulmer opened the New Covington Theater on New Hampshire, in the Warren Building opposite the depot. The best known of the early theaters, the Parkview, was opened by C. S. A. Fuhrmann on May 3, 1913. The building, now occupied by Hebert's Drug Store, still stands at the corner of Boston and New Hampshire streets.

CHAPTER XXIII

Resorts

No picture of life in St. Tammany during this period would be complete without a look at life in the resorts. Probably the two best known and longest lived of the hotels were Claiborne Cottage and Mulberry Grove Hotel.

When Claiborne Cottage opened its doors in 1880, its main building was the old courthouse which had been built in Claiborne in 1818. After the seat of justice was moved, the old building served as a private residence and as a Catholic seminary before being renovated by the Jaufroid family, who managed it as a hotel for a number of years.

In 1831, a famous event in New Orleans had touched on Claiborne Cottage. Madame Lalaurie, the young, beautiful, and wealthy wife of Dr. Lalaurie, was found to be torturing her slaves. Her house was surrounded by an angry mob, from which she escaped in her carriage. She was driven to Bayou St. John, where a schooner was waiting to carry her to the north shore. She took refuge for ten days at the mill house of John Nelden, a young English lumberman, near the old courthouse in Claiborne, after which she departed for Mobile and Paris, where her wealth and beauty made her a great social success.

Claiborne Cottage was later managed by Jules B. Maille. In 1889, an extensive improvement program which included a new main building was commenced. The advertisement in the *Farmer* after the renovation was complete described the new hotel:

CLAIBORNE COTTAGES
Covington, La.
Summer Terms from $10 Per Week
According to Accomodation.

Claiborne Cottage near Covington, Louisiana (*Courtesy The Louisiana State Museum*)

The new Hotel, with nearly a thousand feet of Broad Galleries, a covered Open-air Salon, Drawing room, Dining room, 65 feet long, and large, airy Chambers, is now open for guests. The old buildings have been completely renovated.

Location on a hill overlooking the lovely Bogue Falaya River; flanked by lofty pines. Pure water. Mosquitoes almost unknown. Open to southerly breezes. Good fishing. Boats. Good roads for Driving. Park-like scenery.

Address,   JULES B. MAILLE
                                              Covington, La.
                              East Louisiana Railroad

An article in the *New Orleans Daily States* talks about Claiborne Cottage during that time:

We mentioned above, that the Court House at Claiborne, still stood. That was very soon fitted up as a hotel, as the location had been always recognized as one of the very best in the parish for a sanitarium. It prospered beyond the most sanguine expectations and it was found necessary last year to enlarge its capacity for accommodation. During the past winter, Mr. Jules Maille, the proprietor, built a magnificent addition, after the most modern model. This structure is 500 feet by 60, is two stories in height and has broad galleries its whole length, upstairs and down.

Its bedrooms are, of course, numerous, large and airy, and as it has been built with a view to the accomodation of winter as well as summer guests, every room has its fireplace. Its dining room is capacious, having space for 500 guests, its parlors spacious and the promenades on the side galleries are unrivalled.

Mr. Maille, the proprietor, seems to have been endowed by nature with ability to perform the duties to which he has devoted himself. A gentleman of the old Creole stock, courtesy and politeness are inate with him. Having lived upon the best he naturally provides such for his guests. His patrons are mostly drawn from the ranks of the old families whose names are historic in this State; and one can come nearer seeing the life as it was lived among the "ancient regime," at Claiborne Cottage than any place we know. In contrast with the rush and hurry, the grasping ill-breeding of the Northern and Western watering places, this is positively delicious.

And such a table! Columns have been written about Creole cooking and Creole coffee. Both are to be had in their perfection at the Claiborne Cottage, rendered more delightful by the presence of a society which cannot be excelled in the world, as will be readily seen from the following list of the guests at present sojourning in this most agreeable place.

THE GUESTS

Mrs. George Denegre; Mr. Felix Puig and sister; Col. J. A. Chalaron, wife, daughters and sons; Mr. John N. Baldwin and family; Mr. O. Villere, wife, daughter and sons; Mr. P. L. Cusachs, wife and son; Miss Margot Cusachs; Miss L. Burke; Mr. C. V. Labarre, wife and daughter; Mr. Albert Dufour and wife; Mr. Brode and wife; Mr. George Villere and wife; Mrs. L. V. Labarre; Mr. J. P. Quinault, wife and daughter; Mr. F. Claiborne; Mr. Ben Buchanan; Mr. Jas. Wilson; Mr. Thomas Keefe; Mr. E. Sauter.

There are numerous delightful drives in the neighborhood, and the accomodations in that line, under the management of Messrs. Roubion & Giesen, is in every variety and at exceedingly reasonable prices.

Claiborne Cottage was later run by Mrs. A. C. Wood, and still later by the Domergue family of Covington. It was last used as a hotel under the ownership and management of Dr. Numa M. Hebert. In November 1912, the old hotel burned to the ground, ending a 30-year career as one of the most popular resorts in the state.

Another famous resort was the Mulberry Grove Hotel, which was opened by Charles Thiery in June 1881, on the site of the mulberry tree and silk farm formerly operated by Paul Lacroix. It was as successful as Claiborne Cottage, and when the first season closed in October 1881, construction of several new buildings was begun. Its ad in the *Farmer* the next spring said:

MULBERRY GROVE HOTEL
Near Covington,
St. Tammany Parish, La.
CH. THIERY, PROPRIETOR,

This delightful summer resort is now open for the reception of guests. It is charmingly situated, near the banks of the Bogue Falia, about two miles and a half north of Covington, and is surrounded by a beautiful grove of mulberry trees. The Hotel has recently been thoroughly renovated, and a number of new cottages, single and double, have been erected for the accomodation of families.

MINERAL SPRINGS.—The water of the fine Springs at Mulberry Grove has recently been analyzed by an eminent chemist, and pronounced to be fully equal in its medicinal properties, to that of Abita Springs, and unsurpassed anywhere. Persons desiring to spend the summer in a quiet and attractive place, possessing all the advantages of pure air, fine shade, with both clear and mineral springs; baths, and a table supplied with the very best the market affords, should secure accomodations at once at

MULBERRY GROVE HOTEL.

For further particulars, apply to or address CH. TROUILLY, 132 Canal street, or CHAS. THIERY, Proprietor, Covington, La.

In 1884, the water of "the fine springs" at Mulberry Grove was analyzed by C. L. Kepler, chemist, and Dr. Watkins, and pronounced fully equal in medicinal properties to that of Abita Springs. The hotel was famous for its cuisine, as the following attests:

Mr. Ch. Thiery, the popular proprietor of Mulberry Grove Hotel, added new laurels to his crown as the "Prince of Caterers" last Sunday evening on the occasion of a grand banquet, tendered to a number of invited guests, including "ye editor." The menu was of the choicest variety, and gotten up in the highest style of the culinary art, regardless of expense. The bill of fare included turtle soup, baked fish, stewed chicken and mushrooms, shrimp and roast pig; the dessert consisted of Malaga grapes, pears, apples, almonds and pecans; the feast was brought to a fitting finale with champagne, white wine, cognac, coffee, and the best brand of Havanas. Mr. Thiery and his estimable lady, by their cordial reception and careful attention to minor details, added greatly to the pleasure of the occasion. Mulberry Grove Hotel, under the management of Mr. Thiery, deserves to be liberally patronized by the public, and we hope it will in the future, as in the past, continue to grow in popular favor, as one of the most delightful and healthy summer resorts in the State.

A letter to the *Farmer* gives a good description of the Mulberry Grove Hotel, and of a morning in the country:

It was an inspiration when one of the party said, "tomorrow we will go to Mulberry Grove to breakfast," Covington was hardly awake when the wheels of the buggy rolled out of its streets, and the air in the pine woods had all its dewey freshness. To the resident of this quaint village, the beauties of the surrounding country may be an old story, but to the Northern guest, not a breath of the fragrant pine air but brings a sense of delight. The tall trees are scattered along the road to the bridge, skirting the edge of the forest. The horses travel quickly, and before we realize it, we are on the bridge. Could anything be more charming? On either side the trees bend over the clear water below, the eyes find only the restful green of the foliage everywhere, and in every shade, from the dark needles of the pine to the more vivid shades of the oak and cypress. It is impossible to reproduce the still beauty of the curving river, in whose clear depths we see the fish darting hither and thither. Up the farther bank we dash into a shaded forest-road. The sunbeams throw broken patches of light and shadow upon the hard, smooth road, as we move rapidly onward. The road winds in and out among the cypress, magnolia, gum and pine trees, and we roll down a declivity and climb up the hill from the spring to the open gates of Mulberry Grove. It is quite a little hamlet in itself, the large house with its airy dining-room between the foundation pillars, standing with rows of cottages on either side, all among trees in the ample grounds. The log cabin is the point of attraction for us, for there, we are told our breakfast waits. The brown logs, of almost exactly the same size, form the outer walls. Inside, the interstices between the logs are filled with dressed pine harmonious in color. The interior of the room is truly artistic. Gnarled roots form brackets against the walls, the rustic frames of the pictures are draped with gray moss, and the open windows afford glimpses into the cool depths of the Mulberry Grove, from which the place is named. Upon a large round table the snowy cloth is laid and upon a side table are formidable piles of plates. We stand upon no ceremony and time would fail us to mention the delicious coffee, freshly-laid eggs, tender steaks and other good things, which placed before us rapidly disappear. When we have pronounced it the best breakfast possible, and have found ourselves incapable of further exertion in that direction, we go for a stroll in the woods. The thick shade protects us entirely from the hot sun; but under the trees the eye is charmed everywhere with the beautiful vistas. Along the winding stream we follow the high banks, admiring the shallows or deep pools which lie at our feet. The sand is almost white; but finally, at a bend, we see further in the stream a large bank of pure white sand glistening in the sunlight. Two or three birds wheel in circles over the water but no sound, save our own voices, breaks the silence. We give a last look at all this loveliness, and then turn towards the hotel.

By the sun, it is almost high noon when we turn our faces homeward. We pass swiftly over the wood road, pause a moment on the bridge, and then through the fragrant pines to the hospitable roof which rises among the trees.

Katharine Whiteside

Covington, La.
April 20, 1887.

Eventually, the hotel was sold to Dr. Frank G. Marrero, who operated it as a hotel and as a sanitarium until sometime after 1905. In the ad in the Glass brochure of 1905, Mulberry Grove is said to be 450 feet above sea level, putting it far above all other places in St. Tammany.

CHAPTER XXIV

Entering the Twentieth Century

St. Tammany Parish plunged ahead on a number of fronts during the economic renaissance which accompanied the approach to the modern era. In addition to improvement in transportation, there were also efforts at improved communication.

As early as 1879, attempts were made to establish a telegraph line from Covington to Ponchatoula, but the necessary funds could not be subscribed. The 1850 government survey shows a telegraph line running from the vicinity of present day Pearl River through the swamp to Gainesville, Mississippi, on the Pearl River, and there is a mention of a telegraph line through Apple Pie Ridge, outside of Slidell in 1879. This may have been part of the earlier telegraph line to Gainesville. Apple Pie Ridge, which extends out into the marsh from Indian Village east of Slidell, was one of the earlier settled areas in the east end of the parish, so called originally in jest, because of an old lady who lived on the ridge and who sold cakes and pies. Although the residents preferred to call it "Oakland," the less formal name stuck.

In 1884, a company headed by George Moorman of Mandeville, began the construction of a telephone line from Mandeville to Slidell. The first message over the line took place when it was completed to Bayou Lacombe on June 17, 1884, when General Moorman spoke to Charles Aubry, said to be the leading citizen of Bayou Lacombe. General Moorman spoke to John E. Gusman of Slidell on July 7th, and the first message to New Orleans went through the next day, July 8, 1884.

Inspired by this success, the citizens of Covington raised $500 to have the line extended north from Mandeville. On August 3rd, General Moorman, who had an affinity for leading citizens, spoke to Covington's leading citizen, Judge James M. Thompson. The line was never a commercial success, and, in September 1887, was in such bad shape that the police jury ordered the wires and poles be removed from the public roads of the parish. Of course, by then the East Louisiana Railroad had brought its telegraph line to Covington.

In 1899, the Cumberland Telephone Company began placing poles along the line from Ponchatoula to Covington. By February 24, 1900, the lines had reached Covington, and on April 14, 1900, the telephone system in Covington was in working order. In September of that year there were 79 subscribers.

St. Tammany's burgeoning economy and the spirit of optimism that accompanies such times showed up in its participation in the World Industrial Exhibition at New Orleans in 1885. In 1884, the *New Orleans Times-Democrat* proposed that the Choctaw of St. Tammany Parish, who were said to constitute the bulk of the Indians in Louisiana, send delegates and exhibits to the fair. Different citizens began to get interested, including Messrs. Munsch and Mathieu and Jules B. Maille. Mr. Adam Thompson of Sulphur Springs Plantation sent his prize young Jersey bull, Climax Rex.

A list of the exhibits from St. Tammany appeared in the following letter to the *Farmer*:

> In order to inform our citizens of the status of St. Tammany at the great World's Fair, I will give you a memorandum statement of the articles now on exhibition, and in future letters, will enter more into details:
>
> A beautiful collection of natural fruit, preserved in rosin.
>
> Artistic house and stable, of pine burs, made with mechanical precision, with the aid of a pen-knife only, "Our Cottage Home," with lovely grounds. Both of the above from Miss Nellie B. Kennedy of Mandeville.
>
> A frame of pine burs, "God Bless Our Home," from Miss Mollie J. Kennedy, of Mandeville.
>
> White pierced cocoons, eggs made at Lewisberg.
>
> Samples of raw silk, from cocoons raised at Mr. Chas. Thiery's Mulberry Grove and Lewisberg.
>
> Samples of cocoons raised in Lewisberg, "White Race,"

from Lombardie, Italy, and "Yellow Race," from Salernes Var, France.

Samples of silkworm eggs, made at Lewisberg and Covington.

The above are from Mr. Jules Herbelin, of Lewisberg.

A splendid fire screen, of pine burs, from Miss Jean Trochesset, of Covington.

Herbemont white wine (very fine), and Concord red wine (splendid sample), vintage 1884, from Mr. John T. Munsch, Live Oak Place, near Covington.

Superior red wine, and splendid white wine, vintage 1883, from Mr. Louis E. Mathieu, of Hickory Grove Place, near Covington.

Some wonderfully large turnips and rutabagas, from Mr. Zach Sharp, of Mandeville.

Very large hornet's nest (a great curiosity) from Miss Mary Pitcher, of Lewisberg.

One bale of magnificent cotton and a lot of fine corn, from Hon. J. M. Allison, President Police Jury.

One lot of very large silkworm cocoons, two skeins of spun silk, one bundle of very fine sugar cane, one bundle of splendid ramie and one bundle of gigantic Bermuda grass (22 feet, 6 inches in length) all from Mr. Jules B. Maille, near Covington.

One bale of beautiful cotton from Mr. Hardy H. Smith of Covington.

One bread tray made of tupulo gum, one Indian canoe made of cypress, one section wagon wheel and spokes, one bundle axe helves, one keg of tar, and one package of charcoal, from Mr. T. P. Crawford.

Also one cork tree limb, from the McCann place, in Covington, and the largest collection of timber of all kinds in the building.

The timber exhibit is unusually fine, and has already caused five parties to visit the parish to see our forests, with a view to making purchases.

The above list so far constitutes the roll of honor for our parish, and we are indebted to the exertions of our Lady Commissioner, Mrs. J. M. Thompson, for most of the display we have.

Major E. A. Burke, the Director General, has shown himself to be the most remarkable man of the period.

Geo. Moorman,
Parish Commissioner

At the exhibition, competing against animals from all over the country, Climax Rex won the $50.00 first prize as best Jersey bull, one year and under, and third prize in that category went to Captain Lawless, belonging to G. W. Nott of Mandeville, who was the owner of Fontainebleau Plantation.

The press began to expand during this period, although, with the exception of the *St. Tammany Farmer*, all of the early efforts were abortive.

In 1899, a small newspaper, *The St. Tammany Standard*, which was started by F. W. Smith, and published in New Orleans, was forced to suspend publication after only a few weeks. The *Farmer* got some more competition in July 1903, when the *Covington News*, a weekly paper, began publication with Rev. John B. Kent, owner and editor, and W. P. Fussell as business manager. It apparently enjoyed some success, and in July 1904, the Police Jury bought 1,000 copies of its trade edition to be distributed at the Louisiana Exposition at the World's Fair in St. Louis. However, in June 1908, its press and equipment were sold at public auction to satisfy a judgment, bringing only $50.00. No known copies of the paper have survived.

In May 1909, there was a paper called *The Journal* being published in Covington. It may have been a daily paper, because in June 1910, D. H. Mason and E. D. Kentzel bought the *Farmer* and the *Covington Daily Journal*, planning to continue publication of both papers. It was announced that the first issue of the *Daily St. Tammany* would be published about July 1, 1910. There is no evidence that this event ever took place.

The first newspaper to be published in Slidell, the *Bugle*, made its appearance in mid-1892, with B. B. Garrison as editor. It was probably a short-lived venture, and no copies of it are known to exist.

Two more newspapers appeared in Slidell before the end of the century. In 1897, the Slidell *Item*, Messrs. Johnson and Foote, proprietors, was first published, and in 1899, the Slidell *Brick* came out.

Neither of them lasted very long, the *Item* probably having failed before publication of the *Brick* began, and by 1901, the *Brick* was out of business as well. One issue of the *Brick* survives.

In 1902, E. F. Hailey's *Slidell Advocate* made its appearance. In February 1903, the *Slidell News* began publication. By 1908, when the *Advocate* suspended publication because of the "general financial depression" there was again no newspaper in Slidell. The *Slidell Journal*, in 1910, and the *Slidell American*, in 1912, were other early efforts to get a newspaper going in Slidell.

Mandeville had its second newspaper when the first edition of the *Wave*, edited by E. B. Shanks, hit the street on April 6, 1901. It continued publication for a number of years. An earlier newspaper, also called the *Wave*, had been published in the 1870's.

The *Madisonville Herald*, edited by E. W. Vacher, made its appearance in 1900. Nothing other than the fact of its existence is known about the *Herald*, except that it came out on Wednesday and no known copies survive.

St. Tammany Parish was touched by war for the fourth time when, on April 21, 1898, the Spanish-American War broke out. In the ranks of the Second Louisiana Regiment, which left New Orleans for Mobile in June 1898, were Theodore Zinzer, Zach Bush, Amadee Guyol, Louis Davenport, John D. Talley, and Fernand Parisy, all of Covington.

Colonel Hood's Regiment of Immunes was invited by Judge James M. Thompson to go into camp near Covington, and did so on a large camping ground on the banks of the Tchefuncta River. It was named Camp Caffery after Senator Donelson Caffery. The regiment remained in camp there from May through July 1898, when it left for Santiago for garrison duty.

In September 1898, Zach Bush was home from Mobile on furlough, having been seriously injured when a box of meat fell on him, breaking some ribs. Private Joshua Davis, of Company C of the Second Louisiana, died of the ravages of dysentery at "Alger's Pest Hole" in Miami, apparently the only casualty of the war from St. Tammany. He had enlisted from Mandeville. Others who enlisted from Mandeville were: John Murry, George Schultz, Walter LaGrue, Philip Schultz, Boy Davis, and Peter Berlier.

Approaching the end of the 19th century, the parish as a whole was in an enviable position. The *New Orleans Times Democrat* reported in 1892:

Since the last census the growth and development of St. Tammany parish in Louisiana, has rapidly increased in population, in wealth, in products, in manufactures, and the important position it occupies in the eyes of the world as a health resort, all entitle it to something more than a passing notice.

In the last ten years St. Tammany has doubled her population: between 800 and 1,000 new farms have been opened within her borders: new sawmills have been erected, equipped with the latest and most improved machinery; brickyards have sprung up from one end of the parish to the other, notably among these, and the finest in the state, are those at Slidell, St. Joe, a few miles further in the interior, others on the Abita, one or two on the Boguefalaya, bayou Lacombe and Bonfouca.

The culture of cane has assumed important proportions in the last twenty years. Every farmer has a cane mill and not one of them needs to travel outside of the limits of his own farm for his sugar and molasses, while its export, which is large, is shipped by steamer, schooner and the East Louisiana Railroad.

Its truck farms, with their products of corn, potatoes, fruits and vegetables come to perfection in the parish.

The output of her tar, turpentine, rosin factories, the sand, wood and charcoal industries give profitable and remunerative employment to hundreds of men and fifty or sixty schooners, as witness the statistics of the arrivals and departure of vessels from and to the Old and New Basins daily. The culture of the fleecy staple also has become of no mean importance in adding to the income of the St. Tammany farmer.

The grape is indigenous to the soil, and the vineyards of St. Tammany have attracted the attention of every visitor and stranger, and wine of no mean quality and in paying quantities is produced.

. . . .

Of this crop of 1891, over 400,000 barrels, the parish of St. Tammany has contributed 50,000 barrels, one-half of the total rice crop of the state of South Carolina, which until a few years ago, held the position and was considered as the foremost, the

A still and a turpentine orchard *(Courtesy The Louisiana State Museum)*

Charcoal or tar kiln

banner state of the Union, in this respect. Is not this a just cause of pride, that St. Tammany should produce 50,000, one-eighth of the rice crop of the entire fifty-nine parishes of the state?

In addition to all this, and not least after the most careful research into facts and figures, the United States government's official report as to the health statistics of the United States places St. Tammany at the head of the list in point of health; San Antonio, Tex., second; and Waukesha, third. St. Tammany has for some forty or fifty years been presently held up before the world as a health resort, free, entirely free, from yellow fever, cholera and malaria as witness the certificates and opinions of some of the most distinguished physicians of our own and neighboring states.

St. Tammany during the last four years has been out of debt, pays dollar for dollar to all to whom she may become indebted, has a surplus of some $7,000 or $8,000 in her treasury, has added in that time nearly $600,000 to her assessable property, lowered the rate of taxation from 16 mills to 13 mills and put all its bridges in excellent order.

The police jury of the parish, appointed four years ago, have been mainly instrumental in this good work, and deserve the highest credit. They have, in their every act, kept steadily in view the honor, the prosperity and the advancement of their parish.

. . . .

Property has increased in value all over the parish from 100 to 2000 per cent, according to location, and there is scarcely a foot of public land to be purchased in its length and breadth. Game abounds—the deer, turkey, woodcock, partridge, grassee, kipe lorrien, robin, garde sollef, snipe, duck; while the rivers and bayous swarm with fish, so that the hunter and fisherman will always find ample cause for congratulation that they have not forgotten their rod or gun; while for the love of nature no grander or more diversified forests exist on the planet, no finer specimens of that monarch of the forest, the oak, can anywhere meet the eye; there are no clearer, limpid, lovely and more romantic streams than are to be found here, nor are fairer women or braver men to be met with the world over.

CHAPTER XXV

Covington Grows Up

While all the new settlements and towns were springing up throughout the parish, the established towns and population centers were also developing, generally from the same causes. We know more about Covington because of the *St. Tammany Farmer,* which has been in publication since 1874, and which is the most valuable single historical resource in St. Tammany Parish. The *Farmer* also furnishes much information about the rest of the parish as well.

The first sign of returning life in Covington after reconstruction sprang from its reputation as a health and resort center. It is likely, judging from the sizeable number of doctors for the population, that Covington had long been a haven for people suffering from lung disease. We already know that the town was a haven for refugees from the frequent yellow fever epidemics in New Orleans. There was a major epidemic in 1878, and another, even more serious in 1897. In the latter epidemic literally thousands of refugees crowded the hotels, boarding houses, and private homes of the area. Dr. Sarah Hackett Stephenson, M.D., wrote to the *Chicago Times Herald* and the *Farmer* published her letter:

Chicago, Sept. 30—To the Editor: The statement is made in your paper that Atlanta is the only southern city not quarantined against yellow fever. There is one other exception, namely, the City of Covington, only thirty miles from and in daily communication with New Orleans, north of Lake Pontchartrain, and the terminus of the East Louisiana Railroad.

Covington is one of the oldest cities in the state, yet it has never quarantined against yellow fever; and although refugees from the city flock there by the hundred, there has never been an epidemic. Recently the Mayor of Covington convened the council for the express purpose of considering the quarantine question. The proposition to quarantine was voted down by the aldermen 5 to 1.

Covington is situated in a high, dry, piney region, being surrounded by a belt of long-leaf pine extending 150 miles to the north and east and between forty and fifty miles to the west. The air is filled with the balsamic odor. There is a constant liberation of ozone and no germ disease of any kind has ever gained foothold there. The city has been known and patronized by the old creole families of New Orleans, but as the population is very conservative no plans have been taken to make known the great sanitary advantages of this remarkable place.

New Orleans physicians of the old regime knew of these great sanitary virtues and always sent their consumptive cases to Covington. I myself have seen cases taken on a stretcher that were cured within three months. I am constrained to make these statements that the people who are panic-stricken in regard to yellow fever may possibly read of this city of refuge so near at hand, and so that the tuberculous northerner may know that within twenty-four hours and with small expense he may find a climate where the tubercle bacillus cannot thrive.

Sarah Hackett Stevenson, M.D.

The above is from the Chicago Times-Herald of Oct. 1. The writer, Mrs. Stevenson, is one of the most eminent physicians of Chicago, and has been an occasional visitor to Covington, hence she speaks from actual knowledge of the facts as they exist here. Her timely and favorable comments will do much toward attracting the attention of the people of Chicago to the great advantages offered by our town to invalids, especially those suffering with consumption as well as our attractions as a desirable and healthy summer and winter resort.

Several years before Covington had received the official endorsement of the United States Government as the healthiest spot in

The oldest house in Covington (built ca. 1820)

The Covington depot

the United States. Witness the following news story from the *Daily City Item* of June 29, 1891:

The *Item* called upon Mayor Guyol of Covington, La., yesterday with a view of obtaining data relative to the rapid settlement and development of St. Tammany parish and Covington. In that locality land that was worth $2 an acre two years ago is hardly obtainable at $10 to-day, and is being eagerly taken at that. Mayor Guyol, when questioned as to the causes, stated that they were numerous.

"When the census for the year 1890 was taken," said he, "the returns for the third and fourth wards computed the population at 4000, while 6000 would have been nearer, Covington the third and Mandeville the fourth ward; the population of the remaining wards numbers 6000 souls, thus giving the parish a population of 10,000." When the census commissioner, Mr. A. Fontini, now in the U.S. Mint at New Orleans, forwarded the returns to the bureau, showing a population of 10,000 and only twenty-five deaths, the statistics were returned with a request to the commissioner to go over the territory again as some mistake must have been made, and incidentally advising him that eighty would be a very low death average for the population. Accordingly, the commissioner went over Mandeville and Covington and in the computed population of 4000 inhabitants found that ten deaths—from all causes—had ensued. These points were especially selected because their communication with outside territory was more extended than others—Mandeville by water, Lake Pontchartrain, and Covington by rail.

The commissioner, on this percentage, returned the statistics to the bureau, and his original figures stood. Of the ten deaths, two-thirds were recorded against Mandeville, the majority being aged people. On the percentage Covington ranks as

THE MOST HEALTHY PLACE IN THE UNITED STATES,

with San Antonio second and Waukesha third. Travelers who have journeyed to the Old World compare the climate and temperature with that of Nice, Italy. No matter where you turn in this section you find mineral springs and little or nothing is made of many that Northern sections of the country would advertise and herald the world over.

. . . .

The following statements are supported by the certificates of responsible parties; they cover a period of over twenty-six years, which is certainly long enough to furnish a sufficient test:

Typhoid fever—Since 1860 there has been but one death from typhoid fever in Covington. This case was undoubtedly contracted elsewhere, and the disease did not spread.

Pneumonia—One death. This was the case of a colored man who had been badly wounded and was much exposed during the coldest weather we have ever known at this point.

Small pox—Three imported cases; no deaths and the disease did not spread.

Scarlet fever—Two imported cases; no deaths and the disease did not spread.

Malarial fever—No cases.

Diphtheria—No cases.

Cholera—No cases.

Yellow fever—Two cases imported in 1867. The disease did not spread, although many were in contact with the patients, and the funerals were largely attended.

The water of a number of the wells and springs in the vicinity were reputed to have therapeutic value rivalling that of the famous springs in Abita. It was to be expected that the combination of the ozone air, the water, and the natural beauty of the area would attract visitors, and that accommodations would appear for them. One of the earliest hotels in Covington of which there is a record was Sterling's Hotel. F. B. Martindale had a hotel in the town prior to 1880, as did Calvin G. Joyner, who later bought and operated Martindale's.

Other early hotels in Covington included Rosedale Cottage, operated by Mrs. L. C. LeBreton; Crystal Springs House, kept by Mrs. F. Gonthier; Claudel House; the Bank Hotel; and Ernest's Restaurant and Hotel.

The resort business continued to flourish into the early years of the 20th century. The Riverside Hotel, later Richard's, and today the home of Charles F. Read, was a popular resort. Melrose Cottage, run by Charles L. Smith was accepting guests in 1901. It was a large two-story building, with wide halls and galleries, which could accommodate 30 guests.

In 1902, E. L. Charropin bought the Crystal Springs Hotel, at the foot of Lee Road, from the Gonthier family, and continued the operation of that popular resort. In July of 1902, Dr. Charles O. Farrington of New York and H. C. Ames of Baltimore came here to build and operate a large hotel and sanitarium. They negotiated for the old Mulberry Grove Hotel, but their plans fell through. In 1904, the Mulberry Grove Hotel Company, Ltd., was organized to build a large hotel on the site of the old hotel, with Dr. Marrero as the principal stockholder. A $100,000 hotel was planned, to accommodate 250 guests, but once again, as with all major proposals for large hotels in St. Tammany, the project never got off the ground. The old hotel was repaired and refurbished, however, and continued in business for some time.

In February 1906, plans were announced for the construction of a large modern hotel in Covington, and another, to accommodate 400 guests, was proposed for Sulphur Springs, for the tourist trade. The latter hotel never got out of the announcement stage, but the former, the Southern Hotel, opened its doors on June 1, 1907, on the corner of Boston and New Hampshire Streets, where it still stands. In 1912, Dr. F. F. Young bought the Southern, and turned it into a sanitarium for a few years under the name of the New Fenwick. In 1913, Dr. Young leased The Oaks, a resort hotel, to be used as his sanitarium, and began to operate the Southern as a European-plan hotel. In 1916, he also bought Glen Cottage, another popular resort.

One of the most famous wells in the parish was Roche's Well, which was located on the property now occupied by the Bogue Falaya Plaza and which was famed for its medicinal properties. In 1881, the *Farmer* wrote of a young lad from the city who was cured of chills and fever by water from the well, which, it was said had cured a number of cases of rheumatism, dyspepsia, fever, and ague. In 1886, the water was chemically analyzed and found to contain oxide of sodium, oxide of calcium, oxide of aluminum, oxide of magnesium, oxide of iron, chlorine, sulphuric acid, crenic and apocrenic acid, and silicic acid. In that same year, the well was leased by Caleb Parker, who bottled the water and sold it at Lilienthal's on Canal Street in New Orleans for 75 cents per bottle. In 1889, the well and surrounding property was bought by a group from New Orleans, who planned to build a large hotel and sanitarium there. Like every other scheme for the construction of a large hotel in St. Tammany, it never got past the planning stage.

Covington was growing, with a population in 1890 of 976, and the *Farmer* bragged on her assets, saying that, in 1890, Covington had 15 dealers in general merchandise, 2 bakeries, 3 butchers, 3 blacksmiths, 2 wheelwrights, 1 tannery, 1 barber shop, 4 restaurants, 1 shoe shop, 1 steam pottery, 1 cabinet maker, 15 carpenters, 5 stage lines, 1 drug store, 3 doctors, 4 painters, 2 bricklayers, 1 brickyard, 1 lumber yard, 4 saloons, 1 billiard room, 2 fruit, fish, and vegetable shops, 1 confectionery, 3 well borers, 1 tailor, 1 dentist, 2 lawyers, 1 music teacher, 4 private boarding houses, 2 hotels, 4 white churches, 1 colored church, 4 white schools, 2 colored schools, 1 printing office, 1 millinery store, several warehouses, and livery and feed stables.

Covington also boasted a new town hall, dedicated on Monday, August 25, 1890, which was situated in the ox lot in the middle of the square bounded by Boston, Columbia, Rutland, and Florida streets. That block of Columbia Street was the principal commercial area in the town.

New businesses in Covington did not seem to come in during the 1890's, except for the hotels. Messrs. Giesen and Roubion established a livery, feed, and sale stable in 1890, and a branch of the Southwestern Building and Loan Association opened that same year. In 1894, Frank Rodgers established the first office intended exclusively for handling real estate sales. F. A. Guyol, an attorney, farmer, and hotel keeper, had earlier advertised himself as handling real estate, but Rodgers was the first, of whom there is record, to do so exclusively. He has been followed by a multitude.

Probably the most significant economic development of the decade, not only for Covington but for the parish as a whole, was the establishment of the Bank of Covington, which began doing business on June 6, 1899, in Mr. P. E. Theriot's store. It was an immediate success. In 1903, it changed its name to Covington Bank & Trust Company, increased its capital to $100,000, and voted to open branches in Slidell and Franklinton. Its success inspired the founding of other financial institutions in St. Tammany Parish.

In 1901, the Peoples Building and Loan Association went into business, the first locally chartered homestead in the parish. In June 1905, a meeting was held in the offices of Ellis and White, attorneys, to organize a new bank. The St. Tammany Banking Company and Savings Bank, with 80 persons subscribing $30,000 in capital was duly organized, with Harvey E. Ellis as its first president. It opened its doors on August 22, 1905. Today, following a number of mergers and changes of name it still exists as the First National Bank, the largest bank in the parish.

In 1901, electricity came to Covington when the St. Tammany Ice and Manufacturing Company was awarded the contract to light the town. By June of that year, the plant was in operating condition. In 1904, the Ice Company, as it was called, was given the franchise to provide water to Covington, and in January of 1905 was laying the water mains.

Baseball in Covington had been mentioned by the *Farmer* as early as 1884, but it was not until after 1900 that competitive sports became popular. In 1901, the Covington baseball team was champion of the parish and defeated a number of celebrated teams from New Orleans. A. R. Smith was the captain of the team.

In 1904, there were baseball and football teams at Dixon Academy. Covington High School and St. Joseph's College, established at the new Benedictine monastery at Cedar Hill Plantation, also fielded teams. Basketball also appeared in 1904. There was even a meeting held at Judge James M. Thompson's house in 1902 to discuss the organization of a golf club, and in 1903, the Covington Athletic Club was formed.

The golf club was not to be, but the meeting did result in the formation of the Bogue Falaya Club, which bought the old Presbyterian Church on the corner of New Hampshire and Independence, tore down the old church, and built a "large and handsome building" as their clubhouse. At the time of its grand opening on March 7, 1903, the building had "electric lights, has fine bath-rooms, pool and billiard tables, the latest magazines, periodicals, etc., always on the place. Porter in charge." The first reception and dance at the new club was described as a brilliant social event, with handsome gowns and full dress suits in evidence, and music furnished by the Covington Orchestra. By 1907, however, the club was in receivership, and its building was sold by E. P. Singletary, the Receiver, to the MCB

Club, which established its library there. Today the building is the Episcopal Parish House.

Covington was also the site of the first known street lighting in St. Tammany, when oil fired street lamps were installed there in 1879. In February 1880, the first fire company was organized in Covington, but did not last too long. On February 5, 1881, Covington Fire Company No. One was dissolved by mutual consent.

Another event of interest in the early days was the first celebration of Mardi Gras in Covington, on February 25, 1879. After a buildup of several weeks in the *Farmer*, with royal edicts and bulletins announcing King Rex's progress towards Covington, the King arrived in Ponchatoula by train on February 24, 1879, and was escorted to Covington. On the next day, Mardi Gras, there was a day parade, followed by a night parade and ball. Rex was portrayed by Lord Tinker.

After this, Mardi Gras was regularly celebrated in Covington with varying degrees of formality and elaborateness on some occasions by the adults and on some by the Juvenile Rex Organization. In 1891, the Juveniles had a parade, reception, and ball, presided over by J. L. "Deed" Smith, King, and Miss Adele Pechon, queen. The next year the Knights of Carnival Association had a parade and ball, with Ernest Pechon as king and Miss May Monet, queen. In 1893, Julian Smith and Jennie Pujol presided over the Rex Junior Parade and Ball. In 1894, there was a celebration by the Juvenile Rex Club, but no word as to the king and queen. Master Jules Pechon was king and Miss Frances Heintz, queen, in 1895.

The adults took over again in 1896, when there was a Rex parade with eight floats, followed by a grand masquerade ball in the Town Hall. Charles Stroble was king and Bessie Norman was queen. The next year the parade had six floats and five marching, riding, and bicycling groups with A. L. Pechon as king and Rebecca Strain as queen. A small scale Mardi Gras was held in 1898, with a parade of maskers in the afternoon and a ball at the Town Hall that night. Leon Hebert was king and Miss Philomene Pechon was queen. There were no formal Mardi Gras celebrations in 1899 or 1900.

During the early years of the 20th century, Mardi Gras was not celebrated formally in Covington. In February 1907, however, it started up again with a bang, with a grand industrial display, thou-

Mardi Gras supplement appearing in the March 4, 1911, issue of the St. Tammany *Farmer*

King Rex arrives at Covington on the steamer *Josie*, Mardi Gras 1909

Mardi Gras in Covington, 1909

sands of visitors, and public speaking at the courthouse. Anatole Beaucoudray was king and Linda Alpuente was his queen. Mardi Gras was missed in 1908, but in 1909, there was a parade with 12 floats and a number of marching groups. The king, who arrived in town on Captain Weaver's steamer, *Josie*, was once again Anatole Beaucoudray with Miss Mary Dutsch as queen.

Again, there was no celebration in 1910. Probably the most elaborate of all Mardi Gras celebrations in Covington was held in 1911, however. H. B. Pruden, as Chief Tamanend, was king, and Miss Mae Poole, as an Indian princess, was queen. The parade consisted of nine floats, each representing an Indian legend of St. Tammany Parish. After the parade, a great ball was held at Cantrelle Hall. If there were any formal celebrations of Mardi Gras after 1911, the *Farmer* did not report them.

Covington was to be beset by a number of major fires during this period, the first of which took place on the early morning of November 11, 1898, as described by the *New Orleans Daily States*:

> At one o'clock this morning a disastrous conflagration was started in the new town hall of the little village of Covington which radiated and swept the entire business district, causing a loss which has been estimated in the wide range from $10,000 to $80,000 though a well posted insurance man of this city who is familiar with all the conditions at Covington places the loss as not exceeding $25,000, including buildings and stocks, upon which there appears to be little or no insurance. The town hall sits in the middle of the block bounded by Columbia, Boston, Rutland and Florida streets and beside the loss of the stores the Bank of Covington and the post office is in ruins. It is along Columbia street between Rutland and Boston that the principle stores are ranged on either side, and the following is the list of those who have suffered as far as could be gained; the list is believed to be accurate and complete:
>
> Victor Frederick's drug store; Howard's Bakery; Bogel's tailor shop; the mercantile firms of Cooper & Strain; Hardey Smith (and warehouse adjacent); Ed. J. Fredericks, P. Thiriot, O. V. Richard, C. Laborde, B. Labat, Charles Fredericks, Hanhart & Co., (New Orleans store); Emile Frederick's saloon; the postoffice; Bank of Covington; Mrs. Warren's residence and

John Thebald's blacksmith shop. This takes in the principal business section of the city and the loss in nearly every instance is total. A visit to the various insurance offices of the city failed to locate any insurance, and it is stated on good authority that it is likely that not more than 10 per cent of the loss is covered by insurance, if even that much. Vic Frederick's building is owned by Hosmer and Emile Fredericks; O. V. Richard's building by Mr. Wherli; C. Laborde's building by Mr. Palliot, owned by Hosmer and Amile Fredericks; O. V. Richard's building by Mr. Wherli; C. Laborde's building by Mr. Palliot, of Madisonville; Charles Frederick's building by Mrs. Cahier; B. Labat's by the same; New Orleans store by Mr. Wherli; while Hardey Smith, Emile Fredericks and John Theobald own their own buildings. The post office is owned by Judge Thompson, the Bank of Covington building by the Warren estate and Mrs. Warren's residence by herself.

This tragedy, in which fortunately no injuries were suffered and no lives lost, brought about the establishment of Covington Fire Company No. 1, the first fire protection in the town since the abortive effort of the 1880's.

Covington Fire Company No. 1 organized the new company, ordered a hook and ladder truck and buckets in 1900, and fought their first fire with the new equipment on April 28, 1901, when the town jail caught fire. The *Farmer* reported that, although the jail was destroyed and one prisoner killed, the fire company was soon at the scene, and prevented the fire from spreading.

Apparently neither the new equipment nor the fire company were maintained as operating units. In 1906, there was another serious fire in Covington, which destroyed Preston Burns' store, his two-story residence, a cottage, O. M. Burch's store, the Knights of Pythias Hall, and the Chinese laundry. Miss Serena Jones, one of Judge Jesse Jones' daughters, was an eyewitness to the fire, and described it in a letter to her niece, Mary Hosmer:

> No doubt, you saw in the newspaper this morning, an account of the fire last night—it is supposed to have been caused by an electric wire in Patrick's store which is on the square this side of the grave yard.
>
> At 12 o'clock, the whistles of both ice factories began to

Aftermath of the 1906 fire in Covington (*Photograph from the collection of J. Louis Smith, Jr.*)

The Covington baseball team, parish champions of 1901. First row, second from left: team captain A. R. Smith; third row, second from left: Anatole Beaucoudray; third row, third from left: E. J. "Boss" Frederick; third row, second from right: Leon Hebert; third row, extreme right: J. Louis Smith; in stands above Hebert and to his right: John Mulling (*Photograph from the collection of J. Louis Smith, Jr.*)

blow furiously and several loud pistol shots were fired. I ran to the window and saw the flames which were already of great volume—fortunately, there was no wind, at all. I awoke Laura and after watching the fire from the upstairs gallery about a quarter of an hour, as it seemed to be increasing and spreading, we decided to go and see how near it was. We went as far as Stroble's stable; the streets were full of people looking on. I thought of you, in the last large fire, how useful you were and how hard you worked to help. The Pythian hall was burning and there was great danger of Babington's store and the depot catching. A car had been sent to Greenlaw's mill for dynamite and as soon as it came, they blew up the house next to Dr. Tolson's office, which checked the fire on that side of the street and a large new brick store, on the opposite side, not quite finished yet, stopped it there. It was two o'clock when we came back home as there was no longer any danger. It is a shame that the town has no fire engine or water works. . . .

Apparently, the 1906 fire breathed new life into the volunteer fire teams. In 1909 there was a Fireman's Parade, which included the Hook and Ladder Company, the Chemical Company, and the Jefferson Fire Company No. 1. In November 1909, these organizations got together and formed the Covington Fire Department. In August of that year, 25 fire plugs were to be installed. In October 1909, there was another fire. It was reported that this was the first time the new fire plugs were used, and it turned out that they did not fit the hoses carried by the fire trucks. Five houses were destroyed.

CHAPTER XXVI

The Other Towns

MADISONVILLE

At some time after its original incorporation, Madisonville had ceased to function as a political entity. The decline of the lake trade and the effects of the Civil War had decimated the town economically. Since it did not enjoy the hotel and excursion business which were to breathe life into Covington and Mandeville, the road back was much more difficult for Madisonville.

The first step forward came in 1878 when A. Heisser moved his sawmill to Madisonville, opened a large broom factory, and began the manufacture of all kinds of woodwork. In April 1882, the *Farmer* reported that the shipyards in Madisonville were doing a good business.

Later in 1882, the town was once again incorporated, and elected a slate of officers. William Hanghan was named mayor, and Henry Kaiser, Michael Haas, Pedro Baham, Victor Fauria, Everette Perkins, and Thomas Badeaux were the aldermen.

In 1884, this report appeared in the *Farmer:* "Mayor Wren seems determined to revolutionize this once wicked town, and already his power is feared and respected and our citizens enjoy more peaceable times."

In 1885, it was reported that at Oulliber and Baham's shipyard there had been general employment for two months, and that Theo Jay had erected a new sawmill opposite the town.

In the late 1880's, Madisonville was described in the *New Orleans Times-Democrat* as having two shipyards, Messrs. Oulliber and Baham at the lower end of town and the Cardone Brothers at the upper end; Heisser's sawmill and factory; the large sawmill of Mr.

232

John Jay, just above the town; the brickyards of Messrs. Lancaster, Morgan, Delery, and others; a large business in wood, charcoal, and lumber; large shipment of wool, some cotton, moss, birds, poultry, molasses, and rice; and the business houses of Galatas & Son, Theo. Dendinger, Brinknel, Englehardt, and the Pelloat Brothers.

The old Madison House Hotel was still in business on the river front, and a new town hall was completed in 1891. The shipyard business continued to grow, and by 1895 there were four shipyards in the town: Charles Oulliber's, V. P. Baham's, F. Cardone's, and Louis Baham's. Louis Baham had taken over the Cardone Brothers shipyard, and V. P. Baham was operating the old Drinkwater Shipyard.

The twentieth century started auspiciously for Madisonville, when Jahncke and Baham built the largest marine ways in the south, which could handle the largest river boats. In 1906, the Madisonville Progressive Union was formed and in that same year the Madisonville Bank was fully subscribed and went into business.

A 1907 article in the *Hammond Sun* about Madisonville listed the businesses in the town as Theodore Dendinger's Saw and Planing Mill, the Chas. Oulliber Bros., V. P. Baham and Ernest Lee Jahncke shipyards, the Madisonville Bank, the Madisonville Ice Manufacturing Company, a drug store, hotel, two livery stables, two butcher shops, and five or six mercantile establishments doing a large business. The town council was then planning to place a breakwater on the riverfront and "erect a wharfage that will be a pride to the town and save the oaks."

Mardi Gras celebrations began in Madisonville as early as 1895, where there was a parade and ball, with Eugene Mugnier as Rex, and Miss Lelia Heughan, queen. The next year, there were a number of floats in the parade and a mounted guard. Felix Curro and Frances Clunder were king and queen. In 1899, the Madisonville Carnival Club was organized, with 115 members. Mr. De Mont, "an artist of well known merit from New Orleans," was named general manager. The parade that year was said by the *Farmer* to be "very fine."

A parade and ball for Mardi Gras were held in 1907 in Madisonville, but no other details are known.

The great expansion of the shipyards during World War I, which has been covered elsewhere, was the high water mark for Madisonville. Some estimates put the population of the area in excess of 4,000, as a result of the high employment in the shipyards. With the end of the war, however, Madisonville dropped back to its former population level.

Madisonville today is a peaceful, quiet town. The old shipyards are gone, but the modern yard of Equitable Equipment Company still carries on the traditions of earlier days.

MANDEVILLE

As in the case of Covington, Mandeville's post-Reconstruction recovery was related to the excursion business, which was to be the mainstay of the economy for many years. In 1880, only the Colomes Hotel was in operation in Mandeville, but it was soon followed by Frappart House, on the lake front, which still stands, and is now the property of the Kings Daughters and Sons. It was owned and operated for a time by Denis Bechac, circa 1893, under the name of The Denis Restaurant. The Marquis G. P. de Marigny built the Crescent Hotel and Restaurant in 1887, on the corner of Gerard and Lake streets, which was operated by the Mugnier Brothers.

Another popular resort of the day was Paul's Exchange, operated by Paul Arceneaux, which is now Bechac's Restaurant. Mrs. J. M. Favaron operated a private boarding house on Gerard Street at the foot of the steamer wharf. In 1889, the Lafferanderie Hotel opened in Mandeville.

Mandeville was still the largest town in the parish with an 1890 population of 1,012. In 1893, the town included "5 first class grocery stores, 3 first class hotels, 2 fine bar rooms, 3 butchers, 3 bakers, a daily steamboat, daily train, daily mail, and a telegraph office." On July 14, 1893, in line with her French heritage, Mandeville celebrated Bastille day:

> The French fete, the glorious anniversary of the fall of the Bastile, so dear to every Frenchman's heart, was celebrated at Mandeville this year with unusual pomp and splendor, the scene of the festivities being the beach front of Paul Arceneaux's Exchange. An old cannon found in the Lake, which had been for years in the cellar of Frappart's (now Denis) Hotel, was dragged forth rigged to its carriage, and in a few minutes

boomed out in loud welcome to the day of joy and celebration. Paul's famous Exchange was elaborately decorated with bunting, United States and French flags, and at nightfall gloried in the splendid electric light, while most of the neighboring houses were brilliantly illuminated with Chinese lanterns and decorated with flags. A splendid display of fireworks, consisting of bombs, Roman candles, rockets, etc., added greatly to the effectiveness of the scene, while several large bonfires built on the beach cast a ready glow over the whole of the lovely picturesque little town and presented a most weird and pleasing spectacle. The committee in charge of the celebration were Messrs. Ant. Anglade, chairman, H'y Ricau, artilleryman (who, by the way, was so unfortunate as to have his arm very badly lacerated by the premature discharge of the cannon), Rene Pocheleu, V. B. Angaud, John Devonshire, Paul Arceneaux, Mr. Lafond, Frank Ribava, Depre Bros., Mr. Manau, G. Pascal, M. Lafargue, S. Escoffier, Jr., Denis Bechac, J. P. Zatarain, Mugnier Bros., Isidore Levy, John Smith, Alex Band, A. E. Esquinance. After the fireworks, the committee and their friends repaired to Paul's to partake of a punch brewed by the old reliable Paul himself, and drank to the toast, "Vive la Republique."

It was also in 1893 that the Mandeville Yacht Club took possession of its clubhouse and grounds. The club had almost 200 members, and regularly conducted regattas on Lake Pontchartrain. There had been an earlier yacht club of the same name in Mandeville, which had conducted regattas in 1888 and 1890. The earliest regatta was held on July 27, 1888. Some of the boats entered were the *Krin*, *Pansy*, *Imelda*, *Edna*, *Virgie*, *Nellie J.*, *Clara F.*, *Aida*, *Sallitta*, and *Dude*. By 1893, this first yacht club was no longer in existence. The second yacht club was more successful, but had probably ceased to exist by April 1903, when the club house was foreclosed on.

Mandeville must have been a gay place in those days. The records are replete with accounts of balls, dances, concerts, regattas, and celebrations of all types. In May 1897, a May Pole dance was held, at which Dr. R. B. Paine appeared as Dionysius and Cupid was portrayed by little Miss Ella Paine, "who appeared clothed in the veritable wings of the Love God." In contrast, the first W.C.T.U. chapter in the parish was also formed in Mandeville in 1900, under the leadership of Mrs. R. B. Paine.

The Covington fish market

The Mandeville post office

In 1906, the St. Tammany Banking Company opened a branch in Mandeville, after $5,000 in stock was locally subscribed. Later that year, the Bank of Mandeville, with capital of $10,000, began business.

Mandeville began celebrating Mardi Gras formally in 1907, when there was a grand carnival parade and ball. In 1908, the carnival was a "fine display" with floats decorated by Walter April of New Orleans. There were two kings, P. A. Arceneaux, who presided over the parade and A. Hartman, who was king at the ball. Mr. Hartman's queen was Miss Inez Ribava. Apparently, Mr. Arceneaux did not have a queen. In 1909, Mr. Hartman was king again, with Miss Edna Vix, queen.

On July 27, 1910, the electric lights were turned on in Mandeville for the first time by A. D. Piaggio, president of the Mandeville Electric Light and Ice Company, which had its plant on Villere Street.

In 1913, the town got a boost when Poitevent and Favre built its sawmill on the west end of town, just east of where the causeway meets the lake. In the same year, a contract was let for the construction of a concrete seawall, 7,000 feet long, to be built of slabs two by 12 feet, eight inches thick. For some reason, this contract was not fulfilled, but another contract was let in June 1916, for the seawall which still stands today.

ABITA SPRINGS

Abita Springs, in the late 1870's, was an unincorporated settlement. The fabled spring had long been known for its healthful and therapeutic properties, but little had been done to make it available to the public. Then in 1879, Mrs. F. A. Bossier began to accommodate a few boarders at her home near the springs. In June of 1880, Frank Lenel opened his famous Long Branch Hotel, just across the Abita River from the Springs.

In 1881, the Abita Springs were purchased by Eager and Ellerman, in association with Thomas L. Airey, John J. Gidiere, William Henry, W. G. Coyle, and Adam Thompson, who wanted to develop the Springs into both a winter and summer resort. They proposed a hotel with accommodations for between 100 and 200 people; a railroad from Mandeville to the Springs, with fast steamers in the lake to run between West End and Mandeville. It would take only two and one-half hours to go from New Orleans to Abita.

By 1886, there were three hotels in Abita: Bossier House, the Long Branch, and Labat's. The big plans of Eager and Ellerman had never come to pass, and they sold the springs to William Henry, who planned to continue the project. In May 1887, Henry, in turn sold the tract to Eddie Bossier, Ed Breckenridge, and Poitevent & Favre for $12,000.

Earlier that year, Mr. Bossier, anticipating the arrival of the East Louisiana Railroad, laid out a town near the springs, called Bossier City. A new store was opened by Mr. McEvoy, who also had a telegraph office there. Ira E. Strain opened a meat market. By June 10, 1887, the tracks were only two miles from the waiting town. Construction of a large pavilion was begun.

In short order, there were two more hotels, Simon's and Alexander's, a Catholic Church and a post office, presided over by Thomas H. McEvoy. Poitevent and Favre built a handsome, octagonal, two-story pavilion over the springs, designed by Thomas O. Sully. Sully, a native of Covington, was to become one of the best known architects in New Orleans.

A visit to Abita Springs was described in one of the New Orleans newspapers:

> The season has been one of continued scenes and routines of pleasure in every conceivable form for all have been able to remain long enough to become acquainted and initiated. We eat breakfast at 9 o'clock A.M., when all who can move around light out for a ramble to the springs and through the pine woods, the girls and boys gayly romping over the gargling springs, and far away over hill and dale, filling the woods with the cheery voices of the pleasure-seekers from among the wage-workers and counter hoppers of the great Southern Emporium.
>
> The old crippled vets, both of the wars and baser turmoils, hunting out some radical reminiscence of a fallen foe; some improvise a resting place beneath the deep shade of wild oak groves near the musical bubbles of lympid waters of the far fame Abita, its crystal stream beautiful to behold and refreshing to the thirst of the delighted beholder, or can recline upon the seats of the ample pavillion provided for the rest and amuse-

ment of visitors. Dinner at 3 o'clock, P. M., and then rest and leisure the balance of the evening, or a game of croquet, or music in the parlor agreeable to the taste and inclination.

Night brings the western bound train with the mail. After the discussion of which, and the greeting of fresh arrivals, supper, with the pleasant tete-a-tete of a family circle with the flow of wit and the flow of soul, making all as merry as the marriage bell.

After supper, we have a regular "pitch in" for a jolly good time in the way of music and other parlor entertainment, and as we have had a few theatrical oddities to aid in conducting recitals and dramatical episodes through the whole season, this part of the amusements has been quite a rich treat; the whole concluding with a merry country dance, which each one gives away to the fun and glee in good old country style, trying to out dance his partner. Sometimes we have plays in which both young and old join as "Pleased—or displeased"— "Comparison," or the popular games of "Feather," where all assemble in a circle of chairs, stretching a sheet in the circle, and placing a feather on the sheet, each one blowing the feather away from himself and to his neighbor's side, and he who catches the drop of the feather gives a forfeit to be cancelled by the performance of some frivolous act; generally making the actor the subject for fun for the balance of the party.

As a specimen, a gentleman is required to make love and a proposal to a lady according to the most improved style of the age. This requires much cheek and talent as the getting off of an extem-po on "court occasion."

I have seen the dignified gentry hopping on all fours like a frog, for the amusement of laughing spectators.

It is considered dishonorable to repudiate penalties.

This closes the amusements of the evening, about 10 or 11 o'clock—each one retiring to their cozie cottage room for a night's rest after the innocent frolic of the day.

Sometimes the horses are hitched up to the hacks, and little wagons used in the country, for a jostle over the rough roads, and over the country to the villages and other neighboring watering places (for there are not less than half a dozen in three miles of this place). The trip is made at rattling stride, and back again for breakfast at 9 o'clock, and such is life at Abita Springs.

There are four well kept and commodious hotels in a few hundred yards of the main Artesian Saline Calebian Springs, which has been analized by physicians, and found to contain the various medicinals concomitants of carbonic gases, soda iron, magnesium and sulphur.

Without speaking to the detriment of the other hotels, we cannot refrain from mention of the Bossier House, and recommend the taste and comfort displayed in all of its arrangments, and the proprietor as the prince of gentlemen and hotel keepers.

It can be truly said of him, he is a gentleman, a scholar, and can keep a hotel.

A Visitor.

Stories that a large hotel was to be built at the Springs continued, but none of these was ever to be built, even though the excursion business continued to be brisk. In February 1890, Abita was the site of a prize fight between Vacquelin and the famous heavyweight, Jake Kilrain, who had fought the great John L. Sullivan to a standstill. The fight attracted the following editorial comment from the *New Orleans City Item*:

Two things are becoming painfully evident. One is that the prize fighting nuisance is on the increase and the other that our city authorities are not inclined to handle the subject with that energetic, positive spirit necessary for its suppression. There is, however, a remedy left. Let the legislature at its next session pass an act regulating the matter throughout the state.

Against legitimate sports or amusements the *Item* has no word of complaint. Undoubtedly some of them are a benefit to the community in several ways. Not so with prize-fighting. The hangers on of the ring are non-producers and undesirable citizens in every way. There is much to be lost and nothing to be gained by their presence. And the glove business is more demoralizing than the old-style "London ring rules," because it is continuous and has the quasi sanction of the law, and is defended to a degree by respectable clubs and citizens. In olden days, at long intervals, noted pugilists would arrange matches to come

off in this vicinity. The fight over, the "pugs" and their following departed, those of our people who had the curiosity to see
such sport were gratified, and that was the last of it. Now it is
an every week affair, Sunday being the favorite day, thus
doubly shocking a large part of the community, while third and
fourth rate and fake fighters are becoming too numerous and
brazen for the public peace and decency.

From our sporting columns it will be seen that the quiet,
secluded and law-abiding village of Abita was invaded yesterday
(by a gang composed principally of toughs) who virtually held
sway from 10:30 in the morning until nearly 5 o'clock in the
afternoon. A prize-fight made this possible, an arena within less
than a hundred yards of the centre of the village and about 150
yards from the principal church of the town, in the rear of and
adjoining a saloon, being the scene.

What must have been the feelings of the pious inhabitants of
Abita at this condition of affairs? It may be said that Abita is a
small place and that the sheriff was on the ground to preserve
order; but it does not matter if there was but a single family or
worshipper to be shocked, certainly protection should have
been afforded from any such ruffianly intrusion. No person has
any vested right to do that which annoys, intimidates, or in any
way trespasses upon the rights of another, not even with the
sanction of a sheriff. As there is no law directly forbidding
prize-fighting, any sheriff can permit it to go on without becoming officially liable; but let a legislative enactment be passed
affixing a penalty against such official for dereliction of duty,
and there will quickly be found sufficient deputies to cope with
the plug-uglies.

In 1891, the newly constructed Bossier House burned to the
ground. Eddie Bossier, the proprietor, bought Brown's Hotel, and
stayed in business. An ice factory, the first one on the north shore,
was completed, and went into operation in July 1891. Apparently
the demand for ice was not so great as anticipated, since it failed in
1894. In 1899, Abita Fire Company No. 1 was founded, and fought
its first fire in May of that year. In June 1899, there was a chemical
engine and a hook and ladder company in Abita.

One of the major industries was the Abita Springs Bottling Company, which bottled water for public consumption. It won a medal for the best carbonated water at the World's Fair in St. Louis in 1904, and at the Pan American Exposition at Buffalo, New York.

A number of hotels appeared in Abita during the 1890's, including Martin's Hotel; Morin's Cottage, an eight-bedroom Queen Anne Cottage; Evergreen Cottage, owned by A. A. Cooley; the Abita Springs Hotel, run by Mrs. O. Aubert; Springview Cottage; and the old reliables, the Long Branch and Labat's, the latter soon to become Mutti's Hotel.

The hotel business does not seem to have increased after 1900. The Long Branch Hotel and Mutti's were still in business, and there is mention of the Gem Hotel, the Ozone Belt Hotel, the Ostendorf Hotel, and the Great Northern Hotel. In 1910, Mutti's burned down, but the Labat family rebuilt it on the site of the old hotel.

Abita Springs finally became an incorporated town in 1903, when the citizens of the subdivisions of Abita Springs and Bossier City joined together.

A town meeting was held to select a mayor, aldermen, and a town marshal. Unanimously selected were Henry Strubbe, mayor; John Caubert, Emile Aubert, and Joseph Rausch, aldermen; and Herman Oalman, town marshal. These officials officially qualified on March 3, 1903, and Abita Springs began its life as an incorporated village. In 1910, its population was 365, sufficient to warrant a proclamation making it a town rather than a village.

In April 1903, the people of the town subscribed $200, and the Police Jury put up $100 to build a fine road from Abita to Covington, using the parish road machine. On October 19, 1906, Abita Springs organized a Progressive Union.

On September 27, 1914, at 7:00 p.m. the electric lights were turned on in Abita for the first time. Three years later, in 1917, it had its own motion picture theater, called the Air Dome.

But other progress was not to come. Over the years the number of hotels and tourists declined, until today none of the old resort hotels remain.

SLIDELL

We have already seen how Slidell first came into being as a station on the New Orleans and Northeastern Railroad in 1882. It must have been a rough town, because by March 1884, it was necessary to establish a committee of safety. According to the *Farmer*, the committee held its meetings in public and all the good citizens were invited to join. "The bad ones are leaving town without an invitation," said the *Farmer*. It also reported that the town was more quiet and orderly since the establishment of the committee.

Shortly after the town was established, the energetic Salmen brothers moved into the area and started their brickyard, which, by 1887, was reported to be able to turn out more bricks than all the yards in the parish combined. Later reports do not bear this out. Also operating in Slidell was Fassman's Brickyard. In 1889, however, all was not well. A visitor to the town wrote:

> Slidell is the first station you reach in the piney woods, and is not far from the Lake. There is little worthy of note about this place except the southern portion of it, which bears some evidence of progress and thrift, consisting of a brickyard and store, and a comfortable dwelling-house close by, which present to the traveler a cheerful appearance. The older portion of the town seems to have been badly used, considering the neglected condition of the buildings. A few dollars' worth of lime would alter the appearance of things wonderfully, if applied properly. The jail, which is unique in its structure, seems to be the most recent evidence of mechanical skill that meets the eye.
>
> My friend Gause's buggy was on hand soon after my arrival and being helped to a seat therein, we soon pulled out for his residence. This is a charming place for quietude and the enjoyment of those surroundings, natural and artificial, which go toward making the comforts of a home. A store of general merchandise occupies one corner of the enclosure, and here for several years Mr. Gause has been distributing goods to the citizens of the parish, who have been engaged in different industries. The selling of pine logs is the leading business hereabouts. Mr. Gause deals extensively in this timber, and has men in different parts of the parish employed in preparing it for market.
>
> Now, though St. Tammany has had its share of notices through the press, this particular "neck of the woods" has never been touched upon. The climate is so salubrious that doctors are rarely seen here. The water, both from wells and springs, is

so clear that you can scarcely detect its presence in a tumbler. The range for stock is good, and the soil, with proper management, will produce most of the crops. I learned that the business of catching fish for market had been embarked in by one of the citizens of this locality and that he shipped his fish along the line of the Queen and Crescent road to different points as far up as Meridian, Miss. Besides, trapping has been pursued to some extent, and Mr. Gause shipped recently to St. Louis, Mo., for account of a customer, several otter skins, which brought a good price. So you see, it is evident that "some things can be done as well as others."

I know of no place better circumstanced for spending a quiet time, by those who are seeking a respite from the rough toils of daily life, and no more hospitable hosts can be found anywhere than Mr. Gause and his estimable wife, who will use every endeavor to make a visitor feel at home in their handsome mansion, so that whoever visits them once will want to go again.

Senex Carr.

Despite that somewhat negative report, the town was incorporated that year, with her first official being S. H. Decker, mayor. It shortly boasted a new Catholic Church, Our Lady of Lourdes, the cornerstone of which was laid on September 14, 1890. A. C. Prevost was operating the Pioneer House during 1890.

An attempt to establish a pay school in Slidell, with Mrs. E. Gill as the teacher was made in January 1891, with 21 children in attendance. The school was a financial failure and Mrs. Gill returned to New Orleans, only to be recalled when the Society of the Holy Name came up with the funding to pay the salary of the teacher. The school, which was called St. Aloysius, was free and open to all denominations, and was to be kept open for ten months per year.

The August 18, 1894, town election must have been a dilly. There was a tie vote in the mayor's race between C. F. McMahon and O. L. Dittmar, although the remainder of the McMahon ticket was elected. McMahon was eventually sworn in as mayor.

The *Farmer* said in 1894 that Slidell would be considered a boom town if it were out west: it had 1,500 inhabitants, new buildings going up, and its hotels full of guests from all parts of the country. Hotels mentioned were the Bird Cage Hotel, owned by E. H. Linton, and Mrs. Eunice Carroll's Hotel, which unfortunately burned down only a week after the *Farmer* reported on its prosperity. The Crescent Hotel, owned by Captain Cornelius Cooper, was also in operation in Slidell at that time.

In 1895, a new Methodist church was being built by Horace Rousseaux and Gus McKinney; F. A. Bourgeois and R. Richie built new stores; and the Slidell Brick Works filled an order for 1,000,000 bricks to be used in the construction of the new St. Charles Hotel in New Orleans. Another economic boost was received when Mississippi voted itself dry in 1895. Slidell was reported to be doing a brisk "jug trade" with people from Mississippi. The enterprising William King maintained a bar on a flat boat moored on the Louisiana side of the Pearl River, just across from Pearlington. He is reported to have shot and killed one of his customers in May 1895.

It was also in 1895 that the Slidell-Covington rivalry first manifested itself. A new courthouse was to be built, and the Slidellians felt that it should be located in their town, which they, with some reason, thought to be the most important town, economically, in the parish. However, the courthouse remained in Covington.

In December 1899, there was another close mayor's race in Slidell, resulting in yet another tie vote between J. M. Curry and the indefatigable O. L. Dittmar. This time, the commission as mayor was issued to Mr. Dittmar.

The 1900 census showed that the estimates made of Slidell's population in 1894 were somewhat optimistic, but the town did have an impressive growth, from 364 in 1890 to 1,129 in 1900. The population jumped from 1,129 in 1900 to 2,188 in 1910 and 2,958 in 1920, making it then the largest town in the parish. In 1901, a letter said that it had six churches, five saloons, six stores, three schools, four fruit stands, three barber shops, one saw mill, two brickyards, and "several other things too numerous to mention."

On December 15, 1903, the Slidell branch of the Covington Bank and Trust Company was opened, the first banking institution in the town. This branch soon broke off from its parent and became the Bank of Slidell, which still exists as the First Bank, with branches throughout the parish. By 1907, it had assets of $131,109.24.

The Slidell Progressive League was formed in 1905. The *Farmer* reviewed the growth of Slidell in a 1907 article:

At the present we have: banks, hotels, schools, boating, hunting, fishing, farming, churches, newspaper, telephones, shipyards, lumber mills, brick plants, creosote works, artesian water, electric lights, a $50,000 ice factory, $25,000 school building, a $5,000 new town hall, $20,000 wholesale grocery. A $5,000 steel bridge will be erected in the near future; in fact, work has begun upon all.

. . . .

Two well-kept hotels furnish accomodation to the local and traveling public. Boating in one of the pleasures, there being a number of motor boats. There are also a number of vessels used for extensive commerce, for import and export shipments of bricks and lumber.

Religious denominations are Baptist, Presbyterian, Methodist, Catholic and Episcopal.

Fraternal societies: Knights of Pythias, Woodmen of the World, Masons, I.O.R.M. and others.

Farming is not on a very extensive scale, but sugar cane, rice, potatoes and vegetables are profitable.

A. Provost, who has been a resident of the parish for some 50 years, gives as a result of his experience, 200 bushels of sweet potatoes to the acre.

Dairying is an undeveloped but profitable industry. I. Usanaz has a herd of nearly forty cows. He can produce milk at a cost of 10 cents a gallon. Food is high in price now but cheaper in summer season.

There was still no fire department in Slidell in 1910. Another milestone was reached in 1911, when Slidell had the only accredited high school in the parish. In 1913, a YMCA was organized.

In August 1914, a new shipyard was built in Slidell, and in January 1917, a 229-foot wooden ship was built by the Slidell Shipbuilding Corporation, F. W. Salmen, president. During World War I, as we have seen, the shipbuilding industry in Slidell became really big business. Unfortunately, at the war's end, the Slidell shipyards suffered the same fate as those in Madisonville.

Of course, none of that can compare with the boom which began in the mid-1950's, which has made Slidell the population and commercial center of the parish.

Epilogue

I guess history stops when you begin running into people you know. At any rate, the history of St. Tammany Parish stops for me in about 1920. This history will not contain such items as the great satsuma and tung nut booms, or the effect of the Depression, or the decline of the railroads and the disappearance of the lake trade. Nor will we discuss the coming of the Five Mile Bridge, also known as the Watson-Williams Bridge, also known as the Maestri Bridge, which tied Slidell to New Orleans; or the Lake Pontchartrain Causeway, which did the same to the west end of the parish; or of Interstate Highways 10 and 12; or of the resulting population boom of the 50's, 60's, and 70's which still continues.

I will not write of how the lumber companies despoiled the parish of its greatest asset, its beauty, because the parish has almost restored itself, despite the best efforts of man. Whether it can rise above the efforts of the developers, who yearly encroach more and more on the recently restored land remains to be seen.

When you think that man has for over 250 years extracted from St. Tammany Parish her wildlife, her trees and their products, her water, her clay, her gravel, her shell, her sand; and has dirtied her air and her streams; we must think how fortunate we are that so much remains. Let us hope that we can keep it so.

Notes

PROLOGUE

p. 3   Pierre Le Moyne
        J. F. H. Claiborne, *Mississippi as a Province, Territory and State.*
        Jackson: Power and Barksdale, 1880. Reprint. Baton Rouge:
        Louisiana State University Press, 1964, p. 17.
        Frederick Austin Ogg, *The Opening of the Mississippi.* New York:
        Cooper Square Publishers, Inc., 1968, p. 174.
        Pierre Margry, *Decouvertes et etablissements des francois dans l'ouest et*
            dans le sud de L'Amerique septentrionale. 6 vols. Paris: D.
            Jouaust, 1880, pp. 187, 188.

CHAPTER I

p. 5   The combination of—Background material for this chapter comes
        from:
        Claiborne, *Mississippi as a Province,* p. 17.
        Ogg, *The Opening of the Mississippi,* p. 174.
        Margry, *Decouvertes et etablissements,* pp. 187-188.

p. 9   He then proceeded—Margry, *Decouvertes et etablissements,* pp. 159-160.
        The chief of—*Ibid.,* pp. 172-173.
        When he arrived—*Ibid.,* p. 184.

p. 10   On the evening—*Ibid.,* p. 188.
        On March 28, 1699—*Ibid.,* p. 188.
        On the next—*Ibid.,* pp. 188-189.
        A league, as—*Webster's Third New International Dictionary,* 4th ed., s.v.
        "league."
        After finding the—Margry, *Decouvertes et etablissements,* p. 189.
        Sauvole tells us—Jay Higginbotham, *Journal of Sauvole.* Mobile: Colo-
        nial Books, 1969, p. 34.
        Iberville was looking—Ogg, *Opening of the Mississippi,* p. 181.
        After returning to—Margry, *Decouvertes et etablissements,* p. 192.

p. 11   He had decided—*Ibid.,* p. 194.
        He called it—Jay Higginbotham, *Fort Maurepas.* Mobile: Colonial
        Books, 1968, p. 32.

CHAPTER II

p. 12   In his journal—Margry, *Decouvertes et etablissements,* p. 184.
        If Iberville had—Background material for this chapter is taken from:
        J. Ashley Sibley, Jr., *A Study of the Geology of Baton Rouge and*
            Surrounding Southeast Louisiana Area. Baton Rouge: Claitor's
            Publishing Division, 1972.
        Charles Schuchert and Carl O. Dunbar, *Outlines of Historical*
            Geology, 4th ed. New York: John Wiley & Sons, Inc., 1947.
        Grover E. Murray, *Geology of the Atlantic and Gulf Coastal Province*
            of North America. New York: Harper & Brothers, 1961.

Roger T. Saucier, *Recent Geomorphic History of the Pontchartrain Basin.* Baton Rouge: Louisiana State University Press, 1963. Fred Kniffen, "Nature's St. Tammany," *St. Tammany Historical Society Gazette,* Vol. 2, 1977.

CHAPTER III

p. 15   It is not—William G. Haag, "Louisiana in North American Prehistory," *Melanges,* No. 1, 1971. Baton Rouge: Louisiana State University Press, p. 3.
Remains of the—*Ibid.,* p. 3.
However, some arrowheads—Private collections of Paula Patecek Johnson and Shirley Rester.
There are three—Saucier, *Recent Geomorphic History,* pp. 58-59; Haag, "Louisiana in North American Prehistory," p. 40.
The Archaic Indians—Haag, "Louisiana in North American Prehistory," p. 7.

p. 17   The famous Poverty—Saucier, *Recent Geomorphic History,* p. 59; Haag, "Louisiana in North American Prehistory," p. 40.
The Poverty Point—*Ibid.,* p. 10.
It was first—James A. Ford and George I. Quimby, Jr., "The Tchefuncte Culture, an Early Occupation of the Lower Mississippi Valley," *Memoirs of the Society for American Archaeology,* No. 2. Menasha, Wis.: Society for American Archaeology and Louisiana State University Press, 1945.
It flourished between—Haag, "Louisiana in North American Prehistory," p. 15.
The Marksville—Saucier, *Recent Geomorphic History,* p. 17.
The Coles Creek—*Ibid.,* pp. 81-82; Haag, "Louisiana in North American Prehistory," p. 22.
The famous Pontchartrain—Saucier, *Recent Geomorphic History,* pp. 108-109.
The Plaquemine Historic—*Ibid.,* pp. 85, 87; Haag, "Louisiana in North American Prehistory," p. 26.

p. 18   Apparently, during this—John R. Swanton, *Indian Tribes of North America,* Bulletin 145, Bureau of American Ethnology, Smithsonian Institution. Washington: U.S. Government Printing Office, 1952, p. 196.

CHAPTER IV

p. 19   Shortly after Iberville—Margry, *Decouvertes et etablissement,* p. 200.
The French were—Higginbotham, *Journal of Sauvole,* pp. 24-25.

p. 20   An early chronicle—Glenn R. Conrad, ed., *Historical Journal of the Settlement of the French in Louisiana,* Virginia Koenig and Joan Cain, translators. Lafayette: University of Southwestern Louisiana, 1971, pp. 21, 22.
In May 1700—Ruth Lapham Butler, *Journal of Paul Du Ru.* Chicago: The Caxton Club, 1934, p. 65.

p. 21   Sometime later, probably—Richebourg Gaillard McWilliams, *Fleur de Lys and Calumet.* Baton Rouge: Louisiana State University Press, 1953, pp. 100, 101.

In the spring—*Ibid.,* p. 106.

p. 26   Penicaut was once—*Ibid.,* p. 144.

p. 27   Le Page Du Pratz—Le Page Du Pratz, *History of Louisiana.* London, 1774. Reprint. Baton Rouge: Claitor's Publishing Division, 1972, pp. 193-194.

According to Penicaut—McWilliams, *Fleur de Lys,* p. 219; Charles O'Neill, *Charlevoix's Louisiana.* London and Baton Rouge: Louisiana State University Press, 1977, p. 166.

By 1725, they—Dunbar Rowland and A. G. Sanders, *Mississippi Provincial Archives, 1704-1743,* Vol. III. Jackson: Press of the Mississippi Department of Archives and History, 1927, p. 535.

Shortly thereafter, the—John R. Swanton, *Indians of the Southeastern United States,* Bulletin 137, Bureau of American Ethnology, Smithsonian Institution. Washington: U.S. Government Printing Office, 1946, p. 82.

One Spanish document—A. G. I., Cuba, Legajo 216B, Report to Charles Parent, June 1788.

Other tribes which—Swanton, *Indians of the Southeastern,* pp. 96, 121; Swanton, *Indian Tribes,* pp. 174-180.

p. 29   A 1759 affidavit—"Index to Spanish Judicial Records," LHQ, Vol. 8, pp. 523-524.

In 1761 they—*Rillieux's Heirs v. Singletary,* 17 La. 88 (1841).

In about 1725—Swanton, *Indian Tribes,* p. 136.

The Choctaw were—*Ibid.,* p. 180.

French records indicate—RSC, LHQ, Vol. 19, pp. 768-771.

Spanish records dated—A. G. I., supra. Parent to Gayoso de Lemos, July 18, 1798; Report of June 1788; Letter to Parent, June 9, 1790; Letter from Parent, 1788; Letter from Parent, 1792.

Later they are—Dagmar Renshaw Lebreton, *Chahta Ima.* Baton Rouge: Louisiana State University Press, 1947; David I. Bushnell, Jr., *The Choctaw of Bayou Lacomb, St. Tammany Parish, Louisiana.* Bulletin 44, Bureau of American Ethnology, Smithsonian Institution.

However, as late—Clarence Edwin Carter, ed., *Territorial Papers of the United States, Orleans Territory,* Vol. IX. Washington: U.S. Government Printing Office, 1940, p. 62.

There is also—Dunbar Rowland, ed., *Official Letter Books of W. C. C. Claiborne,* 1801-1816. Jackson: State Department of Archives and History, 1917. Vol. VI, pp. 267, 269, 233, 234.

CHAPTER V

p. 30   In 1718, Bienville—Heloise Hulse Cruzat, "New Orleans Under Bienville," LHQ, Vol. 1, 1918, pp. 77-79.

In 1723, he—*Ibid.,* p. 79.

In August 1699—McWilliams, *Fleur de Lys,* pp. 16-17.

p. 31   The first permanent—Archives, Louisiana State Museum, Petition of
        Pierre Brou to Superior Council, August 22, 1725; RSC, LHQ,
        Vol. 7, 1924, p. 681.
        Brou, whose signature—Charles R. Maduell, Jr., *The Census Tables for
        the French Colony of Louisiana from 1699 through 1732.* Baltimore:
        Genealogical Publishing Co., Inc., 1972, p. 96.
        In 1745, he—Pierre Boyer's Will, RSC, LHQ, Vol. 13, 1930, p. 677.

p. 32   Another early resident—Archives, Louisiana State Museum, "Pe-
        tition of Rene Chairman to Superior Council," January 3, 1726;
        RSC, LHQ, Vol. 3, 1920, p. 141.
        Du Chesne appears in—Maduell, *Census Tables,* p. 96.
        Du Chesne died shortly—RSC, LHQ, Vol. 5, pp. 107-108, 111, 116;
        Vol. 8, p. 141.
        Others who are—Maduell, *Census Tables,* p. 96.
        Jean Vis has—J. Hanno Deiler, *Settlement of the German Coast of Louisi-
        ana and the Creoles of German Descent.* Philadelphia: German
        American Historical Society, 1909. Reprint. Baltimore: Genea-
        logical Publishing Company, 1970, p. 98.
        During its early—John G. Clark, *New Orleans, 1718-1812.* Baton
        Rouge: Louisiana State University Press, 1970, p. 3.
        Among the industries—*Ibid.,* p. 28.
        The method by—du Pratz, *History of Louisiana,* pp. 193-194.

p. 34   In early 1735—RSC, LHQ, Vol. 5, pp. 267-268.
        Originally Bunel and—RSC, LHQ, Vol. 5, p. 259; Vol. 8, p. 119.
        In August 1735—RSC, LHQ, Vol. 5, p. 271.
        We do not—RSC, LHQ, Vol. 8, p. 287.
        A new partner—RSC, LHQ, Vol. 9, pp. 129, 173.
        On October 12, 1737—RSC, LHQ, Vol. 9, p. 518.
        The last mention—RSC, LHQ, Vol. 9, p. 518.
        On June 20, 1736—Archives, Louisiana State Museum, Lease among
        Francois Hamont and Louis Joseph Bizoton and Claude La-
        combe, June 20, 1736; RSC, LHQ, Vol. 8, p. 296.
        The Bizoton-Lacombe—Archives, Louisiana State Museum, Partner-
        ship Agreement between Jean Baptiste de Chavannes and
        Claude Vignon, D^t Lacombe, October 2, 1738; RSC, LHQ, Vol.
        10, p. 123.

p. 35   In April 1739—Archives, Louisiana State Museum, Partnership
        Agreement among Claude Vignon, D^t Lacombe, Jean Baptiste
        de Chavannes, and Jacques Chenier, April 26, 1739; RSC, LHQ,
        Vol. 6, p. 500.
        In March 1739—Archives, Louisiana State Museum, Contract and
        Boat Plans— Charles Lemoine and Jean Moreau with Jean Bap-
        tiste de Chavannes and Claude Vignon, D^t Lacombe, March 9,
        1739; RSC, LHQ, Vol. 6, p. 305.
        Unfortunately, the builders—RSC, LHQ, Vol. 6, p. 672, 678.
        It was in—RSC, LHQ, Vol. 7, p. 499.
        On January 4, 1739—RSC, LHQ, Vol. 6, p. 288.
        In fact, the—RSC, LHQ, Vol. 6, p. 310.

Alas, for true—RSC, LHQ, Vol. 10, p. 424, 430.
In 1745, Lacombe—RSC, LHQ, Vol. 14, pp. 452, 454.
On March 6, 1746—RSC, LHQ, Vol. 15, pp. 515, 516.
On March 9, 1748—RSC, LHQ, Vol. 17, p. 560; Vol. 18, p. 448.
Lacombe had made—"Nuncupative Will of Vignon, So-called Lacombe," LHQ, Vol. 3, p. 567; RSC, LHQ, Vol. 18, p. 714.

p. 36   Other than the—RSC, LHQ, Vol. 7, p. 494.
Jaffre was living—"Early Census Tables of Louisiana," Jay K. Ditch, trans. LHQ, Vol. 13, p. 215.
Although he was—Maduell, *Census Tables*, p. 96.
In 1728, he—RSC, LHQ, Vol. 4, p. 500.
La Liberte had a—RSC, LHQ, Vol. 7, p. 491.
On January 16, 1740—RSC, LHQ, Vol. 10, pp. 271-272, 423-429; Archives, Louisiana State Museum, Inventory, Succession of Jaffre, March 18, 1740.

p. 37   Mme. Jaffre did—RSC, LHQ, Vol. 10, p. 413.
Antoine Aufrere operated—RSC, LHQ, Vol. 19, p. 710.
In April 1735,—RSC, LHQ, Vol. 5, p. 264.
He was originally—RSC, LHQ, Vol. 5, pp. 401-403, 421; Archives, Louisiana State Museum, Inventory, Succession of St. Julien, October 9, 1736.
Aufrere's next partnership—RSC, LHQ, Vol. 10, pp. 103, 123, 126.
In December 1738—RSC, LHQ, Vol. 6, p. 287.

p. 38   In January 1739—RSC, LHQ, Vol. 6, p. 295.
In one case—RSC, LHQ, Vol. 7, p. 492.
The interrogation of—RSC, LHQ, Vol. 19, p. 768.
The north shore—RSC, LHQ, Vol. 3, p. 444.
Francois Hery, called—RSC, LHQ, Vol. 15, pp. 515, 516.
He called it—Mary A. Petersen, "British West Florida: Abstracts of Land Petitions," LGR, Vol. 18, No. 4, pp. 318, 336.
Jean Baptiste Baudreau—RSC, LHQ, Vol. 18, p. 722; RSC, LHQ, Vol. 21, pp. 887-892.

p. 39   Jacques Milhet and—RSC, LHQ, Vol. 25, p. 562.
As early as—*Rillieux's Heirs v. Singletary*, #495, 8th Judicial District Court, St. Tammany Parish; 17 La. 83 (1841); Jay Higginbotham, *Family Biographies*. Mobile: Colonial Books, 1967, p. 24.
After Francois' death—Walter Lowrie, *American State Papers*, Vol. V, pp. 533, 534. Washington: Duff Green, 1834.
Since they neglected—*Heirs of Vincent Rillieux v. The United States*, No. 18, U. S. District Court, Eastern District of Louisiana.

p. 40   Francois Rillieux's son—Higginbotham, *Family Biographies*, p. 25.
The family sold—*Heirs of Vincent Rillieux to John Gusman*, October 27, 1838, Book G-1, p. 100. Office of the Clerk of Court, St. Tammany Parish.
Another large tract—Lowrie, *American State Papers*, Vol. V, p. 533.
Besides running a—*Succession of Vincent Rillieux*, No. 112 ¾, Probate Court, St. Tammany Parish.

CHAPTER VI

p. 42   In 1755, the—Background material for this chapter comes from:

William L. Langer, *Encyclopedia of World History*. Boston: Houghton-Mifflin Company, 1948.

Samuel Eliot Morison and Henry Steele Commager, *Growth of the American Republic*. New York: Oxford University Press, 1942.

Claiborne, *Mississippi As a Province*.

Ogg, *Opening of the Mississippi*.

By a proclamation—"Proclamation Respecting New Governments in America," LHQ, Vol. 13, p. 611.

p. 43   In 1776, Montfort—Mary A. Petersen, "Montfort Browne, Soldier and Lieutenant Governor," LGR, Vol. 18, p. 231.

Captain Harry Gordon—"New Orleans and Bayou St. John in 1766," LHQ, Vol. 6, p. 19.

In his "Observations—Jacob Blackwell, "A Contemporary English View on the Trade and Prospects of New Orleans at the Close of the French Dominion," extract from "Observations on West Florida." LHQ, Vol. 6, p. 221.

p. 46   The earliest British—Petersen, "British West Florida," LGR, Vol. 18, p. 336.

A few British—All information on British settlers is taken from article by Petersen, which appears in the *Register* from Vol. 18, 1971 through Vol. 20, 1973.

CHAPTER VII

Background material from this chapter was taken from:

John Walton Caughey, *Bernardo de Galvez in Louisiana, 1776-1783*. Gretna: Pelican Publishing Company, 1972.

Frederick Stephen Ellis, "American Activity in Louisiana during the Revolutionary War," *St. Tammany Historical Society Gazette*, Vol. 1, 1975.

James Alton James, *Oliver Pollock, The Life and Times of an Unknown Patriot*. New York and London: D. Appleton-Century Company, 1937.

p. 50   As early as—Pollock to the President of Congress, September 18, 1782, Records and Papers of the Continental Congress, Vol. 50, pp. 1-13; Sparks Ms., Vol. 41, The Houghton Library, Harvard University.

In 1776, Oliver—Pollock to Congress, October 10, 1776, Sparks Ms., The Houghton Library, Harvard University, Vol. 41; Pollock to the President of Congress, September 18, 1782, supra.

Pollock, an unsung—Pollock to the President of Congress, September 18, 1782, supra.

In April 1777—Galvez to Galvez, May 12, 1777, A.G.I., Sto. Domingo, Legajo 2596; British Merchants to Lloyd, A.G.I. Cuba, Legajo 188.

p. 51   Galvez seized all—Galvez to Galvez, May 12, 1777, supra.

Among the vessels—Pollock to Congress, May 4, 1777, Sparks Ms., supra; Review of Proceedings, A.G.I. Sto. Domingo, Legajo 2652.

When the goods—Pollock to Congress, April 1, 1778; July 6, 1778, Sparks Ms., supra; December 15, 1778, Records and Papers of the Continental Congress; Pollock to the President of Congress, September 18, 1782, supra.

p. 52   In retaliation for—Burdon to Galvez, April 21, 1778, A.G.I. Cuba, Legajo 191; Galvez to Nunn, April 22, 1778, A.G.I., Sto. Domingo, Legajo 2547; Galvez to Nunn, April 29, 1778, A.G.I. Cuba, Legajo 191.

He resolved to—Galvez to Navarro, August 18, 1779 and October 16, 1779, A.G.I., Cuba, Legajo 2358.

Be that as—Pickles to Piernas, September 12, 1779, A.G.I. Cuba, Legajo 192.

p. 53   Lieutenant Rousseau wrote—Pierre Rousseau, Relacion du Combat de la Goelette Taindre de la Frigate Maurice Capne Guillaume Pickles Americaine, contre le Bateau Le Ouest Floride de Panzacol Capitainne Painne, September 12, 1779, A.G.I. Cuba, Legajo 2358.

p. 54   Captain Pickles shortly—Caughey, *Bernardo de Galvez,* p. 160.

p. 55   Shortly before the—Caughey, *Bernardo de Galvez,* p. 161.

Captain Pickles continued—Presa Hecha por el Corsario La Corbeta de la Fragata La Moreis de los Estados Unidos de America su Capn Guillermo Pickles, 1779, A.G.I., Cuba, Legajo 701.

On September 21st—Capitulation of the Inhabitants of the Settlements on Lake Pontchartrain, October 16, 1779, Records and Papers of the Continental Congress, supra; Claiborne, *Mississippi as a Province,* p. 122.

p. 56   It is doubtful—Galvez to Navarro, October 16, 1779, supra.

CHAPTER VIII

p. 58   It was during—All inferences regarding population patterns are drawn from information gleaned from Walter Lowrie, *American State Papers,* Vols. IV and V; U.S. Government Surveys of St. Tammany Parish.

Shortly after the—Pintado map.

The first commandant—Ethel Boagni, "The Commandant of the Tchefuncta," *St. Tammany Historical Society Gazette,* Vol. 1, September, 1975, p. 22.

Parent's major business—Archives of the Spanish Government of West Florida, Vol. VIII, p. 313.

p. 60   In 1788, he—Unsigned order, June 7, 1788, A.G.I., Cuba, Legajo 216.

In 1790, Parent—Unsigned order, June 9, 1790, A. G. I., Cuba, Legajo 216.

Parent was also—Unsigned orders, March 21, 1794; 1793 (date illegible); 1793 (date illegible); October 15, 1792; 1790 (date illegible); May 14, 1793; April 28, 1794, A.G.I., Cuba, Legajo 216.

Another suit for—Unsigned order, 1792, A.G.I., Cuba, Legajo 216.

Others who suffered—Order Baron de Carondelet to Parent, August 7, 1794; unsigned order, date illegible; unsigned order, date illegible, A.G.I. Cuba, Legajo 216.

Parent was also—Unsigned order, date illegible; unsigned order, February 3, 1792, A.G.I. Cuba, Legajo 216.

He also was—Parent to Baron de Carondelet, September 27, 1793; unsigned order, September 11, 1793; unsigned order, May 11, 1798, A.G.I. Cuba, Legajo 216.

He also had—Unsigned order, date illegible; unsigned order, October 23, 1798, A.G.I., Cuba, Legajo 216.

On two occasions—Letter from Parent, January 4, 1789; letter, 1792, A.G.I., Cuba, Legajo 216.

Other names mentioned—Parent to Gayoso de Lemos date illegible, unsigned order, October 18, 1792; unsigned order, May 20, 1794, unsigned order, date illegible, A.G.I., Cuba, Legajo 216.

p. 63   The Spanish maintained—Unsigned order, date illegible, A.G.I., Cuba, Legajo 216.

Parent died in—Succession of Charles Parent, Archives of the Spanish Government of West Florida, Vol. VIII, p. 304.

Parent's son, Charles—Boagni, *The Commandant*, p. 26.

Some of the—Lowrie, *American State Papers*, Vols. IV and V.

CHAPTER IX

p. 65   Even before the—William E. Myer, *Indian Trails of the Southeast.* Forty-second Annual Report of the Bureau of American Ethnology. Washington: U.S. Government Printing Office, 1929.

There must have—Blackwell, "A Contemporary English View," p. 221.

In 1804, a—*Pintado Papers*, Book IV, pp. 195-196.

p. 66   A contemporaneous survey—*Pintado Papers*, Book VII, pp. 34, 39.

Another 1804 survey—*Pintado Papers*, Book V, pp. 25, 26, 29.

On October 18, 1804—*Spanish West Florida Records*, Vol. VIII, p. 336.

In October 1803,—Clarence Edwin Carter, *Territorial Papers of the United States*, Vol. IX. Washington: U.S. Government Printing Office, 1940, p. 72.

In November 1803—*Ibid.*, p. 113.

A final piece—Report of Anchorage Fees of Bayou St. John for 1803 by Don Juan de Castanedo. Records of City Council of New Orleans, 1794-1803, Book 4087, p. 92.

p. 67   Boat building, another—Ship Registers and Enrollments of New Orleans, Louisiana, Vol. 1, 1804-1820. Baton Rouge: Louisiana State University Press, 1941.

The policy of—Carter, *Territorial Papers*, Vol. IX, p. 193.

p. 68   An interesting survey—*Pintado Papers,* Book VII, p. 74.

p. 69   However, it did—Lowrie, *American State Papers.*
The most active—Succession of Charles Parent, *Records of the Spanish Government of West Florida,* Vol. VIII, p. 304.
Another action was—*Ibid.,* Vol. XIV, p. 264.

p. 70   The Succession of—*Ibid.,* Vol. XIV, p. 229.
Another 1808 proceeding—*Ibid.,* Vol. XIV. p. 42.
The Spanish records—*Ibid.,* XIII, p. 48.

CHAPTER X

p. 71   As time passed—Background material for this chapter is taken from Isaac Joslin Cox, *The West Florida Controversy, 1798-1813.* Baltimore: The Johns Hopkins Press, 1918.
Finally, on July—*Ibid.,* p. 346; James A. Padgett, ed., "Official Records of the West Florida Revolution and Republic," LHQ, Vol. 21, p. 688.
The "District of—Cox, *West Florida Controversy,* p. 346; Padgett, "Official Records of the West Florida Revolution," LHQ, Vol. 21, p. 688.
The convention, which—Padgett, "Official Records of the West Florida Revolution," LHQ, Vol. 21, pp. 690-691.

p. 72   Other grievances were—*Ibid*
On August 24, 1810,—*Ibid.,* p. 710.

p. 73   On August 29th—*Ibid.,* p. 715.
On October 24th—*Ibid.,* p. 746.
Cooper refused to—Cox, *West Florida Controversy,* p. 386.
Cooper, for his—James A. Padgett, "West Florida Revolution of 1810," LHQ, Vol. 21, p. 187; Padgett, "Official Records of the West Florida Revolution," LHQ, Vol. 21, p. 688n, 731; Cox, *West Florida Controversy,* p. 412.
It was not—Cox, *West Florida Controversy,* p. 408.
Colonel Philemon Thomas—Padgett, "Official Records of the West Florida Revolution," LHQ, Vol. 21, p. 720.

p. 74   The officers of—*Ibid.,* p. 721.
The convention then—*Ibid.,* p. 730.
On September 30th—*Ibid.,* p. 730.
General Thomas was—*Ibid.,* p. 731.

p. 75   General Thomas, at—*Ibid.,* p. 739.
Under the new—*Ibid.,* pp. 755, 766, 767.
On November 19th—*Ibid.,* pp. 755, 766.

p. 77   On November 22nd—*Ibid.,* pp. 756, 770.
Among less momentous—*Ibid.,* pp. 758, 759, 760, 771, 772, 774, 775, 776, 779.
On October 27th—Cox, *West Florida Controversy,* p. 489.
On December 7th—*Ibid.,* p. 501.

CHAPTER XI

p. 78   On December 22,—Rowland, *Official Letter Books,* Vol. 5, p. 64.

p. 79   The name is—H. G. Morgan, Jr., "Tammany, Origin of Name," Publications of the Louisiana Historical Society, Vol. V, p. 54.

On April 24th—Act of Territorial Legislature, April 24, 1811.

Writing to Colonel—Carter, *Territorial Papers,* p. 908.

p. 81   Shortly thereafter, a—Powell A. Casey, "Military Roads and Camps in or near Covington and Madisonville, Louisiana," *St. Tammany Historical Society Gazette,* Vol. 2, p. 59.

In 1813, the—Henry Marie Brackenridge, *Views of Louisiana.* (1st ed., Pittsburgh, 1841). Chicago: Quadrangle Books, Inc., 1962.

In addition a—Casey, "Military Roads and Camps," p. 62.

On June 26,—*Ibid.,* p. 63.

p. 82   Writing to Robert—Rowland, *Official Letter Books,* Vol. 5, p. 62.

Despite that problem—Carter, *Territorial Papers,* Vol. IX, pp. 983-985.

Outside of the—*Ibid.*

After an extended—Lillie Richardson, "The Admission of Louisiana into the Union," LHQ, Vol. 1, p. 333.

In the more—LGR, Vol. XVIII, No. 3, p. 247.

p. 85   On the other—*Ibid.,* Vol. XVI, No. 4, p. 336.

In his message—Rowland, *Official Letter Books,* Vol. VI, p. 150.

Claiborne continued to—*Ibid.,* Vol. VI, p. 161.

The 1811-1812—Original tax roll, Archives, Office of the St. Tammany Parish Clerk of Court.

The 1812 tax—Original tax roll, Archives, Office of the St. Tammany Parish Clerk of Court.

p. 86   There were also—*Ibid.*

The sale of—Sale, John Gustavus to Packwood & Price, August 31, 1812, COB A-1, Folio 37, Conveyance Records, Office of the St. Tammany Parish Clerk of Court.

As to immigration—Lowrie, *American State Papers.*

CHAPTER XII

p. 87   In September 1812—Letter, Claiborne to Holmes, September 21, 1812. Rowland, *Official Letter Books,* Vol. VI, p. 182.

In the spring—Letter, Claiborne to Armstrong, April 14, 1813. Rowland, *Official Letter Books,* Vol. VI, p. 233.

Governor Claiborne later—Rowland, *Official Letter Books,* Vol. VI, p. 267.

Jacques Dreux, who—*Pintado Papers,* Book IV, p. 29.

Possibly as early—Adrian D. Schwartz, *Sesquicentennial in St. Tammany,* Covington City Council, 1963.

In 1813, the—Sale, Dreux to Collins, May 13, 1813, COB A-1, Folio 283, Conveyance Records, St. Tammany Parish.

p. 88   By legislative act—Act of the Louisiana Legislature, March 11, 1816.

One of these—*Louisiana Progress,* April 15, 1938, p. 12.

The other story—Powell A. Casey, "Military Roads in the Florida
   Parishes of Louisiana," Louisiana History, Vol. XV, p. 320n.
The first election—*Farmer,* May 15, 1915.
In 1798, a—*Pintado Papers,* Book VII, p. 34.
In 1814, a—Copy of original map of McCarty made by H. Curtis,
   September 2, 1841, Archives, Clerk of Court, St. Tammany Par-
   ish.
Madisonville was incorporated—Act of Louisiana Legislature, Feb-
   ruary 18, 1817.
In 1813, a—Brackenridge, *Views of Louisiana,* p. 281.

p. 90   By legislative act—Act of Louisiana Legislature, March 25, 1813.

p. 91   In 1817, an—Act of Louisiana Legislature, February 18, 1817.
         The people must—Act of Louisiana Legislature, March 16, 1818.
         This location was—Bond, Ligon et al to Parish Judge, July 10, 1818,
            COB A-1, folio 240, Records of St. Tammany Parish.
         Despite his otherwise—Letter, Claiborne to Flournoy, September
            29, 1813. Rowland, *Official Letter Books,* Vol. VI, p. 271.

p. 93   In early 1814—Howard I. Chapelle, *American Sailing Navy.* New York:
            Norton, 1949, p. 292.
         Some historians believe—Casey, "Military Roads and Camps," p. 62.
         A bomb ketch—Powell A. Casey, *Louisiana in the War of 1812,* 1963,
            p. 10.
         On December 16—*Ibid.,* p. 19.
         The 13th Regiment—*Ibid.,* pp. 38, 39.
         The commanding officer—*Ibid.,* p. 39.
         Elements of the—Powell A. Casey, *The Battle of New Orleans.* The
            Battle of New Orleans, 150th Anniversary, Committee of Louisi-
            ana, 1965, p. 75.
         The 13th Regiment—Casey, *Louisiana in the War of 1812,* pp. xi-xiv.
         After the British—Order Book, Louisiana Militia, Louisiana State
            Library, General Order of March 7, 1815.
         An affidavit made—Archives, St. Tammany Historical Society.

p. 94   The same cannot—"General David B. Morgan's Defense of the Con-
            duct of the Louisiana Militia in the Battle on the Left Side of the
            River," LHQ, Vol. 9, p. 16.

p. 95   When General Jackson—*Major Howell Tatum's Journal while Acting
            Topographical Engineer (1814) to General Jackson,* Smith College
            Studies on History, Vol. VII, October 1921 to April 1922, John
            Spencer Bassett and Sidney Bradshaw, eds. Northampton,
            Mass.: Department of History, Smith College.

p. 96   Alston's is the—Sale, Alston to Chappell, April 22, 1818, COB A-1,
            folio 318; sale, Alston to Chappell, April 22, 1818, COB A-1,
            folio 320; sale, Alston to Chappell, July 19, 1819, COB A-1, folio
            340, Conveyance Records, St. Tammany Parish, Louisiana.

p. 97   It was here—Act of Louisiana Legislature, January 13, 1821; U.S.
            Government Survey, T4S, R12E.
         One hundred and—Lowrie *American State Papers.*

In 1819, Washington—Act of Louisiana Legislature, March 6, 1819.
In the next—U.S. Census of 1820.

p. 99 Boat building had not—Ship Registers and Enrollments of New Orleans, Louisiana, Vol. 1, 1804-1820, Louisiana State University, 1941.
One last look—Lowrie, *American State Papers,* Vol. III, p. 475.

CHAPTER XIII

p. 101 The direct route—Casey, "Military Roads in the Florida Parishes," p. 237.
The road was—Act of Louisiana Legislature, March 24, 1822.

p. 102 There must have—Act of Louisiana Legislature, February 14, 1821.
An indication of—Act of Louisiana Legislature, January 13, 1821.
In those days—C. M. Kerr, "Highway Progress in Louisiana," Minutes, St. Tammany Parish Police Jury. LHQ, Vol. 2, p. 67.
In the middle—U.S. Government Survey.

p. 103 This second survey—*Ibid.*
There is no—Minutes, St. Tammany Parish Police Jury, June 4, 1833, Louisiana State University Library.
The Mandeville-Bayou—Survey in case of *Letchworth v. Bartell,* No. 225, 8th Judicial District Court, St. Tammany Parish.
In the years—Ship Registers and Enrollments of New Orleans, Louisiana, Vol. II, 1821-1830, Louisiana State University, 1942.
The years 1830—*Ibid.,* Vol. III, 1831-1840, 1942.
The first steamboat—Letter. W. H. Seymour, *Farmer,* August 17, 1901.

p. 104 In 1832, William—Ship Registers, Vol. III, p. 51.
In 1833, William—*Ibid.,* p. 174.
Another steamboat was—*Ibid.,* p. 24.
On Sunday morning—*New Orleans Bee,* April 14, 1834.
The same group—Ship Registers, Vol. III, pp. 17-19.
The increase in—Lighthouses of the United States, Document No. 62, pp. 100-101; Department of Transportation, United States Coast Guard, Lighthouses and Light ships of the Northern Gulf of Mexico, p. 28.

p. 105 The Bonfouca light—*Ibid.,* p. 31.
The keeper of—Correspondence, Fifth Auditor of the Treasury Department, 1820-1852; *Journal 1842,* Tchefuncta Lighthouse, 1842, Archives, Louisiana State University Library.
It has been—*New Orleans Daily States,* July 7, 1890, p. 2, col. 1.
John M. Tate—J. M. Tate, "Covington Years Ago," *Farmer,* October 21, 1911.
The population of—U.S. Census, 1840.

p. 106 One old document—Map of Bayou Bonfouca, Succession of Pierre Thomas Robert *et ux,* No. 9 ¾, Probate Court, St. Tammany Parish.
During the decade—U.S. Census, 1840.

Mr. Hennen was—Tate, "Covington Years Ago," December 2, 1911.
Major Tatum mentioned—Bassett, *Major Howell Tatum's Journal,* pp. 94-96.
In 1821, Jeremiah—Act of Louisiana Legislature, January 9, 1821.
Two other early—U.S. Census, 1830, 1840, 1850.
By 1850, the—U.S. Census, 1850.

p. 108   The 1850 agricultural—U.S. Agricultural Census, 1850.

p. 109   An unusual crop—Advertisement, *Louisiana Advocate,* August—, 1839, photocopy in Archives, St. Tammany Historical Society.
These were sold—Sale, Lacroix to Trois, *et al.,* September 27, 1839, Archives, Clerk of Court, St. Tammany Parish.
Also in 1839—Lease, Louise Tabymaun to Richard H. Crawford, February 18, 1839, MOB G, folio 76, Mortgage Records, St. Tammany Parish.
In 1850, Jules—U.S. Census, 1850.

CHAPTER XIV

p. 110   There were no—U.S. Abstract Book, Office of Clerk of Court, St. Tammany Parish.
During the mid-1820s—Sale, Bonnabel to Marigny, June 29, 1829, COB B-1, folio 498; Sale, Bonnabel to Marigny, June 29, 1829, COB B-1, folio 503, Conveyance Records, St. Tammany Parish.
The stories that—W. Adolphe Roberts, *Lake Pontchartrain.* Indianapolis and New York: The Bobbs-Merrill Company, 1946, p. 105.
In the 1830s—Clarence L. Johnson, "The Family of Marigny de Mandeville and the Fountainebleau Plantation," *Louisiana Conservation Review,* Vol. 8, pt. 4, Summer, 1939, p. 40. Louisiana Department of Conservation.

p. 111   In July 1837—*The New Orleans Bee,* July 11, 1837.
Lewisburg, which lies—Plat of Lewisburg, Archives, Clerk of Court, St. Tammany Parish.
Another real estate—Sale, Hart to Jacobs, November 22, 1836, COB E-1, folio 575, Conveyance Records, St. Tammany Parish, and other sales by Hart.
Another early attempt—COB D-1, folio 346, Conveyance Records, St. Tammany Parish.
In 1819, the—Background information on early attempts at education is taken from James W. Mobley, "The Academy Movement in Louisiana," LHQ, Vol. 30, p. 738; Act of Louisiana Legislature, March 6, 1819.
Probably in answer—Sale, Gibson to Trustees of the Covington School, November 10, 1820, COB A-1, folio 502, Conveyance Records, St. Tammany Parish.
Two years later—Sale, Collins to Covington School, September 18, 1812, COB A-1, folio 624, Conveyance Records, St. Tammany Parish.

p. 113   In 1823, the—Timothy Flint, *Recollections of the Last Ten Years in the*

Valley of the Mississippi. Boston: Cummings, Hilliard and Company, 1826 (Southern Illinois University Press Reprint, 1968) p. 227.

In 1820, the—Act of Louisiana Legislature, February 16, 1820.

Then, by Act—Act 10 of 1828, Louisiana Legislature.

Another step forward—Act 103 of 1837, Louisiana Legislature.

Reverend S. B. Hall—Tate, "Covington Years Ago," October 28, 1911; *Farmer,* February 23, 1907.

p. 114   Another school was—Act 86 of 1837, Louisiana Legislature.

The 1840 census—U.S. Census, 1840.

The school system—U.S. Census, 1850.

In 1844, Mandeville—Mobley, "The Academy Movement," pp. 916-917.

p. 115   In 1853, records—Unsigned and untitled document, Archives, Clerk of Court, St. Tammany Parish.

The earliest formal—E. Russ Williams, *Kinsmen All,* Bogalusa, 1964.

In 1823, Reverend—Flint, *Recollections of the Last Ten Years,* p. 227.

p. 118   The present Presbyterian—Adrian D. Schwartz, *Sesquicentennial in St. Tammany,* Covington City Council, Covington, 1963, p. 37.

The Presbyterian church—*New Orleans Times-Picayune,* November 13, 1944, p. 16, col. 6.

The Methodist church—Robert C. Carter, *Methodist Historical Commemoration,* p. 6 (unpublished typewritten manuscript); Schwartz, *Sesquicentennial,* p. 37.

Christ Episcopal Church—Mrs. Amos Neff and others, Christ Episcopal Church; *Farmer,* March 25, 1916.

In the census—U.S. Census, 1850.

In 1832, the—James Rees, *Tales and Sketches,* Vol. III, 1852. Unpublished manuscript in possession of Mrs. Amos Neff.

p. 119   The original agreement—Agreement among Joseph D. Davenport and others, undated, Archives, Clerk of Court, St. Tammany Parish.

On July 21,—Rees, *Tales and Sketches.*

p. 120   Rees's "Journal of—*Ibid.*

p. 121   We also learn—*Ibid.*

The *Palladium* tells—*Ibid.*

The *Palladium* of—*Ibid.*

p. 122   In 1833, Joseph—Sale, Davenport to Mortee, September 17, 1833, Archives, Clerk of Court, St. Tammany Parish.

By 1839, Mr.—Clipping from *Louisiana Advocate,* August 1839, photocopy in Archives of St. Tammany Historical Society.

The 1850 census—U.S. Census, 1850.

One business that—*Eugene Lamuloniere v. His Creditors,* No. 788, 8th Judicial District Court, St. Tammany Parish.

In 1853, another—Tate, "Covington Years Ago," October 28, 1911.

p. 123   In 1850, two—*Deutsch Zeitung,* New Orleans, August 21, 1850, p. 3, col. 4.

One visitor described—*New Orleans Daily Picayune,* August 15, 1855, p. 2, col. 2.

p. 124   Probably foremost among—Affidavit of Jesse R. Jones, in Succession of Robert Badon, *et ux,* No. 84, Probate Court, St. Tammany Parish.

His original homestead—Lowrie, *American State Papers;* U.S. Government Survey, Township 6 South, Range 11 East; *Louisiana Progress,* April 15, 1938.

p. 125   Judge Jones was—*Farmer,* May 15, 1915; Judicial Archives, Office of Clerk of Court, St. Tammany Parish; Norma D. Core, Lists of Public Officials in St. Tammany Parish, Archives, Clerk of Court, St. Tammany Parish.

His letter to—Letter, Jones to Police Jury, May 29, 1830, Archives, Clerk of Court, St. Tammany Parish.

p. 126   Judge Jones operated—Brickyard Account for 1867, Jones-Hosmer-Buck Papers, Manuscript Department, Special Collections Division, Tulane University Library.

He also operated—*Louisiana Progress,* April 15, 1938.

He owned a—Numerous acquisitions, Conveyance Records, St. Tammany Parish.

Another important early—Letter, Claiborne to Warner, July 18, 1811, quoted in Williams, *Kinsmen All,* p. 9.

Judge Warner was—*Ibid.*

He was certainly—*Ibid.,* p. 8.

His daughter, Tabitha—*Ibid.,* p. 91.

p. 127   The Penn family—Core, Lists of Public Officials; James Calhoun, ed., *Louisiana Almanac,* 1975-1976. Gretna: Pelican Publishing Company, 1975, p. 358.

Penn's Mill, one—Tate, "Covington Years Ago," February 3, 1912.

He was successful—U.S. Census, 1830, 1840, 1850; Appointment as Justice of the Peace, Miscellaneous Collection, Louisiana State Museum; Core, Lists of Public Officials.

Other men whose—Core, Lists of Public Officials.

CHAPTER XV

p 129   The *Louisiana Advocate*—*Farmer,* February 23, 1907.

In 1851, a—*Ibid.;* Lee Lanier, "Bloody Tangipahoa," *Amite News Digest,* November 20, 1975, November 27, 1975, December 4, 1975.

The census of—U.S. Census, 1860.

p. 130   Not surprisingly, considering—U.S. Agricultural Census, 1860.

p. 131   On December 20—Chambers, *History of Louisiana,* Vol. 1, p. 626.

CHAPTER XVI

p. 132   Many of the—Records of assistance to families of soldiers, Archives, Clerk of Court, St. Tammany Parish.

Other companies which—Andrew B. Booth, *Records of Louisiana Confederate Soldiers and Louisiana Confederate Commands,* New Orleans, 1920, Vol. 1, pp. 12, 15.

Another company which—*Franklinton Era-Leader,* October 13, 1910.

The St. Tammany Regiment—Letter, Penn to Morgan, Coquillon and Lovering, June 27, 1861, Archives, Clerk of Court, St. Tammany Parish.

It was commanded—*Strength and Organization,* St. Tammany Regiment, Louisiana Militia, August 1862, Archives, Clerk of Court, St. Tammany Parish.

p. 133   By April 1862—Petition of Mortee, *et al.,* to Judge Geo. Wm. Martin, April 1862, Archives, Clerk of Court, St. Tammany.

In 1863, the—Petition of Penn *et al.,* to President, Police Jury, Archives, Clerk of Court, St. Tammany Parish.

The wife, father—Letter, Penn to Police Jury, April 1863, Archives, Clerk of Court, St. Tammany Parish.

Unionist sentiment in—Order No. 1, Geo. H. Penn, March 15, 1862, Archives, Clerk of Court, St. Tammany Parish.

In 1862, the—*Standard History of New Orleans, Louisiana,* Henry Rightor, ed. Chicago: Lewis Publishing Company, 1900, p. 155; John Smith Kendall, *History of New Orleans.* Chicago and New York: Lewis Publishing Company, 1922, Vol. I, p. 244; Henry E. Chambers, *History of Louisiana,* Chicago and New York: American Historical Society, Inc., 1925, Vol. I, p. 633.

p. 134   Only a week—O.R.N., Series I, Vol. 18, p. 453.

The next day—*Ibid.,* p. 451.

On May 13, 1862—*Ibid.,* p. 452.

A number of—"Parish Residents Fail in an Attempt to Trade with New Orleans," *St. Tammany Historical Society Gazette,* Vol. 1, p. 60.

They received this—*Ibid.,* p. 61, Archives, St. Tammany Historical Society.

p. 136   Later in 1862—O.R., Series I, Vol. 15, p. 124.

p. 138   Actually, there were—*Ibid.,* p. 786.

Martial law had—General Order No. 2., H. Q. 1st District, Dept. No. 1, Brigadier General Ruggles, July 2, 1862, Ms. 16, Ella Paine Collection, Archives, St. Tammany Historical Society.

In September 1862—O.R., Series I, Vol. 15, p. 705.

The *New Orleans*—*New Orleans Daily Delta,* September 2, 1862, p. 2.

p. 140   By October 22,—*Ibid.,* p. 841.

The only other—*Ibid.,* p. 188.

In December 1862—*Daily Picayune,* December 16, 1862, p. 2, col. 5.

The first group—*Ibid.*

By December 10,—O.R.N., Series F. Vol. 19, p. 399.

The U.S.S. *New London*—*Ibid.,* pp. 494, 585.

Shortly thereafter, the—*Ibid.,* Vol. 20, p. 439.

On August 26—*Ibid.,* p. 484.

p. 141   On December 10—O.R.N., Series I, Vol. 20, pp. 855, 856.

On December 28—*Ibid.,* p. 738.

The enterprise proved—O.R., Series I, Vol. 34, pt. 2, p. 83.

p. 142   One of these—O.R., Series I, Vol. 34, pt. 1, p. 104.
           A second expedition—*Ibid.*, p. 136.

p. 143   The occupation of—Matt A. Morgan, "A Village Ransacked," *St. Tammany Farmer,* April 13 and 22, 1893.
           One resident described—*Ibid.*

p. 144   In December 1863—*Wanderer,* Vol. 1, No. 15, Archives, Clerk of Court, St. Tammany Parish.

p. 145   Between April 1st—O.R., Series I, Vol. 34, pt. 1, p. 869.
           On May 3—O. R., Series I, Vol. 34, pt. 2, p. 235.
           She was involved—*Ibid.*, p. 281.

p. 146   Other correspondence shows—Letter, Edwards to Officer Commanding Port at Mandeville, May 16, 1864, copy in Archives, St. Tammany Historical Society.
           At the request—Letter, Bouny to Edwards, May 16, 1864; Edwards to Bouny, May 16, 1864; copies in Archives, St. Tammany Historical Society.

p. 147   Lieutenant Bouny replied—Copy of letter, Bouny to Edwards, Archives, St. Tammany Historical Society.
           There is more—Morgan, "A Village Ransacked," *Farmer,* April 15, 22, 29, May 6, 13, 27, 1893.
           Matt M. Morgan—*Ibid.*, May 13 and 27, 1893.
           On April 23—Letter Taylor to F. Cousin *et al.,* April 23, 1864, Archives, St. Tammany Historical Society.

p. 148   On October 13—O.R., Series I, Vol. 34, pt. 2, p. 685.
           In the next—*Ibid.*, p. 742.

CHAPTER XVII

p. 150   With the surrender—T. Harry Williams and A. Otis Hebert, Jr., *The Civil War in Louisiana, A Chronology.* (n.p.): Louisiana Civil War Centennial Commission, p. 8; Chambers, *A History of Louisiana,* p. 657.
           J. Madison Wells—Proclamation, Archives, Clerk of Court, St. Tammany Parish.

p. 153   St. Tammany Parish—*New Orleans Times,* August 12, 1865, p. 2, col. 2.

p. 155   In August, it—*New Orleans Tribune,* August 25, 1865, p. 2, col. 2.
           Another story in—*Ibid.*, September 23, 1865, p. 2, col. 2.
           In November 1865—*Ibid.*, November 9, 1865, p. 2.
           St. Tammany lost—Louisiana Legislature, Act 54 of 1869.
           The 1870 census—U.S. Census, 1870.

p. 157   The agricultural census—U.S. Agricultural Census, 1870.
           In 1868, the—Chambers, *History of Louisiana,* p. 667.
           Poitevent & Favre—U.S. Abstract Book, Archives, Clerk of Court.
           In the decade—U.S. Census, 1880.

p. 159   The *Farmer* had—*Farmer,* August 21, 1880.

In 1870, in—Mobley, "The Academy Movement," LHQ, Vol. 30, p. 913.

In 1875, the—Annual Report of the State Superintendent of Public Education, 1875. New Orleans, 1876, p. 372.

There were nine—*Ibid.*, pp. 327, 361

p. 160   Of these, 370—*Ibid.*, p. 304.

The 1880 census—U.S. Census, 1880.

In 1882, Covington—*Farmer*, April 29, 1882.

The private school—*Farmer*, May 6, 1882.

CHAPTER XVIII

p. 163   As early as—*Farmer*, October 26, 1878.

Probably the most—*Ibid.*

Originally built in—*New Orleans Daily Picayune*, April 17, 1899, p. 10, col. 5; *New Orleans Times-Picayune*, January 18, 1920, Sec. 2, p. 1, col. 4.

Another well known boat—*Farmer*, October 26, 1878.

In July 1879—*Ibid.*, July 5, 1879.

This brisk business—*Ibid.*, July 5, 1879.

Charles Frederick's Stage—*Ibid.*

Apparently the principal—U.S. Census, 1870, 1880.

p. 164   The population figures—U.S. Census, 1880; *Louisiana Almanac,* James Calhoun, ed. Gretna: Pelican Publishing Company, 1975, p. 116.

One visitor painted—*Farmer*, June 18, 1887.

p. 166   As early as—*Ibid.*, April 17, 1880.

In May 1881—*Ibid.*, May 7, 1881.

The road was—*Ibid.*, March 17, 1883.

Finally, on October—*Ibid.*, October 20, 1883.

In October of—*Ibid.*, October 25, 1884, August 29, 1885.

p. 167   In 1885, the—*Ibid.*, November 14, 1885.

On June 26—*Ibid.*, June 25, 1887.

Finally, on May—*Ibid.*, May 19, 1888.

The next step—*Ibid.*, May 14, 1892.

This line was—*Ibid.*, May 21, 1892.

Then in 1902—*Ibid.*, November 29, 1902.

It was completed—*Ibid.*, June 20, 1903.

p. 168   By December 1903—*Ibid.*, December 5, 1903.

Sometime during the—*Ibid.*, April 27, 1904.

Meanwhile, the Salmen—*Ibid.*, April 27, 1904, quoting story from the *Mandeville Wave.*

It was in—J. S. Glass., pub., *St. Tammany Parish*, New Orleans, 1905, p. 75. Private collection of the Charles Koepp family.

In 1904, the—*Farmer*, September 10, 1904; October 1, 1904; February 4, 1905.

By August 1—*Ibid.*, August 4, 1906.

In September 1906—*Ibid.*, September 8, 1906.

On January 17—*Ibid.,* January 17, 1909; May 15, 1909.
At about the—*Ibid.,* October 10, 1908.

p. 171 In February 1908—*Ibid.,* February 15, 1908.
It was never—*Ibid.,* March 18, 1911.
The last attempt—*Ibid.,* May 5, 1906; June 9, 1906; July 14, 1906;
July 13, 1907; August 24, 1907; October 10, 1908; January 23,
1909; Brochure of St. Tammany and New Orleans Railway and
Ferry Company, Archives, St. Tammany Historical Society.
Despite the revenues—*Farmer,* June 8, 1918.
Its assets were—*Ibid.,* August 31, 1918.

p. 172 Or that glorious—*Ibid.,* May 20, 1903.

CHAPTER XIX

p. 173 In 1908, when—*Farmer,* August 8, 1908.
The only notice—*Ibid.,* April 7, 1906.
The 1880 census—U.S. Census, 1880.

p. 175 Another early mill—*Farmer,* January 18, 1879.
The Messrs. Hamlet—*Ibid.,* March 18, 1882; February 14, 1891.
W. T. Jay—*Ibid.,* June 4, 1881.
By 1885, he—*Ibid.,* November 14, 1885.
The Sunnyside Sawmill—*Ibid.,* April 10, 1886.
In 1891, J. H.—*Ibid.,* April 18, 1891; July 5, 1891.
In 1893, the—*Ibid.,* March 11, 1893.
In 1894, the—*Ibid.,* July 14, 1894.
J. A. Barker—*Ibid.,* August 17, 1895.
W. T. Jay—*Ibid.,* May 18, 1895.
The area around—*Ibid.,* January 4, 1902.
In 1906, the—*Ibid.,* September 15, 1906.
Another early mill—*Ibid.,* October 28, 1893; September 22, 1894;
May 4, 1895.
In 1913, Poitevent—*Ibid.,* July 19, 1913.
Another well-known mill—J. S. Glass, pub. *St. Tammany Parish,* New
Orleans, 1905, p. 77.

p. 176 The largest of—*Ibid.,* p. 75.
The other was—*Farmer,* May 2, 1891; August 11, 1894.
In addition to—*Ibid.,* September 5, 1891.
In 1893, Southern—*Ibid.,* June 10, 1893.
In 1899, when—*Ibid.,* May 27, 1899.
The St. Tammany—*Ibid.,* November 23, 1907; September 5, 1908.
In addition to—*Ibid.,* November 3, 1888; December 15, 1898; Sep-
tember 5, 1891; October 7, 1893.

p. 177 St. Tammany clay—*Ibid.,* March 21, 1908; June 19, 1915; July 3,
1915; January 8, 1916.
In addition, much—*Ibid.,* February 27, 1915; March 11, 1916.
As late as—*Ibid.,* November 4, 1899.
Foremost among these—*Ibid.,* January 6, 1906.
In July 1906—*Ibid.,* May 5, 1906; July 21, 1906.

In 1909, after—*Ibid.,* February 20, 1909.
In 1907, four—*Ibid.,* June 1, 1907.
The *Margaret,* which—*Ibid.,* March 27, 1909.
A second *Pineland—Ibid.,* April 7, 1909.

p. 178   The sidewheel excursion—*Ibid.,* March 19, 1910.
A second steamer—*Ibid.,* May 28, 1910.
The same company—*Ibid.,* August 13, 1910; April 22, 1911.
Daily boat service—*Ibid.,* February 24, 1912.
In 1913, the—*Ibid.,* August 23, 1913.
In June 1914—*Ibid.,* June 27, 1914.
Renamed the *Mandeville—Ibid.,* April 29, 1916.
As late as—*Ibid.,* March 6, 1920.
In the late—*Ibid.,* August 13, 1887.
By 1895, there—*Ibid.,* September 7, 1895; October 5, 1895.
Louis Baham had—*Ibid.,* May 25, 1895; June 1, 1895.
In 1907, Charles—*Ibid.,* April 6, 1907.
In 1913, A. D.—*Ibid.,* March 1, 1913
World War I—*Ibid.,* April 21, 1917

p. 179   The Baham shipyard—*Ibid.,* May 12, 1917.
In March 1918—*Ibid.,* March 2, 1918.
Another shipyard was—*Ibid.,* May 12, 1917.
The big government—*Ibid.,* March 18, 1919.
During the war—*Ibid.,* September 27, 1919.
In August 1914—*Ibid.,* August 29, 1914.
In January 1917—*Ibid.,* January 6, 1917.
Slidell's shipyards were—*Ibid.,* March 8, 1919.

CHAPTER XX

p. 180   One important part—Agricultural statistics in this chapter are compiled from: *Crop Reports of the Louisiana State Board of Agriculture
and Immigration* for the applicable years; U.S. Agricultural Cen-
suses; and *St. Tammany Parish: Resources and Facilities,* St. Tammany Parish Development Board, 1950.
The *Times-Democrat—Farmer,* July 25, 1891.

p. 181   On January 6—*Ibid.,* January 23, 1892.
Grape culture became—*Ibid.,* July 12, 1879; August 2, 1879.

p. 182   In 1884, John—*Ibid.,* July 5, 1884; August 16, 1884.
Another wine maker—*Ibid.,* December 13, 1884; April 1, 1885.
Other varieties of—*Ibid.,* July 11, 1885; July 18, 1885; August 8,
1885; August 14, 1886; September 3, 1887.
His farm was—*Ibid.,* September 6, 1884.
Another wine grape—*Ibid.,* October 23, 1886; July 30, 1887.

p. 183   In 1881, the—*Ibid.,* May 7, 1881.
The *Farmer* ran—*Ibid.,* April 21, 1883; June 16, 1883; April 26, 1884;
June 14, 1884; February 7, 1885; November 7, 1885.
In 1884, Mr.—*Ibid.,* April 26, 1884.
In 1885, Mr.—*Ibid.,* February 21, 1885.

As early as—*Ibid.*, April 21, 1883.

In 1884, he—*Ibid.*, June 14, 1884.

Then in November—*Ibid.*, November 7, 1885.

p. 184 Apparently, Mr. Herbelin—*Ibid.*, January 30, 1886; May 22, 1886; August 7, 1886.

After the sheriff's—*Ibid.*, August 14, 1886.

The *Farmer* described—*Ibid.*, October 9, 1880.

p. 185 Harry Dutsch of—*Ibid.*, August 18, 1883.

Jules Cahier's Pecan—*Ibid.*, August 6, 1887.

In 1894, there—*Ibid.*, August 11, 1894.

p. 186 In Covington, Havana—*Ibid.*, July 4, 1903.

The only commercial—*Along the Line of the New Orleans Great Northern Railroad,* The Southern Manufacturer, New Orleans, c. 1910. (Reprinted in 1978 for Poole Lumber Company of Covington, by W. T. Kentzel, Printers, Covington.)

CHAPTER XXI

p. 187 Some early post—*Farmer,* April 7, 1883; August 8, 1903; August 22, 1903; January 2, 1886.

In 1894, Matthew—*Ibid.*, August 11, 1894; September 22, 1900.

Talisheek was originally—*Ibid.*, September 4, 1880.

Because of a—*Ibid.*, December 21, 1907.

Chinchuba, between Covington—*Ibid.*, January 16, 1892.

It was the—*Ibid.*, August 23, 1890.

On September 24—*Ibid.*, September 27, 1890.

For the first—*Ibid.*, February 17, 1900.

p. 188 Another place of—*Ibid.*, September 1, 1894; May 18, 1895; May 30, 1896.

There were post—*Ibid.*, November 1, 1890; September 26, 1896; August 3, 1895.

In the 1840s—*Ibid.*, October 28, 1893.

However, by 1893—*Ibid.*, October 28, 1893.

p. 189 In 1894, F. M.—*Ibid.*, September 22, 1894.

In 1879, Honey—*Ibid.*, February 8, 1879; February 9, 1895.

However, disastrous flooding—*Ibid.*, February 8, 1902.

Thomasville, which was—*Ibid.*, May 21, 1892; September 16, 1893.

In 1892, a—*Ibid.*, May 21, 1892.

The advent of—*Ibid.*, March 18, 1882.

p. 190 Another new town—*Ibid.*, November 14, 1885.

In August 1886—*Ibid.*, August 18, 1886.

p. 191 In 1888, the—*Ibid.*, July 14, 1888.

About five and—*Ibid.*, February 28, 1888.

A post office—*Ibid.*, May 26, 1888.

A Catholic church—*Ibid.*, May 2, 1891; December 19, 1891.

In 1892 there—*Ibid.*, January 9, 1892.

The post office—*Ibid.*, June 25, 1904.

St. Joe Station—*Ibid.*, May 2, 1891; August 11, 1894.

The town of—*Ibid.*, September 26, 1891; August 1, 1903; January 2, 1904.

Along the N.O.G.N.—U.S. Geological Survey.

Maud, which was—*Farmer*, December 21, 1907; March 14, 1908.

Probably the most—*Ibid.*, August 4, 1900; November 10, 1900; November 17, 1900.

On Saturday, March—*Ibid.*, March 2, 1901; March 9, 1901.

p. 193   How big is—*Ibid.*, April 27, 1901.

In December 1901—*Ibid.*, December 28, 1901

St. Tammany Health—*Ibid.*, March 1, 1902.

A large two-story—*Ibid.*, April 26, 1902.

A big pavilion—*Ibid.*, June 28, 1902.

In October 1902—*Ibid.*, October 18, 1902.

In 1905, St.—*Ibid.*, January 14, 1905.

In November, plans—*Ibid.*, November 11, 1905.

In 1907, the—*Ibid.*, October 12, 1907.

Originally known as—*Ibid.*, July 4, 1903; July 25, 1903.

The name of—*Ibid.*, July 4, 1903.

After the lumber—*Ibid.*, September 17, 1904.

In 1907, the—*Ibid.*, January 12, 1907; November 23, 1907.

In 1908, there—*Ibid.*, June 13, 1908.

p. 194   By 1910, Ramsay—U.S. Census, 1910.

In 1912, however—*Farmer*, January 6, 1912.

A somewhat more—*Ibid.*, June 18, 1904.

A depot was—*Ibid.*, April 22, 1905; May 30, 1908.

In June 1908—*Ibid.*, June 6, 1908; June 27, 1908.

There was even—*Ibid.*, August 29, 1908.

In addition, the—*Ibid.*, September 5, 1908; September 12, 1908.

On May 14—*Ibid.*, May 10, 1913.

In May 1916—*Ibid,* May 6, 1916.

CHAPTER XXII

p. 195   In September 1882—*Farmer*, September 9, 1882.

This school lasted—*Ibid.*, August 30, 1884.

In the same—*Ibid.*

There were also—*Ibid.*, October 4, 1884.

The public school—*Ibid.*, January 31, 1885.

In 1886, St.—*Ibid.*, April 10, 1886.

Its grounds were—*Ibid.*, June 11, 1887.

p. 196   Other private schools—*Ibid.*, October 2, 1886; January 15, 1887; January 5, 1889; January 17, 1889.

In 1890, one—*Ibid.*, November 1, 1890; January 24, 1891; February 7, 1891.

Citizens in Madisonville—Petition, April 19, 1892; undated petition; Archives, Clerk of Court, St. Tammany Parish.

In February 1891—*Farmer*, February 21, 1891.

Mandeville in that—*Ibid.*, January 31, 1891.

In April 1891—*Ibid.*, May 2, 1891; August 8, 1891.

Other private schools—*Ibid.*, October 17, 1891; January 9, 1892; October 22, 1892.

There was also—*Ibid.*, April 9, 1892.

p. 197 St. Francis Xavier—*Ibid.*, July 1, 1893.

By 1893, the—*Ibid.*, July 22, 1893.

In 1897, Misses—*Ibid.*, January 2, 1897.

In September 1898—*Ibid.*, August 27, 1898.

It was operated—*Ibid.*, September 10, 1898.

Miss Eva Ward—*Ibid.*, January 28, 1899; September 9, 1899.

In November, that—*Ibid.*, November 25, 1899.

The most important—*Ibid.*, September 30, 1899; October 7, 1899.

In 1900, Dixon—*Ibid.*, July 7, 1900; September 15, 1900.

About ten years—*Ibid.*, July 23, 1911.

At about the—*Ibid.*, January 4, 1902.

In conjunction with—*Ibid.*, October 18, 1902.

The public school—*Ibid.*, April 20, 1901; October 19, 1901.

There could be—*Ibid.*, May 5, 1900; December 2, 1905.

p. 199 Another indication of—*Ibid.*, March 23, 1901.

There was a—*Ibid.*, June 6, 1903.

In 1904, the—*Ibid.*, October 8, 1904.

The first reported—*Ibid.*, April 2, 1910.

George E. Sears—*Ibid.*, May 10, 1910.

In 1911, Deed—*Ibid.*, July 1, 1911.

Mr. Smith, something—*Ibid.*, September 6, 1913.

Mr. Sears made—*Ibid.*, June 11, 1910.

p. 200 On July 7, 1907—*Ibid.*, July 7, 1907.

In May 1908—*Ibid.*, May 23, 1908.

The New Rink—*Ibid.*, March 18, 1916.

Victor H. Frederick—*Ibid.*, June 28, 1913, August 2, 1913.

On September 7,—*Ibid.*, September 7, 1912.

The best known—*Ibid.*, May 10, 1913.

CHAPTER XXIII

p. 201 When Claiborne Cottage—*Farmer*, March 27, 1880; April 24, 1880; May 1, 1880.

In 1831, a—*Ibid.*, February 15, 1890; *New Orleans Daily Picayune*, March 13, 1892, p. 16, col. 1.

Claiborne Cottage was—*Farmer*, January 15, 1887; June 25, 1887.

In 1889, an—*Ibid.*, November 30, 1889.

The advertisement in—*Ibid.*, June 7, 1890.

p. 203 An article in—*New Orleans Daily States*, July 7, 1890; p. 2, col. 1.

p. 204 Claiborne Cottage was—*Farmer*, June 11, 1892; August 10, 1895.

It was last—*Ibid.*, March 28, 1896.

In November 1912—*Ibid.*, November 2, 1912.

Another famous resort—*Ibid.*, June 25, 1881.

It was as—*Ibid.*, October 22, 1881; October 27, 1881; April 29, 1882.

Its ad in—*Ibid.*, May 20, 1882.

p. 205   In 1884, the—*Ibid.*, August 30, 1884.
          The hotel was—*Ibid.*, September 27, 1884.

p. 206   A letter to—*Ibid.*, April 23, 1881.

p. 207   Eventually, the hotel—*Ibid.*, July 6, 1895.

CHAPTER XXIV

p. 208   As early as—*Farmer*, August 16, 1879.
          The 1850 government—U.S. Government Survey.
          Apple Pie Ridge—*Farmer*, October 4, 1879.
          In 1884, a—*Ibid.*, June 21, 1884.
          The first message—*Ibid.*
          General Moorman spoke—*Ibid.*, July 12, 1884.
          Inspired by this—*Ibid.*, June 28, 1884.

p. 209   On August 3rd—*Ibid.*, August 9, 1884.
          The line was—*Ibid.*, September 24, 1887.
          In 1899, the—*Ibid.*, October 21, 1899.
          By February 24—*Ibid.*, February 24, 1900; April 14, 1900.
          In September of—*Ibid.*, September 22, 1900.
          In 1884, the—*Ibid.*, November 8, 1884.
          Different citizens began—*Ibid.*, December 13, 1884.
          A list of—*Ibid.*, January 3, 1885.

p. 211   At the exhibition—*Ibid.*, March 7, 1885.
          In 1899, a—*Ibid.*, September 2, 1899.
          The *Farmer* got—*Ibid.*, July 11, 1903.
          It apparently enjoyed—*Ibid.*, July 30, 1904.
          However, in June—*Ibid.*, June 20, 1908.
          In May 1909—*Ibid.*, May 1, 1909.
          It may have—*Ibid.*, June 11, 1910.
          The first newspaper—*Ibid.*, August 6, 1892.
          Two more newspapers—*Ibid.*, May 15, 1897; September 2, 1899.

p. 212   Neither of them—*Ibid.*, September 28, 1901.
          In 1902, E. F.—*Ibid.*, August 2, 1902.
          In February 1903—*Ibid.*, February 28, 1903.
          By 1908, when—*Ibid.*, July 4, 1908.
          The *Slidell Journal*—*Ibid.*, April 2, 1910; August 31, 1912.
          Mandeville had its—*Ibid.*, April 13, 1901.
          The *Madisonville Herald*—*Ibid.*, June 23, 1900.
          St. Tammany Parish—*Ibid.*, April 23, 1898.
          In the ranks—*Ibid.*, June 4, 1898.
          Colonel Hood's Regiment—*Ibid.*, May 21, 1898.
          The regiment remained—*Ibid.*, July 23, 1898; July 30, 1898.
          In September 1898—*Ibid.*, September 10, 1898.
          Private Joshua Davis—*Ibid.*, August 20, 1898.
          Others who enlisted—*Ibid.*, June 18, 1898.

p. 213   The *New Orleans*—*New Orleans Times-Democrat*, January 18, 1892.

CHAPTER XXV

p. 216   There was a—*Farmer,* October 2, 1897; October 9, 1897.
Dr. Sarah Hackett—*Ibid.,* October 9, 1897.

p. 219   Witness the following—*Ibid,* July 11, 1891; *New Orleans Daily City Item,* June 29, 1891.

p. 220   One of the—*Farmer,* January 17, 1891.
F. B. Martindale—*Ibid.,* April 26, 1879; June 11, 1881.
Other early hotels—*Ibid.,* May 20, 1882; April 28, 1883; April 24, 1886; July 16, 1887; March 2, 1889.
The Riverside Hotel—*Ibid.,* March 30, 1901; March 17, 1906.
Melrose Cottage, run—*Ibid.,* April 27, 1901.

p. 221   In 1902, E. L.—*Ibid.,* March 28, 1902.
In July of—*Ibid.,* July 12, 1902.
In 1904, the—*Ibid.,* March 19, 1904.
In February 1906—*Ibid.,* February 17, 1906; March 17, 1906.
The latter hotel—*Ibid.,* June 8, 1907.
In 1912, Dr.—*Ibid.,* June 15, 1912
In 1913, Dr.—*Ibid.,* September 13, 1913; July 4, 1908.
In 1916, he—*Ibid.,* June 10, 1916; April 10, 1897.
In 1881, the—*Ibid.,* August 13, 1881.
In 1886, the—*Ibid.,* May 22, 1886.

p. 222   In 1889, the—*Ibid.,* June 29, 1889.
Covington was growing—*Ibid.,* January 4, 1890; U.S. Census, 1890.
Covington also boasted—*Farmer,* August 23, 1890; August 30, 1890.
Messrs. Giesen and—*Ibid.,* April 12, 1890; May 3, 1890.
In 1894, Frank—*Ibid.,* January 13, 1894.
F. A. Guyol—*Ibid.,* June 12, 1886.
Probably the most—*Ibid.,* June 4, 1898.
In 1903, it—*Ibid.,* September 19, 1903.

p. 223   In 1901, the—*Ibid.,* March 30, 1901.
In June 1905—*Ibid.,* June 17, 1905.
It opened its—*Ibid.,* August 26, 1905.
In 1901, electricity—*Ibid.,* January 12, 1901; March 20, 1901; June 1, 1901.
In 1904, the—*Ibid.,* November 5, 1904; January 14, 1905.
Baseball in Covington—*Ibid.,* June 21, 1884.
In 1901, the—*Ibid.,* June 29, 1901.
A. R. Smith—*Ibid.,* June 29, 1901.
In 1904, there—*Ibid.,* April 23, 1904; June 4, 1904; December 12, 1904.
Basketball also appeared—*Ibid.,* February 6, 1904.
There was even—*Ibid.,* April 5, 1902; December 26, 1903.
The golf club—*Ibid.,* May 24, 1902; July 19, 1902.
At the time—*Ibid.,* March 14, 1903.
The first reception—*Ibid.,* April 4, 1903.
By 1907, however—*Ibid.,* November 23, 1907; December 28, 1907.

p. 224   Covington was also—*Ibid.,* August 16, 1879.
In February 1880—*Ibid.,* February 28, 1880.

On February 5—*Ibid.*, February 5, 1881.
Another event of—*Ibid.*, March 1, 1879.
In 1891, the—*Ibid.*, February 14, 1891.
The next year—*Ibid.*, March 5, 1892.
In 1893, Julian—*Ibid.*, February 18, 1893.
In 1894, there—*Ibid.*, February 10, 1894.
Master Jules Pechon—*Ibid.*, March 2, 1895.
The adults took—*Ibid.*, February 22, 1896.
The next year—*Ibid.*, March 6, 1897.
A small scale—*Ibid.*, February 26, 1898.
In February 1907—*Ibid.*, February 16, 1907.

p. 227   Mardi Gras was—*Ibid.*, February 27, 1909.
Probably the most—*Ibid.*, March 4, 1911.
Covington was to—*Ibid.*, November 12, 1898; *New Orleans Daily States*, November 12, 1898, p. 1.

p. 228   This tragedy, in—*Farmer*, April 1, 1899.
Covington Fire Company—*Ibid.*, June 23, 1900; May 4, 1901.
In 1906, there—*Ibid.*, August 25, 1906.
Miss Serena Jones—Letter, Jones to Hosmer, August 24, 1906, Jones-Buck-Hosmer Papers, Tulane University Library.

p. 231   In 1909 there—*Farmer*, March 20, 1909.
In November 1909—*Ibid.*, November 20, 1909.
In August of—*Ibid.*, August 14, 1909.
In October 1909—*Ibid.*, October 30, 1909.

CHAPTER XXVI

p. 232   The first step—*Farmer*, December 21, 1878.
In April 1882—*Ibid.*, April 15, 1882.
Later in 1882—*Ibid.*, November 4, 1882.
In 1884, this—*Ibid.*, October 4, 1884.
In 1885, it—*Ibid.*, November 14, 1885.
In the late—*Ibid.*, August 13, 1887.

p. 233   The old Madison—*Ibid.*, December 1883; February 14, 1891; June 20, 1891.
The shipyard business—*Ibid.*, September 7, 1895; October 5, 1895.
Louis Baham had—*Ibid.*, May 25, 1895; June 1, 1895.
In 1895, W. T.—*Ibid.*, June 8, 1895.
The area around—*Ibid.*, January 4, 1902.
The twentieth century—*Ibid.*, August 21, 1900.
In 1906, the—*Ibid.*, April 18, 1906.
The Houlton Lumber—*Ibid.*, September 15, 1906.
A 1907 article—*Ibid.*, April 6, 1907.
Mardi Gras celebrations—*Ibid.*, March 9, 1895.
The next year—*Ibid.*, February 22, 1896.
In 1899, the—*Ibid.*, January 28, 1899.
The parade that—*Ibid.*, February 18, 1899.
A parade and—*Ibid.*, February 16, 1907.

p. 234   In 1880, only—*Ibid.*, March 8, 1879; July 4, 1885.
It was owned—*Ibid.*, May 20, 1893; July 29, 1893.
The Marquis G. P.—*Ibid.*, April 9, 1887; June 11, 1887.
Another popular resort—*Ibid.*, July 23, 1887; February 9, 1889.
Mrs. J. M. Favaron—*Ibid.*, September 22, 1888.
In 1889, the—*Ibid.*, March 30, 1889; June 7, 1890.
Mandeville was still—U.S. Census, 1890.
In 1893, the—*Farmer*, June 23, 1893.
On July 14—*Ibid.*, July 29, 1893.

p. 235   It was also—*Ibid.*, July 8, 1893; July 29, 1893.
There had been—*Ibid.*, July 2, 1888; August 4, 1888; August 9, 1890.
The second yacht—*Ibid.*, April 25, 1903.
In May 1897—*Ibid.*, May 22, 1897.
In contrast, the—*Ibid.*, March 31, 1900.

p. 237   In 1906, the—*Ibid.*, April 18, 1906.
Later that year—*Ibid.*, September 22, 1906.
Mandeville began celebrating—*Ibid.*, February 2, 1907.
In 1908, the—*Ibid.*, November 30, 1907; March 7, 1908.
In 1909, Mr.—*Ibid.*, February 27, 1909.
On July 27—*Ibid.*, July 30, 1910.
In 1913, the—*Ibid.*, July 19, 1913.
In the same—*Ibid.*, October 8, 1913.
For some reason—*Ibid.*, June 24, 1916.
Then, in 1879—*Ibid.*, May 31, 1879.
In June of—*Ibid.*, December 6, 1879; March 27, 1880; June 5, 1880; June 19, 1880.
In 1881, the—*Ibid.*, June 18, 1881.

p. 238   By 1886, there—*Ibid.*, April 3, 1886.
The big plans—*Ibid.*, March 6, 1886.
In May 1887—*Ibid.*, May 14, 1887.
Earlier that year—*Ibid.*, February 5, 1887.
A new store—*Ibid.*, June 11, 1887.
Construction of a—*Ibid.*, June 18, 1887.
In short order—*Ibid.*, June 11, 1887; August 20, 1887; January 21, 1881.
Poitevent and Favre—*Ibid.*, June 9, 1888.
A visit to—*Ibid.*, October 20, 1888.

p. 240   Stories that a—*Ibid.*, December 22, 1888.
In February 1890—*Ibid.*, February 1, 1890.
The fight attracted—*Ibid.*, February 15, 1890.

p. 241   In 1891, the—*Ibid.*, March 21, 1891.
Eddie Bossier, the—*Ibid.*, January 9, 1892.
An ice factory—*Ibid.*, July 11, 1891.
Apparently the demand—*Ibid.*, April 14, 1894.
In 1899, Abita—*Ibid.*, April 29, 1894; May 20, 1899; May 27, 1899.
In June 1899—*Ibid.*, June 24, 1899.

p. 242   It won a—*Ibid.*, October 22, 1904.
A number of—*Ibid.*, April 18, 1891; May 27, 1893; September 2,

1893; April 13, 1895; March 26, 1898; May 7, 1898; September 10, 1898.

The Long Branch—*Ibid.*, July 27, 1901; March 31, 1900; April 8, 1903; May 7, 1904; September 2, 1905; March 12, 1910.

In 1910, Mutti's—*Ibid.*, December 10, 1910; May 6, 1911.

Abita Springs finally—*Ibid.*, January 24, 1903; January 31, 1903.

A town meeting—*Ibid.*, February 14, 1903.

These officials officially—*Ibid.*, March 7, 1903.

In 1910, its—*Ibid.*, September 3, 1910; U.S. Census, 1910.

In April 1903—*Farmer*, April 18, 1903.

On October 19—*Ibid.*, October 27, 1906.

On September 27—*Ibid.*, September 26, 1914.

Three years later—*Ibid.*, April 7, 1917.

We have already—*Ibid.*, March 18, 1882.

It must have—*Ibid.*, March 29, 1884.

p. 243   Shortly after the—*Ibid.*, September 24, 1887.

Also operating in—*Ibid.*, October 22, 1887.

A visitor to—*Ibid.*, March 30, 1889.

p. 244   Despite that somewhat—*Ibid.*, April 13, 1889; September 5, 1896.

It shortly boasted—*Ibid.*, September 27, 1890.

A. C. Prevost—*Ibid.*, November 1, 1890.

An attempt to—*Ibid.*, January 24, 1891.

The school was—*Ibid.*, February 7, 1891; May 2, 1891.

The August 18—*Ibid.*, August 18, 1894.

McMahon was eventually—*Ibid.*, September 1, 1894.

The *Farmer* said—*Ibid.*, August 18, 1894; September 1, 1894.

p. 245   The Crescent Hotel—*Ibid.*, December 15, 1894.

In 1895, a—*Ibid.*, March 30, 1895; April 20, 1895.

Slidell was reported—*Ibid.*, May 18, 1895.

It was also—*Ibid.*, November 23, 1895.

In December 1899—*Ibid.*, December 2, 1899; December 16, 1899.

The 1900 census—U.S. Census, 1890, 1900.

The population jumped—U.S. Census, 1900, 1910, 1920.

In 1901, a—*Farmer*, May 18, 1901.

On December 15—*Ibid.*, November 28, 1903.

By 1907, it—*Ibid.*, December 21, 1907.

The Slidell Progressive—*Ibid.*, December 2, 1905.

The *Farmer* reviewed—*Ibid.*, November 16, 1907.

p. 246   We know there—*Ibid.*, October 8, 1910; October 29, 1910.

Another milestone was—*Ibid.*, January 7, 1911.

In 1913, a—*Ibid.*, February 22, 1913.

In August 1914—*Ibid.*, August 29, 1914; January 6, 1917.

Bibliography

Act of Territorial Legislature, April 24, 1811.

Acts of Louisiana Legislature, March 25, 1813; March 11, 1816; February 18, 1817; March 16, 1818; March 6, 1819; February 16, 1820; January 9, 1821; January 13, 1821; February 14, 1821; March 24, 1822; Act 10 of 1828; Act 103 of 1837; Act 86 of 1837; Act 54 of 1869.

Along the Line of the New Orleans Great Northern Railroad. New Orleans: The Southern Manufacturer, c. 1910. Reprint (for Poole Lumber Company). Covington: W. T. Kentzel, Printers, 1978.

Archives, Clerk of Court, St. Tammany Parish.

Archives, Louisiana State Museum.

Archives, St. Tammany Historical Society.

Archivo General de Indias.

Bassett, John Spencer and Sidney Bradshaw, eds. *Major Howell Tatum's Journal while Acting Topographical Engineer (1814) to General Jackson.* Smith College Studies on History, Vol. VII, October 1921 to April 1922. Northampton: Department of History of Smith College.

Boagni, Ethel. "The Commandant of the Tchefuncta," *St. Tammany Historical Society Gazette.* Vol. 1, September 1975.

Booth, Andrew B. *Records of Louisiana Confederate Soldiers and Louisiana Confederate Commands.* New Orleans, 1920. Vol. 1.

Brackenridge, Henry Marie. *Views of Louisiana* (1st ed., Pittsburgh, 1841). Chicago: Quadrangle Books, Inc., 1962.

Bushnell, David I. *Choctaw of Bayou Lacomb, St. Tammany Parish, Louisiana.* Bulletin 44, Smithsonian Institution, Bureau of American Ethnology. Washington: Government Printing Office, 1909.

Butler, Ruth Lapham. *Journal of Paul Du Ru.* Chicago: The Caxton Club, 1934.

Calhoun, James, ed. *Louisiana Almanac, 1975-1976.* Gretna: Pelican Publishing Company, 1975.

Carter, Clarence Edwin, ed. *The Territorial Papers of the United States.* Washington: U.S. Government Printing Office, 1940.

Carter, Robert C. *Methodist Historical Commemoration.* (Unpublished typewritten manuscript.)

Casey, Powell A. *Battle of New Orleans. Louisiana at the Battle of New Orleans.* Battle of New Orleans, 150th Anniversary, Committee of Louisiana, 1965.

———. *Louisiana in the War of 1812.* (n.p.) 1963.

———. "Military Roads and Camps in or Near Covington and Madisonville, Louisiana." *St. Tammany Historical Society Gazette,* Vol. 2, 1977.

———. "Military Roads in the Florida Parishes of Louisiana," *Louisiana History,* Vol. XV.

Caughey, John Walton. *Bernardo de Galvez in Louisiana, 1776-1783.* Gretna: Pelican Publishing Company, 1972.

Chambers, Henry E. *A History of Louisiana.* Chicago and New York: American Historical Society, Inc., 1925. Vol. 1.

Chapelle, Howard I. *American Sailing Navy.* New York: Norton, 1949.

Claiborne, J. F. H. *Mississippi as a Province, Territory and State.* Jackson: Power and Barksdale, 1880. Reprint. Baton Rouge: Louisiana State University Press, 1964.

Clark, John G. *New Orleans, 1718-1812.* Baton Rouge: Louisiana State University Press, 1970.

Commager, Henry Steele and Samuel Eliot Morison. *Growth of the American Republic.* New York: Oxford University Press, 1942.

Conrad, Glenn R., ed. *Historical Journal of the Settlement of the French in Louisiana.* Translated by Virginia Koenig and Joan Cain. Lafayette: University of Southwestern Louisiana, 1971.

Core, Norma D. *Lists of Public Officials in St. Tammany Parish.* Archives, Clerk of Court, St. Tammany Parish.

Cox, Isaac Joslin. *West Florida Controversy, 1798-1813.* Baltimore: Johns Hopkins Press, 1918.

Crop Reports of the Louisiana State Board of Agriculture and Immigration.

Cruzat, Heloise Hulse. "New Orleans under Bienville," *Louisiana Historical Quarterly,* I (1918).

Daily Picayune, December 17, 1862, p. 2.

Deiler, J. Hanno. *Settlement of the German Coast of Louisiana and the Creoles of German Descent.* Philadelphia: German American Historical Society, 1909. Reprint. Baltimore: Genealogical Publishing Company, 1970.

Deutsch Zeitung. New Orleans, August 21, 1850.

Ditch, Jay K., translator. "Early Census Tables of Louisiana," *Louisiana Historical Quarterly,* XIII (1930) p. 215.

Dunbar, Carl O. and Charles Schuchert. *Outlines of Historical Geology,* 4th ed. New York: John Wiley and Sons, Inc., 1947.

Du Pratz, Le Page. *History of Louisiana.* 1774. Reprint. Baton Rouge: Claitor Publishing Division, 1972.

Ellis, Frederick Stephen. "American Activity in Louisiana during the Revolutionary War," *St. Tammany Historical Society Gazette,* I (1977) p. 3.

Flint, Timothy. *Recollections of the Last Ten Years in the Valley of the Mississippi.* Boston: Cummings, Hilliard and Company, 1826. Reprint. Carbondale and Edwardsville: Southern Illinois University Press, 1968.

Ford, James A. and George I. Quimby. "Tchefuncte Culture, An Early Occupation of the Lower Mississippi Valley." *Memoirs of the Society for American Archaeology,* Vol. II. Menasha, Wis.: Society for American Archaeology and Louisiana State University Press, 1945.

Franklinton Era-Leader, October 13, 1910.

Glass, J. S. pub. *St. Tammany Parish.* New Orleans, 1905, p. 75. Private collection of the Charles Koepp family.

Gove, Philip Babcock, ed. *Webster's Third New International Dictionary.* Springfield: G. & C. Merriam Company, 1966.

Green, James Kimmins, "Louisiana Politics, 1845-1861." *Louisiana Historical Quarterly,* XII (1929) p. 617.

Haag, William G. "Louisiana in North American Prehistory." *Melanges.* Vol. 1. Baton Rouge: Louisiana State University Press, 1971.

Higginbotham, Jay. *Family Biographies.* Mobile: Colonial Books, 1967.

————. *Fort Maurepas.* Mobile: Colonial Books, 1968.

————, ed. *Journal of Sauvole.* Mobile: Colonial Books, 1969.

"Index to Spanish Records." *Louisiana Historical Quarterly.*

James, James Alton. *Oliver Pollock, the Life and Times of an Unknown Patriot.* New York and London: D. Appleton-Century Company, 1937.

Johnson, Clarence L. "The Family of Marigny de Mandeville and the Fontainebleau Plantation." *Louisiana Conservation Review.*

Johnson, Paula Patecek, Private collection.

Jones-Hosmer-Buck Papers. Manuscript Department, Special Collections Division, Tulane University Library.

Journal 1842, Tchefuncta Lighthouse, 1842. Archives, Louisiana State University.

Kendall, John Smith. *History of New Orleans.* Chicago and New York: Lewis Publishing Company, 1922, Vol. I, p. 244.

Kerr, C. M. "Highway Progress in Louisiana." *Louisiana Historical Quarterly* II (1919) p. 57.

Kniffen, Fred. "Nature's St. Tammany," *St. Tammany Historical Society Gazette* II (1977) p. 1.

Knox, Dudley W., Captain, U.S.N. (Ret.). *Official Records of the Union and Confederate Navies in the War of the Rebellion.* Washington: Government Printing Office, 1927. Series I, Vol. 18, p. 453; Series F, Vol. 19, p. 399; Series I, Vol. 20, p. 855, 856.

Langer, William L. *Encyclopedia of World History.* Boston: Houghton Mifflin Company, 1948.

Lanier, Lee. "Bloody Tangipahoa." *Amite News-Digest,* November 20, 1975; November 27, 1975; December 4, 1975.

Lebreton, Dagmar Renshaw. *Chahta-Ima.* Baton Rouge: Louisiana State University Press, 1947.

Lighthouses and Light ships of the Northern Gulf of Mexico. Department of Transportation, United States Coast Guard, p. 28.

Lighthouses of the United States, Document No. 62, pp. 100-101.

Louisiana Advocate, August --, 1839. Photocopy in Archives, St. Tammany Historical Society.

Louisiana Genealogical Register, Vol. 18, No. 3; Vol. 16, No. 4, p. 336.

Louisiana Militia Order Book. Louisiana State Library. (General Order of March 7, 1815.)

Louisiana Progress, April 15, 1938.

Lowrie, Walter. *American State Papers.* Washington: Duff Green, 1834.

McWilliams, Richebourg Gaillard. *Fleur de Lys and Calumet.* Baton Rouge: Louisiana State University Press, 1953.

Maduell, Charles R., Jr. translator. *Census Tables for the French Colony of Louisiana from 1699 through 1732.* Baltimore: Genealogical Publishing Co., Inc., 1972.

Margry, Pierre, ed. *Decouvertes et etablissements des Francais dans l'ouest et dans le sud de l'Amerique septentrionale.* Vol. IV. Paris: D. Jouaust, 1880. 1880.

Minutes, St. Tammany Parish Police Jury. June 4, 1833. Louisiana State University Library.

Mobley, James W. "The Academy Movement in Louisiana." *Louisiana Historical Quarterly,* XXX (1947) 916-17.

Morgan, H. G., Jr. "Tammany, Origin of the Name." Publications of the Louisiana Historical Society, Vol. 5, p. 54.

Morgan, Matt A. "A Village Ransacked." *St. Tammany Farmer*, April 13, 1893; April 22, 1893.

Murray, Grover E. *Geology of the Atlantic and Gulf Coastal Province of North America*. New York: Harper & Brothers, 1961.

Myer, William E. *Indian Trails of the Southeast*. Forty-second Annual Report of the Bureau of American Ethnology. Washington: U.S. Government Printing Office, 1929.

Neff, Mrs. Amos, and others. "Christ Episcopal Church." *St. Tammany Farmer*. March 25, 1916.

New Orleans Bee. April 14, 1834; July 11, 1837.

New Orleans Daily City Item, June 29, 1891.

New Orleans Daily Delta, September 2, 1862, p. 2.

New Orleans Daily Picayune, August 15, 1855, p. 2, col. 2; December 16, 1862; March 13, 1892, p. 16, col. 1; April 17, 1899, p. 10, col. 5.

New Orleans Daily States, July 7, 1890, p. 2, col. 1; November 12, 1898, p. 1.

New Orleans Times, August 12, 1865, p. 2, col. 2.

New Orleans Times-Democrat, January 6, 1892.

New Orleans Times-Picayune, January 18, 1920, p. 1, col. 4; November 13, 1944, p. 16, col. 4.

New Orleans Tribune, August 25, 1865.

Ogg, Frederick Austin. *Opening of the Mississippi*. New York: Cooper Square Publishers, Inc., 1968.

O'Neill, Charles E. *Charlevoix's Louisiana*. Baton Rouge and London: Louisiana State University Press, 1977.

Padgett, James A., ed. "Official Records of the West Florida Revolution and Republic." *Louisiana Historical Quarterly* XXI (1938) p. 688.

————. "West Florida Revolution of 1810." *Louisiana Historical Quarterly*, XXI (1938), p. 187.

Paine, Ella, Collection. Archives, St. Tammany Historical Society.

Petersen, Mary A. "British West Florida: Abstracts of Land Petitions." *Louisiana Genealogical Register*, XVIII, No. 4, pp. 318, 336.

————. "Montfort Browne, Soldier and Lieutenant Governor." *Louisiana Genealogical Register*, XVIII, No. 3, p. 231.

Pintado Papers, Books IV, V, VII, and VIII.

Records of Assistance to Families of Soldiers. Archives, Clerk of Court, St. Tammany Parish.

"Records of the Superior Council of Louisiana." *Louisiana Historical Quarterly*.

Rees, James. *Tales and Sketches*. Unpublished manuscript in possession of Mrs. Amos Neff.

Report of Anchorage Fees of Bayou St. John for 1803 by Don Juan de Castanedo. Records of City Council of New Orleans, 1794-1803. Book 4087, p. 92.

Rester, Shirley. Private Collection.

Richardson, Lillie. "Admission of Louisiana into the Union." *Louisiana Historical Quarterly* I (1918), p. 333.

Rightor, Henry, ed. *Standard History of New Orleans, Louisiana*. Chicago: Lewis Publishing Company, 1900.

Roberts, W. Adolphe. *Lake Pontchartrain*. Indianapolis and New York: Bobbs-Merrill Company, 1946.

Rowland, Dunbar, ed. *Official Letter Books of W. C. C. Claiborne, 1801-1816.* Jackson: State Department of Archives and History, 1917.

Rowland, Dunbar and A. G. Sanders. *Mississippi Provincial Archives,* 1704-1743. Vol. III. Jackson: Press of the Mississippi Department of Archives and History, 1927.

St. Tammany Farmer.

St. Tammany and New Orleans Railway and Ferry Company. (Brochure) Archives, St. Tammany Historical Society.

St. Tammany Parish: Resources and Facilities. St. Tammany Parish Development Board, 1950.

Saucier, Roger T. *Recent Geomorphic History of the Pontchartrain Basin.* Baton Rouge: Louisiana State University Press, 1963.

Schuchert, Charles and Carl O. Dunbar. *Outlines of Historical Geology.* 4th ed. New York: John Wiley & Sons, Inc. 1947.

Schwartz, Adrian D. *Sesquicentennial in St. Tammany.* Covington: Covington City Council, 1963.

Ship Registers and Enrollments of New Orleans, Louisiana. Baton Rouge: Louisiana State University Press, 1941. Vol. I, 1804-1820; Vol. II, 1821-1830; Vol. III, 1831-1840.

Sibley, J. Ashley, Jr. *A Study of the Geology of Baton Rouge and Surrounding Southeast Louisiana Area.* Baton Rouge: Claitor's Publishing Division, 1972.

Simoneaux, N. E., and Clarence L. Johnson. "The Family of Marigny de Mandeville and the Fontainebleau Plantation, 1700-1938." *Louisiana Conservation Review.* Autumn, 1938; Winter, 1938-1939; Spring, 1939; Summer, 1939. Louisiana Department of Conservation.

Spanish West Florida Records.

State Superintendent of Education, Annual Report of, 1875, New Orleans, 1876, p. 372.

Swanton, John R. *Indians of the Southeastern United States.* Bulletin 137. Bureau of American Ethnology. Smithsonian Institution. Washington: U.S. Government Printing Office, 1947.

————. *Indian Tribes of North America.* Bulletin 145. Bureau of American Ethnology. Smithsonian Institution. Washington: U.S. Government Printing Office, 1952.

Tate, J. M. "Covington Years Ago." *St. Tammany Farmer.*

U.S. Abstract Book. Archives, Clerk of Court, St. Tammany Parish.

U.S. Agricultural Census, 1850, 1860, 1870.

U.S. Census, 1830, 1840, 1850, 1860, 1870, 1880, 1890, 1900, 1910, 1920.

U.S. Geological Survey.

U.S. Government Surveys.

War of the Rebellion, a Compilation of the Official Records of the Union and Confederate Armies. Washington: Government Printing Office, 1901.

Webster's Third New International Dictionary. Springfield: G & C. Merriam Company, 1966.

Weekly Wanderer. Vol. I, No. 15. Archives, Clerk of Court, St. Tammany Parish.

Williams, E. Russ. *Kinsmen All.* Bogalusa, 1964.

Williams, T. Harry and A. Otis Hebert, Jr. *Civil War in Louisiana, A Chronology.* (n.p.) Louisiana Civil War Centennial Commission, p. 8.

Index